Speaking of
WASHINGTON

Speaking of WASHINGTON

Facts, Firsts, and Folklore

John L. Moore

 CONGRESSIONAL QUARTERLY INC.

Washington, D.C.

Copyright ©1993 Congressional Quarterly Inc.
1414 22nd Street, N.W., Washington, D.C. 20037

Book design by Kachergis Book Design,
Pittsboro, North Carolina.

Printed and bound in the United States of America.

Photo credits and permissions for copyrighted materials begin on page 285, which is to be considered an extension of
the copyright page.

Library of Congress Cataloging-in-Publication Data

Moore, John Leo, 1927–
    Speaking of Washington: Facts, Firsts, and Folklore /
John L. Moore ; foreword by Elizabeth Drew.
        p.   cm.
        Includes index.
        ISBN 0-87187-762-7   ISBN 0-87187-741-4 (pbk.)
        1. United States—Politics and government—Miscel-
lanea.
        2. Washington (D.C.)—History—Miscellanea.   I.
Title.
        E183.M78 1993
        975.3—dc20   93-30363
                                                         CIP

To Dorothy
  and
  Jack, Chris, and Meredith

*F*oreword

No matter how much one knows about Washington, there's always more to know. And then there are those things that one once knew, and—exasperatingly—forgot. *Speaking of Washington* is the place to look them up. And in the process, the reader will learn things he or she had never known. Things one did know are put in a new and fresh context.

Did you know that the first presidential wife to be called "First Lady" was Julia Grant? Did you know that Thomas Jefferson, under a pseudonym, submitted an architectural design for the White House? (It lost the contest.) Or that the Millard Fillmores installed the first White House cookstove?

One of the most fascinating things about Washington is the dynamic of some things changing and evolving—from the cabinet to the buildings to the White House staff to the interrelationship between the president and Congress—and others, such as the ambitions and calculations of politicians that remain the same, though adapted to changing circumstances and issues. It's that dynamic that makes Washington such an endlessly interesting subject.

There are many levels to the things one might want to know about Washington: grand history and the smallest bit of trivia; how it works. It's all here.

This book fills a variety of needs. It's an invaluable source for anyone who writes and talks about politics. Speechwriters will find a treasury of material. It will resolve many dinner-table arguments. And, with its brief nuggets and delightful pictures and drawings, it makes for wonderful browsing.

Elizabeth Drew

Contents

Preface

My father had a little game he played with us when we were kids. He'd say, "My brother and I know everything. Ask me a question." So we'd ask, say, "who was the tallest president?" And Dad would answer, "That's one of the things my brother knows."

Of course, he did this only when his brother, my real-life Uncle Sam, was not around to prove or disprove my father's playful exaggeration that the Moore brothers knew *everything*. It was all the more fun because my father loved history, and joke or no joke, he knew an awful lot about many things.

That's somewhat the way it is with this book, *Speaking of Washington: Facts, Firsts, and Folklore.* To say that it contains every imaginable fact about the government in Washington or the people who run it would be stretching the truth. Just as no one or two persons could know everything, no one or two books could contain all the facts worth knowing about a subject so rich and diverse as our system of government and the people—good and bad, smart and not so smart—who have made it work during its first two centuries.

Although *Speaking of Washington* doesn't pretend to be comprehensive in its coverage, it comes closer to that achievement than many books on the subject, and it may even surpass some that set out to be all-inclusive. Readers will find a useful source of information about the ways and wonders of Washington, as well as an interesting read. Along with the trivia (the tallest and shortest presidents? Abraham Lincoln and James Madison, p. 106), there are sections on how laws are made, what presidents do, and how the Supreme Court works.

The book begins with chapters on the foundation blocks of the federal system: the Constitution and its making; the states and their growing role; and the seat of government—Washington, D.C., which for people around the world stands for gleaming white marble, leadership, power, and above all, freedom.

The three major branches of government—executive, legislative, and judicial are given double-barrel coverage: first as institutions and second as groups of people we know as presidents and first ladies, vice presidents, members of Congress, and robed justices of the Supreme Court. Some of them are pretty colorful characters.

Recognizing that the institutions do not work in a vacuum, the book also covers the political and electoral apparatus through which those who govern are selected, as well as the groups that influence the governing process—the unelected power brokers (lobbies, news media, and such) and the Frankenstein's monster of big government, the bureaucracy.

Compiling *Speaking of Washington* has been hard, sometimes frustrating, but always rewarding work. Time and again I've been struck by the difficulty in finding in basic sources what would seem to be the essential bits of Americana—a list, for example, of the Confederate states and when they seceded from the Union. My editor and I finally found it in two different sources that disagreed on dates. (You'll find our reconciled version on p. 21). *Speaking of Washington* may then perform a very real service for general readers, trivia buffs, students, and reference librarians in pulling together thousands of scattered nuggets of information about the U.S. government.

Research and writing, though lonely work, is not single-handed work. I've had a lot of help. My thanks go first to Jeanne Ferris of the Congressional Quarterly book acquisitions staff, who conceived of the project, fed me hundreds of suggested items to include, and set high standards of quality.

The editor-in-chief of CQ books, David R. Tarr, supported *Speaking of Washington* and gave it the benefit of his many years of covering Congress. Nancy A. Lammers, the director of editorial design and production, worked closely with photo researcher Lisa Hartjens and designer Joyce Kachergis to give the book its distinctive, lively appearance.

The folks at CQ also gave me the best editor they could have chosen, Sabra Bissette Ledent. A North Carolinian living in Quebec, Sabra brought just the right touch of humor and background to the project. She organized and reorganized my random collection of facts into a coherent whole, spotted and filled dozens of omissions, and mercilessly kept me going until we had both achieved a work we could be proud of. My special thanks to Sabra.

Production editor Ann O'Malley brought all these pieces together into a book with her usual wit and skill. Carolyn Goldinger pitched in with careful, knowledgeable reading of the proofs. Freelancer Julia Petrakis created the index. And CQ library director Kathleen Walton provided invaluable help in unearthing many hard-to-find pieces of information.

I'm also grateful to Elizabeth Drew for writing the foreword. It's encouraging to know that even a Washington expert like Liz Drew could learn something from this book.

If I neglected to thank anyone, it's probably because of the mental overload of carrying the facts and anecdotes that went into this book. If there are errors, and I'm sure there are, there is no one to blame but me.

Speaking of WASHINGTON

Constitutionally Speaking

We the People

. . ." opens the preamble to the United States Constitution. When those words were written at Philadelphia in 1787 Americans were a much different lot than they are today—far less diverse ethnically and quite a bit fewer in number. Then, blacks (mostly slaves) accounted for about 19 percent of a population that numbered almost 4 million in 1790. Today, African-Americans make up a little over 12 percent of the country's 256 million population, and other minority races account for 3.5 percent.

Geographically, the country was a shadow of its present self in the late 1780s. It stretched over a mere 867,980 square miles versus the sprawling 3.7 million square miles it occupies today.

To accommodate this growth, the government grew as well—indeed, some might say ballooned. The national debt, $77 million or $19.25 for each American in 1789, soared to $4 trillion or $15,625 per person by 1993. As for Congress, the first one had 91 members—26 senators and 65 representatives from thirteen states. Today, the fifty states are represented by 100 senators and 435 representatives. And what happened to the supporting bureaucracy? That's a story unto itself. For most of the first 150 years of its existence, the United States got along with fewer than a half million federal civilian workers. In the next fifty years that number more than quintupled.

Despite these and other far-reaching changes in the mosaic of American life, the United States is still governed by the same remarkable document, the Constitution. In fact, it has proven to be such a stalwart companion of democracy that it is little changed in most respects since the first ten amendments, the Bill of Rights, were added in 1791.

For their part, thousands of Americans flock each year to the National Archives in Washington, D.C., to view the preserved original copies of the Constitution and its famous predecessor the Declaration of Independence. And, although certain other documents have been far less touted, they deserve attention as well, as they too helped to shape the American experiment in government of the people, by the people, and for the people.

■ Albany Plan of Union

Americans might still be British subjects if a 1754 Albany gathering had gone along with a plan suggested by statesman and inventor Benjamin Franklin. He called for a colonial government patterned after the Iroquois confederacy of tribal leaders. The Parliament-granted government, administered by a Crown-appointed president-general, would have had a council of delegates elected by the colonies.

Worried about loss of Indian support if French pressure along the colonies' northern border escalated into war, the British had called the Albany Congress to ensure a united front against the French. Seven northern colonies took part. But in the end neither the British nor any of the thirteen colonies accepted the Albany Plan.

Franklin later wrote that he still felt "it would have been happy for both sides of the water if it had been adopted." But its rejection increased the pressure for Americans to have their own government.

To warn of the danger that France posed in 1754 unless the colonies got together, Franklin published what is generally regarded as the first American editorial cartoon. It depicts the colonies as separate parts of a reptile captioned "Join, or Die."

■ Declaration of Independence

On June 7, 1776, Richard Henry Lee of Virginia, delegate to the Constitutional Convention, proposed that the colonies break with the British Crown. The assignment of drafting a declaration fell to a committee of five that included prominent patriots John Adams and Thomas Jefferson—although it was Jefferson who actually did most of the writing.

The text that was finally produced recited the colonists' grievances against England's unpopular King George III, but the preamble stated a political philosophy with wide popular appeal, holding that "all men are created equal" with "unalienable Rights" to life, liberty, and the pursuit of happiness.

The Continental Congress actually declared independence on July 2, 1776, but it did not approve the wording of the document until two days later, when twelve of the thirteen delegations endorsed Jefferson's draft with few changes (they took out his condemnation of the British slave trade). New York later made the approval unanimous.

Formal signing of the parchment copy took place on August 2. Fifty signatures were affixed then—including the famous one of John Hancock— and the remaining six delegates signed later.

Upon affixing his signature to the Declaration of In-dependence in a large, bold hand, John Hancock remarked, "That is my defiance."

Lee's Resolve

The resolution that Richard Henry Lee proposed to the Contintental Congress on June 7, 1776, contained wording incorporated in the more famous document that resulted—the Declaration of Independence. The Lee Resolution said: "Resolved:

Jefferson's original four-page draft of what would become the Declaration of Independence is still preserved at the Library of Congress.

That these United Colonies are, and of a right ought to be, free and independent States, that they are absolved from all allegiance to the British Crown, and that all political connection between them and the State of Great Britain is, and ought to be, totally dissolved."

Congress postponed a final vote on the resolution, but before recessing it set in motion the drafting of the historic declaration that set the colonies free.

On the Move

Today the original engrossed copies of the Declaration of Independence, the Constitution, and the Bill of Rights rest securely on a movable platform at the National Archives in Washington, D.C. Every night after the last visitor has left these "Charters of Freedom" are lowered twenty feet into a fifty-five-ton vault designed to withstand a nuclear blast.

But the cherished documents have not always had such loving care. The Declaration of Independence, particularly, endured less-than-ideal handling during its many travels since August 2, 1776, when it was signed in Philadelphia.

Travels 1776-1814

The early whereabouts of the Declaration of Independence are not definitely known, but the rolled-up parchment likely went with Congress in its twelve moves to eight different cities until it settled in the permanent capital, Washington, D.C., in 1800. There the document was kept in three different locations until it was hidden at Leesburg, Virginia, in August-September 1814 during the War of 1812. For many years the document was in the care of the secretary of state, beginning with Thomas Jefferson, its principal author. Another future president, James Monroe, was the secretary of state who protected the parchment from the British raid on Washington.

From 1814 to 1841 the Declaration moved with the State Department to three locations in Washington. The document's itinerary since then follows:

☞ 1841–1876—On public display at the Patent Office Building until the building burned while the Declaration was temporarily exhibited in Philadelphia at the American Centennial Exposition.

☞ 1876–1894—On display at the State, War, and Navy Building, now the Old Executive Office Building next to the White House.

☞ 1894–1921—Kept in a State Department vault because of its deteriorating condition.

☞ 1921–1941—Transferred to Library of Congress custody by President Warren G. Harding and displayed in the library's Great Hall, along with the Consti-tution.

☞ 1941–1944—Stored at Fort Knox, Kentucky, during World War II.

☞ 1944–1952—Returned to the Library of Congress and both documents preserved in 1951 in sealed, helium-filled cases.

☞ 1952–present—Both documents enshrined, along with the Bill of Rights, on their movable pedestal at the National Archives.

Dunlap's Broadsides

On the night of July 4, 1776, John Dunlap, Congress's official printer, turned out numerous large poster copies (called "broadsides") of the Declaration of Independence, which had just been approved. Today, Dunlap's broadsides are scarce and valuable. Only twenty-four are known to exist. Most are held by such institutions as the National Archives and Library of Congress, with a few owned by private collectors.

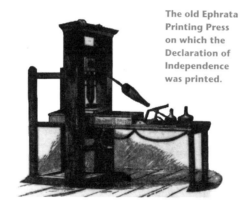

The old Ephrata Printing Press on which the Declaration of Independence was printed.

At Death They Did Part

John Adams and Thomas Jefferson, the only presidents who signed the Declaration of Independence, died within hours of each

Thomas Jefferson from an engraving done while he was in Paris.

John Adams from a portrait by Gilbert Stuart.

other on the fiftieth anniversary of America's independence. Jefferson, eighty-three, died first on July 4, 1826, but the news did not reach his ninety-year-old former rival. Adams's last words reportedly were: "Thomas Jefferson still survives."

Though they died as friends, the two men were political enemies in 1800, when Vice President Jefferson defeated President Adams who was seeking a second term. Adams boycotted Jefferson's inauguration out of bitterness.

■ Articles of Confederation

The first framework for governing the new American states emerged from the same Congress that declared the colonies' independence from Britain. The Articles of Confederation, adopted November 15, 1777, set up a weak government with no

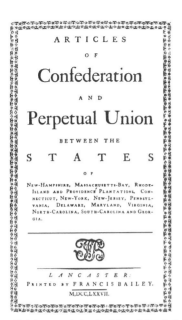

This official copy of the Articles of Confederation was published in Lancaster, Pennsylvania,
where Congress met in 1777. Though the
Confederation lasted only eight years, the document proclaimed a "perpetual union."

executive and a Congress with few powers.
The former colonists still feared centralized power.

That turned out to be a mistake. Once
the British were defeated in 1783, the articles proved not up to the job of soothing the
country's postwar economic and trade
chaos.

One product of this turmoil was Shays's
Rebellion, an uprising of Massachusetts
farmers led by Daniel Shays in 1786. Unable
to meet debt payments because of their
service in the Revolution, the farmers were
angry about losing their farms. The state

militia quickly put down the rebellion, but
the crisis strengthened the national push for
governmental reform and changes in the Articles of Confederation.

The Constitution
The Philadelphia Story

The thirty or so men who convened in Philadelphia in May
1787 were supposed to suggest amendments to the ten-year-old Articles of
Confederation. But they and the delegates
who arrived later went further and in four
months produced an entirely new set of articles—the Constitution of the United
States. By June 21, 1788, the necessary nine
states had ratified their handiwork.

George Washington and James Madison,
both of Virginia, were the only future presidents to sign the Constitution. Other signers
represented each of the thirteen original
states except Rhode Island, which sent no
delegates to the convention. In all, seventy-
four delegates were appointed, but only fifty-
five took part, with attendance averaging
about thirty. Each state had one vote.

Washington presided over the sessions,
which were secret. Little was known about
them until Madison's notes were made
public in 1840.

Some of the most prominent men of the
day were not delegates, including John
Adams and Thomas Jefferson, who were
serving as envoys abroad—Adams to England and Jefferson to France.

In this detail of a Howard
Chandler Christy painting
that hangs in the U.S.
Capitol, George Washing-
ton presides at the Cons-
titutional Convention of
1787. The eighty-one-
year-old Benjamin Frank-
lin (seated, center fore-
ground) worked toward
agreement among the
convention's factions.
Alexander Hamilton
(seated to the left of
Franklin) and James Madi-
son (seated to the right)
played critical roles in se-
curing ratification.

The Founding of a New Nation

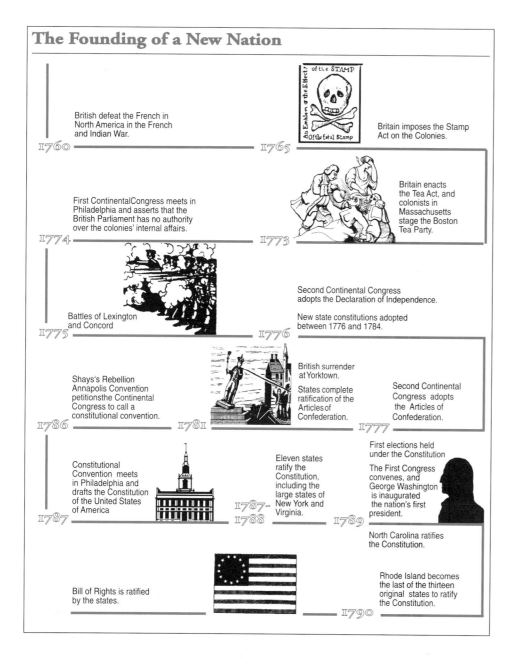

British defeat the French in North America in the French and Indian War.
1760

Britain imposes the Stamp Act on the Colonies.
1765

First ContinentalCongress meets in Philadelphia and asserts that the British Parliament has no authority over the colonies' internal affairs.
1774

Britain enacts the Tea Act, and colonists in Massachusetts stage the Boston Tea Party.
1773

Battles of Lexington and Concord
1775

Second Continental Congress adopts the Declaration of Independence.

New state constitutions adopted between 1776 and 1784.
1776

Shays's Rebellion
Annapolis Convention petitionsthe Continental Congress to call a constitutional convention.
1786

British surrender at Yorktown.

States complete ratification of the Articles of Confederation.
1781

Second Continental Congress adopts the Articles of Confederation.
1777

Constitutional Convention meets in Philadelphia and drafts the Constitution of the United States of America
1787

Eleven states ratify the Constitution, including the large states of New York and Virginia.
1787-1788

First elections held under the Constitution

The First Congress convenes, and George Washington is inaugurated the nation's first president.
1789

North Carolina ratifies the Constitution.

Bill of Rights is ratified by the states.

Rhode Island becomes the last of the thirteen original states to ratify the Constitution.
1790

The Founding Fathers

Although it has fallen out of favor in recent years, the term *Founding Fathers* fits; there were no "Founding Mothers" in the all-male delegation who took part in the Constitutional Convention at Philadelphia during the hot, humid summer of 1787.

Forty-two of the fifty-five delegates were current or former members of Congress; eight had signed the Declaration of Independence. Twenty-one were veterans of the Revolutionary War. Two (Washington and Madison) became president. More than half were lawyers, and almost all the rest were in other professions: medicine, finance, planting, trading.

Some owned large numbers of slaves. Several others owned at least one slave. Most of the slave owners were from southern tobacco- or rice-growing states.

The majority of the delegates were young, averaging forty-three. Jonathan Dayton of New Jersey was the youngest (twenty-six), and Benjamin Franklin of Pennsylvania was the oldest (eighty-one). All were Christians, including two Roman Catholics.

How Hot Was It?

Northerners in their woolen clothes were particularly uncomfortable in

The Old Statehouse in 1776

Philadelphia's muggy heat during the summer of 1787. To make matters worse, the windows in the Pennsylvania State House (now Independence Hall) remained closed because of the pesky black flies.

Scared Silent

An incident later related by William Pierce of Georgia illustrates the convention's obsession with secrecy: A delegate apparently dropped his copy of a paper containing one of the major proposals, the Virginia Plan of Union. Another delegate found it and turned it over to the presiding officer, George Washington. Just before adjourning for the day, Washington admonished the delegates about carelessness

and tossed the paper on the table saying, "Let him who owns it take it." Washington then left the room "with a dignity so severe that every Person seemed alarmed," Pierce wrote. But no one owned up to losing the paper.

Pierce himself briefly panicked because he had left his own paper at home. Although his notes (along with Madison's) helped historians to understand what happened at the convention, Pierce was not among the thirty-nine delegates who signed the completed Constitution on September 17, 1787. He had returned to Congress in New York.

Political Thinkers

As educated men (twenty-six had college degrees), most of the delegates to the Constitutional Convention were familiar with the major works then influencing political thinking in Europe and America, such as British philosopher John Locke's *Second Treatise on Civil Government* and French philosopher Baron Charles de Montesquieu's *The Spirit of Laws*. James Madison of Virginia, in particular, came to the convention armed with his own voluminous research into the forms of democracy.

Whether any one school of thought guided the Framers more than another has

long been argued among historians. What is known, however, is that most Americans of the time shared the delegates' beliefs in the need for a written constitution because the unwritten British constitution had failed to protect the colonists' basic rights.

Baron Charles de Montesquieu

Locke (1632–1704) espoused constitutional law and Montesquieu (1689–1755) originated the concept of separate legislative, executive, and judicial powers. Other writers who championed the causes of freedom and representative government included Thomas Hobbes (1588–1679), British author of *Of Commonwealth;* Jean Jacques Rousseau (1712–1778), who wrote *The Social Contract,* which helped to inspire the American and French revolutions; and Thomas Paine (1737–1809), the American

John Locke

pamphleteer whose *Common Sense* built support for the Revolutionary War.

Virginia and New Jersey Plans

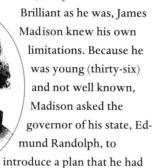

Brilliant as he was, James Madison knew his own limitations. Because he was young (thirty-six) and not well known, Madison asked the governor of his state, Edmund Randolph, to introduce a plan that he had formulated before the convention opened.

The Virginia Plan, as it came to be known, contained several features the Founders embodied in the Constitution—a central, three-branch government with a bicameral (two-body) legislature. It called, however, for seats in both chambers to be allocated according to population, which led to a revolt by the smaller states.

A group led by William Paterson offered the New Jersey Plan, a retooling of the weak Articles of Confederation to give each state an equal voice in Congress. The plan was voted down in favor of total reform, with the matter of apportionment to be decided. One stumbling block, whether to count slaves as people, was resolved with a concession to the South: in calculating populations to determine the number of House seats for each state, three-fifths of the slave population would be added to the state's whole number of free citizens.

The larger big-state versus small-state dispute was settled by the Great Compromise.

The Great Compromise

Also known as the Connecticut Compromise, this agreement saved the Constitutional Convention and created the Senate as it is today. Fearing they would be weak sisters to the more populous states if both chambers were apportioned by population (as proposed for the House), smaller states held out for and won equal representation in the Senate. In return the House, with members elected every two years by popular vote, was given sole power to originate money bills.

To insulate the Senate from popular sentiments, each state's two senators would be chosen by the state legislature for six-year terms. In the words of George Washington, the Senate would be "the saucer where the political passions of the nation are cooled."

Final Product

The Constitution completed by the Framers on September 17, 1787, turned out to be amazingly short. The original charter consisted of only a brief preamble and seven articles. The first three articles set out the powers and structure of the legislative, executive, and judicial branches; the others covered state powers, amendment procedures, constitutional authority (including a ban on religious tests for officials), and ratification requirements. Indeed, as finally published, it was a unique blend of national powers and states' rights, based on republican principles of representative and limited government. It provided for a central government strong enough to function independently of the states. Yet it addressed the concerns of states' rights supporters by providing a system of checks and balances to prevent the tyranny of any one branch.

The very fact that the Constitution was in writing distinguished it from the unwritten British constitution, which supplied many of the concepts on which the Framers built. Other novel features included the single elected president, the flexibility for change as needed, and the clear separation of church and state.

By the time the final copy of the Constitution was ready for signing, only forty-two delegates were still in town. Thirty-nine signed the document. The three who refused to sign were Edmund Randolph

A 'Constitutionary'

As applied to the American system of government, "checks and balances" have nothing to do with bank accounts. The phrase is related to another, "separation of powers," which means that the government's powers are divided among the legislative, executive, and judicial branches. Each one serves as a check on the other to prevent any branch from becoming tyrannical.

Here are the meanings of some other terms associated with the Constitution, but not necessarily mentioned in it (just as "checks and balances" is not specifically used in the document):

Civil rights—a citizen's rights, especially those guaranteed by the Constitution, such as freedom of speech and religion.

Due process of law—the following of established laws and procedures, especially in actions that punish individuals. The Fifth, Sixth, and Fourteenth amendments guarantee that no person shall be deprived of rights without due process of law.

Federalism—the sharing of power between a national government, on the one hand, and subunits, such as states, on the other.

States' rights—any rights that the Constitution does not reserve for the federal government or withhold from the states.

Supreme law of the land—the Constitution or laws and treaties made in accordance with it.

Left to right, George Mason, Edmund Randolph, and Elbridge Gerry refused to sign the Constitution.

and George Mason, both of Virginia, and Elbridge Gerry of Massachusetts.

Franklin's 'Rising Sun'

Benjamin Franklin—old and infirm, and next to Washington the most esteemed delegate—viewed the work of the Constitutional Convention with the skepticism of age and the optimism of youth.

Too frail to speak at length, he closed

the convention with remarks read by fellow Pennsylvanian James Wilson. After confessing that "there are several parts of this constitution which I do not approve," Franklin concluded that he consented "because I expect no better, and because I am not sure it is not the best."

As the delegates were signing the document, Franklin mused, in words recorded by James Madison, that during the session he often looked at the painting behind the president's chair, not certain whether it showed a sunrise or a sunset. "But now at length I have the happiness to know that it is a rising and not a setting sun."

The first coin minted for the United States in 1787 was the so-called fugio cent. One side of the coin displays thirteen interlocking circles—one for each state in the new union. On the other is a sundial with the Latin word "fugio," symbolizing the flight of time. Benjamin Franklin has been credited with the sensible admonition, "Mind Your Business" that appears under the sundial.

Publius the Federalist

Before the proposed Constitution could take effect, it had to be ratified by at least nine states. To help win this approval (especially New York's), Alexander Hamilton, James Madison, and John Jay wrote eighty-five newspaper articles under the pseudonym "Publius" to explain and defend the provisions. Gathered together later as the *Federalist,* the articles provided valuable insight into the reasoning of the Framers during their secret deliberations. As secretary of foreign affairs (before the State Department was created), Jay—unlike Hamilton and Madison—had not attended the Philadelphia convention, but he had followed the proceedings closely and was strongly in favor of ratification.

■ Changing the Constitution

Failed Amendments Galore

In more than two hundred years, the Constitution has been amended only twenty-seven times. The first ten amendments, ratified December 15, 1791, make up the so-called Bill of Rights. More than ten thousand amendments to the Constitution have been proposed since 1789, but few more than a handful have succeeded in winning serious consideration from Congress. Of the thirty-three that Congress saw fit to submit to the states, six failed to win ratification.

All twenty-seven amendments that were ratified came about through one of the two possible ratification methods set forth in the Constitution: proposal by two-thirds majority votes of each house of Congress and ratification by three-fourths of the states. Under this method, Congress calls on the states to ratify an amendment either through their state legislatures or through state conventions. Only once, for the Twenty-first Amendment repealing Prohibition, did ratification come from state conventions.

The other method for changing the Constitution is to call a constitutional convention, which Congress must do if requested by two-thirds (thirty-four) of the states. But this has never happened, largely out of fear that a runaway convention would lead to chaos. Ironically, the 1787 convention that produced the original Constitution far exceeded its mandate and still wrote a remarkable document. A convention of the 1990s, many fear, might not be so responsible.

Bit Players in the Amending Process

As for the other possible actors in the amending process, the president cannot veto constitutional amendments, nor can governors nullify their legislatures' ratification of amendments. Presidents and governors, however, can influence public sentiment for or against an amendment.

In the 'Pending' and 'To File' Baskets

As of early 1993 six of the thirty-three proposed amendments approved by Congress had not been ratified by the states.

Amendment	Year Amendment Submitted to States
Distribution of House seats	1789
Ban on gifts or titles of nobility from foreign powers	1810
Ban on congressional interference with slavery	1861
Empowerment of Congress to regulate child labor	1924
Equal rights for sexes (Equal Rights Amendment)	1972 with a seven-year time limit that was extended thirty-nine months in 1978
Voting representation in Congress for the District of Columbia	1978 with a seven-year time limit

Of the six amendments, only the ERA and D.C. representation proposals carried time limits for ratification. Both fell short of the thirty-eight states needed for approval before the time expired, but the ERA came closer, with thirty-five states by the June 1982 deadline. Sixteen states approved the D.C. amendment before the August 1985 deadline.

The other four proposed amendments could be considered pending, but the chances of their being revived and approved are extremely remote.

Bill of Rights

The ten amendments making up the Bill of Rights are considered practically a part of the original document because Congress and the states acted almost immediately to add them to the Constitution after it was ratified on June 21, 1788. All ten amendments were ratified on December 15, 1791.

The Bill of Rights guarantees the most fundamental of American freedoms, including some that are still hotly debated because of differing interpretations of what the constitutional language means.

Reborn Amendment

Congress approved two other proposed amendments in September 1789 along with the Bill of Rights. One of them, dealing with the apportionment of House members, fell one state short of the eleven required for ratification. The other, barring midterm congressional pay raises, finally gained ratification in 1992 as the Twenty-seventh Amendment.

But other miracle rebirths like that of the congressional pay raise amendment are not likely. In recent years Congress has adopted the habit of attaching time limits to amendments sent to the states. One of these, the Equal Rights Amendment (ERA), died on June 30, 1982, even though Congress extended the original 1979 deadline

Bill of Rights

First Amendment — Guarantees freedom of religion, speech, the press, peaceable assembly, and the right to petition the government.

Second Amendment — One of the most controversial amendments, it states in full: "A well regulated Militia, being necessary to the security of a free State, the right of the people to keep and bear Arms, shall not be infringed."

Third Amendment — Restricts government power to quarter soldiers in private homes.

Fourth Amendment — Bars unreasonable searches of an individual's person, home, records, or belongings.

Fifth Amendment — Requires indictment of persons before they can be tried for serious crimes; forbids trying a person twice for the same offense or compelling self-incrimination; protects against losing life, liberty, or property without due process of the law; and requires just compensation for private property taken for public use.

Sixth Amendment — Ensures defendants a speedy and public trial by an impartial jury, and the rights to be informed of the charges, face an accuser, compel testimony by defense witnesses, and have legal counsel.

Seventh Amendment — Provides for jury trial in all common-law suits involving more than $20.

Eighth Amendment — Bars excessive bail or fines and "cruel and unusual punishment."

Ninth Amendment — Makes it clear that a right may exist even if it is not spelled out in the Constitution.

Tenth Amendment — Declares that the states or the people have all powers that the Constitution does not specifically give to the federal government or deny to the states.

to give the states more time to consider the proposed amendment. The ERA fell three states short of ratification, despite strong pressure for approval from women's groups. The unsuccessful Equal Rights Amendment stated simply: "Equality of rights under the law shall not be denied or abridged by the United States or any state on account of sex."

Right to Vote

Several amendments to the Constitution have removed restrictions on who can vote. Among them and the groups they enfranchised: the Fifteenth (1870), newly freed slaves; the Nineteenth (1920), women; the Twenty-third (1961), residents of the District of Columbia (in presidential elections); Twenty-fourth (1964), persons barred by the poll tax (which the amendment abolished); and the Twenty-sixth

CELEBRATION AT BALTIMORE ON MAY 19th 1870.

(1971), persons between eighteen and twenty-one years of age.

Fastest Approval

The states acted quickly in 1971 to lower the voting age to eighteen. Ratification of the Twenty-sixth Amendment took only 107 days—less than half the time needed to ratify any other amendment.

One reason for the haste: states would have needed two sets of voting rules for the 1972 presidential election. The Supreme Court ruled in *Oregon v. Mitchell*

that a federal eighteen-year-old-voting law did not apply to state elections. Thus, persons under twenty-one could have voted for federal offices, but in most states they would have been barred from electing state and local officials.

Ho Hum

Young people eighteen to twenty years old have shown a decided lack of interest in voting since they gained that right under the Twenty-sixth Amendment. Their participation in presidential elections has de-

clined from 48.3 percent in 1972 (the first one in which they were eligible to vote) to 36.8 percent in 1992.

Slowest Approval

The Twenty-seventh Amendment wins hands down as the one that took the longest to win ratification by three-fourths of the states: 202 years from the time James Madison proposed it until it was finally adopted in 1992. Under its terms, Congress cannot give itself a midterm pay raise. A congressional election must intervene before the raise takes effect, giving the voters an opportunity to throw out the members who approved it.

Although Congress nowadays tacks time limits on the ratification of constitutional amendments, usually seven years, there were none on the pay amendment. When the New Jersey and Michigan legislatures gave their approval on May 7, 1992, they put the amendment over the thirty-eight-state minimum with one state to spare.

From 1873 to 1983 Madison's proposal had languished with only seven state approvals. But in 1982 Gregory D. Watson of Austin, Texas, discovered that the amendment was just dormant, not dead. He launched a one-man effort to revive it, and first one state (Maine) and then another began joining the support parade. Controversy over a late-night Senate pay boost in 1991 gave Watson's campaign added thrust. The raise brought senators' salaries to the $129,500 House level.

National archivist Don W. Wilson determined that the 1992 ratification was valid, and the Twenty-seventh Amendment became part of the Constitution. It states: "No law varying the compensation for the services of Senators and Representatives shall take effect until an election of Representatives have intervened." After the 1992 House election intervened, congressional salaries automatically rose to $133,600, effective January 1, 1993.

Change of Heart

Only one amendment to the Constitution, the Eighteenth, has been repealed outright, but several amendments have in effect voided or revised parts of earlier amendments.

The Twentieth Amendment, ratified in 1933, changed part of the Twelfth Amendment, ratified in 1804, which provided for separate electoral college votes for president and vice president. The newer amendment changed the beginning of presidential terms from March to January.

The Twentieth Amendment in turn was

Other Amendments to the Constitution

Besides the Bill of Rights, seventeen other amendments to the Constitution have been successful.

Amendment		Year of Ratification
Eleventh	Lawsuits against states	1795
Twelfth	Manner of choosing the president and vice president	1804
Thirteenth	Abolition of slavery	1865
Fourteenth	Civil rights, due process, support of rebellion	1868
Fifteenth	Voting rights for all races	1870
Sixteenth	Federal income tax	1913
Seventeenth	Popular election of senators	1913
Eighteenth	Outlawing of intoxicating liquors (Prohibition)	1919
Nineteenth	Voting rights for women	1920
Twentieth	Terms of office (Lame-Duck Amendment)	1933
Twenty-first	Repeal of Prohibition	1933
Twenty-second	Two-term limit for presidents	1951
Twenty-third	Presidential vote for D.C. residents	1961
Twenty-fourth	Abolition of poll taxes	1964
Twenty-fifth	Presidential succession	1967
Twenty-sixth	Voting rights for eighteen-year-olds	1971
Twenty-seventh	Ban on midterm congressional pay raises	1992

revised in part by the Twenty-fifth Amendment of 1967, which set up procedures in case of presidential disability or a vacancy in the vice presidency.

Prohibition, the ban on alcoholic beverages enacted in 1919, was repealed in its entirety by the Twenty-first Amendment in 1933. The fourteen-year "noble experiment" with a "dry" America had been an enforcement disaster. The public refused to comply and bootlegging flourished.

The repeal amendment, however, left it up to the states to decide whether to outlaw intoxicating beverages. Today, of the fifty states, Utah with its large population of Mormons (Church of Latter-Day Saints) comes the closest to still having Prohibition sixty years after it was repealed nationally.

The Twenty-sixth Amendment, which lowered the federal election voting age to eighteen in 1971, affected the "twenty-one years of age" mentioned in the Fourteenth Amendment of 1868, which barred denial of citizens' rights without due process of law.

■ Founding Fallacies

Some of the most beloved legends about the birth of the United States and its democratic government are, sad to say, not true. They are myths, hazy in origin and often debunked, that refuse to die.

The First Flag

There was a Betsy Ross (full name Elizabeth Griscom Ross Ashburn Claypoole), and she was a seamstress who lived in Philadelphia at the time of the American Revolution. But no one knows who actually sewed the first Stars and Stripes. The legend that Betsy Ross did, at George Washington's request, was started by her grandson William Canby. He was only eleven when his grandmother died in 1836 at age eighty-four. Historians think Canby may have embellished a true story he heard as a child about a pennant Betsy Ross sewed for the Pennsylvania navy in 1777.

Taking the Pledge

The pledge of allegiance to the United States flag has been around so long that many people think it dates back to the beginning of the Republic and is spelled out in the Constitution or one of Congress's first laws. Not so. A Baptist preacher named Francis J. Bellamy wrote the pledge in 1892 as part of the four-hundredth observance of Christopher Columbus's arrival in America.

As originally published it read: "I pledge allegiance to my Flag and to the Republic for which it stands: one Nation indivisible, with Liberty and Justice for all." The words "my Flag" were changed to "the flag of the United States of America" during the 1920s. Congress added the pledge to the official Flag Code in 1945 and inserted the words "under God" in 1954.

Meanwhile, the Supreme Court ruled in 1943 that no one could be forced to recite the pledge, ending what had been a morning ritual for millions of schoolchildren.

WHEN THEY BECAME STATES

DELAWARE

Delaware proudly calls itself "the first state" with good reason. It was the first of the thirteen original states to ratify the Constitution, on December 7, 1787, and thus is number one in the chronological order in which the fifty states gained admittance to the Union.

State	Date of Admittance to Union	Chronological Ranking	State	Date of Admittance to Union	Chronological Ranking
Alabama	December 14, 1819	22	Nebraska	March 1, 1867	37
Alaska	January 3, 1959	49	Nevada	October 31, 1864	36
Arizona	February 14, 1912	48	New Hampshire★	June 21, 1788	9
Arkansas	June 15, 1836	25	New Jersey★	December 18, 1787	3
California	September 9, 1850	31	New Mexico	January 6, 1912	47
Colorado	August 1, 1876	38	New York★	July 26, 1788	11
Connecticut★	January 9, 1788	5	North Carolina★	November 21, 1789	12
Delaware★	December 7, 1787	1	North Dakota	November 2, 1889	39
Florida	March 3, 1845	27	Ohio	March 1, 1803	17
Georgia★	January 2, 1788	4	Oklahoma	November 16, 1907	46
Hawaii	August 21, 1959	50	Oregon	February 14, 1859	33
Idaho	July 3, 1890	43	Pennsylvania★	December 12, 1787	2
Illinois	December 3, 1818	21	Rhode Island★	May 29, 1790	13
Indiana	December 11, 1816	19	South Carolina★	May 23, 1788	8
Iowa	December 28, 1846	29	South Dakota	November 2, 1889	40
Kansas	January 29, 1861	34	Tennessee	June 1, 1796	16
Kentucky	June 1, 1792	15	Texas	December 29, 1845	28
Louisiana	April 30, 1812	18	Utah	January 4, 1896	45
Maine	March 15, 1820	23	Vermont	March 4, 1791	14
Maryland★	April 28, 1788	7	Virginia★	June 25, 1788	10
Massachusetts★	February 6, 1788	6	Washington	November 11, 1889	42
Michigan	January 26, 1837	26	West Virginia	June 20, 1863	35
Minnesota	May 11, 1858	32	Wisconsin	May 29, 1848	30
Mississippi	December 10, 1817	20	Wyoming	July 10, 1890	44
Missouri	August 10, 1821	24			
Montana	November 8, 1889	41			

★One of the original thirteen states.

Uncle Sam's Building Blocks: The States

The name—the United *States* of America—says it all. It is a nation made up of fifty individual states, each with its own constitution, united in a federal system that strengthens the whole while retaining the uniqueness of each part.

At first, in 1789, the national government took a back seat to the states. The Tenth Amendment, added to the Constitution in 1791, says, "The powers not delegated to the United States by the Constitution, nor prohibited by it to the States, are reserved to the States respectively, or to the people."

But over the two last centuries the central government at Washington has come to dominate the federal system, touching off sporadic battles over "states' rights," particularly the slavery issue before the Civil War and racial segregation afterward. Gradually, the Supreme Court handed down decisions that enhanced the federal government's powers. The Tenth Amend-

ment, the Court said in 1941, merely states a constitutional "truism"—you keep what you haven't given up.

All this being said, one more truism is worthy of note. The states have continued to play a strong role in the federal system, thereby helping to preserve the cultural, economic, and political diversity of the United States of America.

■ How the States Became States

Only the thirteen original states—the colonies that broke away from England and won the War for Independence—started out that way, as states. They gained admittance to the Union as they ratified the Constitution, the last being Rhode Island on May 29, 1790.

The other thirty-seven states began as other entities and were admitted by Congress in accordance with Article IV, section 3, of the Constitution. Most (thirty) were territories, areas belonging to the United

States but not as part of any state. Much of the nation's expansion came from the addition of territories by purchase, by conquest, or by treaties with France, Spain, Russia, or other former owners.

When a territory felt ready to join the Union, its citizens petitioned Congress through its territorial assembly, and Congress authorized the assembly to draft a constitution. If Congress approved the constitution, it admitted the new state by an act signed by the president, who then proclaimed the state's admission. Once Congress accepts a state, it cannot revoke the act, nor can a state secede from the Union.

Five states—Vermont, Maine, Kentucky, Tennessee, and West Virginia—were formed from land originally part of the first thirteen states. West Virginia was created after Virginia joined the Confederacy in 1861. The western counties of Virginia formed their own state later in 1861 and adopted a constitution the following year. All the donor states agreed to the divisions, although Virginia did not formally agree to the loss of West Virginia until after the Civil War.

Three states were foreign soil before they became states. Texas was the Republic of Texas from 1836, when it won secession from Mexico, until it became a state in 1845. California, carved from land ceded by Mexico, had its own government for a year until it joined the Union in 1850. Hawaii, formerly the Sandwich Islands, became a kingdom in 1810 and a republic in 1883. It was annexed as a U.S. territory in 1898 and became the fiftieth state in 1959.

■ The Confederate States

Eleven southern states seceded from the Union in 1860–1861, defying the North and the law and setting the stage for the Civil War.

The last to leave were Virginia, Arkansas, North Carolina, and Tennessee, which did not secede until after the first shots of the Civil War were fired at Fort Sumter in Charleston harbor, South Carolina. The fort fell to Confederate forces on April 14, 1861.

By 1870, five years after the war ended, all of the states now known as the "Old South" had repealed their acts of secession and had been readmitted to the Union.

An Ordinance.

To dissolve the Union between the State of South Carolina and other States united with her under the compact entitled, "The Constitution of the United States of America."

We, the People of the State of South Carolina, in Convention assembled, do declare and ordain, and it is hereby declared and ordained,

That the Ordinance adopted by us in Convention, on the twenty-third day of May, in the year of our Lord one thousand seven hundred and eighty-eight, whereby the Constitution of the United States of America was ratified, and also, all Acts and parts of Acts of the General Assembly of this State, ratifying amendments of the said Constitution, are hereby repealed; and that the union now subsisting between South Carolina and other States, under the name of "The United States of America," is hereby dissolved.

EVANS & COGSWELL, PRINTERS, CHARLESTON.

The Confederate States and When They Seceded

South Carolina	December 20, 1860
Mississippi	January 9, 1861
Florida	January 10, 1861
Alabama	January 11, 1861
Georgia	January 19, 1861
Louisiana	January 26, 1861
Texas	February 1, 1861
Virginia	April 17, 1861
Arkansas	May 6, 1861
North Carolina	May 20, 1861
Tennessee	June 8, 1861

■ Yankee and Border States

Twenty-three states remained in the Union during the Civil War, along with the western counties of Virginia (which in 1863 became the state of West Virginia). Most of the Union states were in the North, Midwest, and West. They included industrial powerhouses such as New York and Massachusetts, which put the Confederacy at a disadvantage in heavy weaponry.

The slave states of Missouri, Kentucky, Maryland, and Delaware fought for the Union, even though they were below the Mason-Dixon line and generally thought of themselves as southern rather than Yankee. The addition of West Virginia brought the total number of border states to five.

The Mason-Dixon line, traditional demarcation line between the North and South, was named for two English surveyors, Charles Mason and Jeremiah Dixon, who established the line in the 1760s as the border between Pennsylvania and Maryland. For years until then the border had been in dispute between the families of the original owners, William Penn and Lord Baltimore. A westward extension of the line roughly separated the free and slaveholding states.

Some historians trace the South's nickname of "Dixie" or "Dixie's Land" to the Mason-Dixon line.

■ Would-Be States

'New Columbia'

Although it is not part of any state, the District of Columbia is not considered a territory in the normal sense of the word. The Framers of the Constitution wanted it to be kept separate as the seat of the federal government, and the District, formerly part of Maryland, has remained that way.

This unusual status has complicated the District's campaign to gain full representation in Congress. The District has had a nonvoting delegate in the House of Representatives since 1971, and in 1993 the delegate gained the right to vote on the floor when the House meets as the Committee of the Whole to take preliminary action on bills. A constitutional amendment to give Washington, D.C., full representation died in 1985. Only sixteen of the required thirty-eight states approved the amendment.

Meanwhile, supporters of statehood for the District have kept their campaign alive. The city's voters by a bare majority approved a proposed constitution for the state of New Columbia in 1982, and in 1990 they elected two "shadow" senators—one of whom was African-American leader Jesse Jackson—and a "shadow" representative. California and five former territories had successfully used the shadow tactic,

DISFRANCHISEMENT.

CINDERELLA.

The District of Columbia sits in the ashes of disfranchisement while her political sisters go to the ball this evening and, in fact, every evening.

Controversy over the political powerlessness of the District of Columbia has deep roots, as this 1887 cartoon by an unidentified artist depicts. It was not until passage of the Twenty-third Amendment in 1961 that citizens living in the District could vote for president.

and in four cases the Senate accepted the unofficial senators as full-fledged members after statehood was achieved.

In the 1992 presidential campaign, Bill Clinton pledged to support D.C. statehood.

Puerto Rico

The issue of statehood or independence for Puerto Rico has a long and sometimes bloody history. Puerto Rican nationalists were involved in an attempted assassination of President Harry S. Truman and a shooting in the House of Representatives. Other Puerto Ricans have resisted any change in the island's status as a commonwealth of the United States, which has been in effect since 1952.

In 1988 the statehood and commonwealth parties agreed to put the status issue to a vote. They wanted Congress to authorize a referendum that would be binding on the federal government, but the referendum legislation died in 1990.

Commonwealths and Plantations

Four states call themselves commonwealths: Kentucky, Massachusetts, Pennsylvania, and Virginia. *Commonwealth* means a largely self-governing unit, but the term has no legal significance as applied to the four states. Puerto Rico, however, is a commonwealth of the United States and not a state at all.

The full name of the smallest state is "Rhode Island and Providence Plantations."

■ Governors

Terms and Salaries

Governors are elected for four-year terms in all states except Rhode Island and Vermont, where the term is two years.

Before he was elected president, Arkansas's Bill Clinton was the lowest-paid governor—$35,000 a year. Another Democratic governor, New York's Mario M. Cuomo, received the highest salary—$130,000 a year.

Religion

The first Roman Catholic governor was Edward Douglass White, Sr., of Louisiana, who served from 1835 to 1839. In 1894, his son and namesake, Edward Douglass White, became the second Catholic appointed to the Supreme Court. The younger White later became chief justice of the United States.

David Emanuel of Georgia was the first Jewish governor. He served less than a full year in 1801.

Woman Governors

The first female governors were elected in 1924, only five years after women won the right to vote in every state. Elected that year were Nellie Tayloe Ross of Wyoming and Miriam "Ma" Ferguson of Texas. Both succeeded their husbands.

It would be forty-two years before another woman made it to the governor's chair, and again she followed her spouse. Lurleen Wallace was elected Alabama governor in 1966 when her husband, George C.

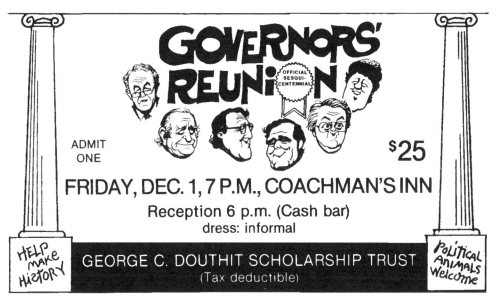

When Arkansas governors get together, the tickets must be cheap—they are the lowest paid governors in the country. From left, Sidney McMath, Orval Faubus, Dale Bumpers, David Pryor, Frank White, and Bill Clinton are featured on this ticket to the 1986 reunion.

Governor Joan Finney (D)

Senator Nancy Landon Kassebaum (R)

Representative Jan Meyers (R)

Wallace, was ineligible for another term.

The first woman governor whose husband had not previously held the office was Ella Grasso of Connecticut, elected in 1974. She was followed in 1976 by Dixy Lee Ray of Washington, also elected in her own right.

By the 1980s female governors were no longer a novelty. In 1993 women headed the government in three states (Kansas, Oregon, and Texas). Other states that had woman governors in recent years included Arizona, Kentucky, Nebraska, New Hampshire, and Vermont.

Seven states had woman lieutenant governors in 1992.

The Women of Kansas

In 1991 Kansas became the first state to have a woman governor (Joan Finney, Democrat), a woman senator (Nancy Landon Kassebaum, Republican), and a woman representative (Jan Meyers, Republican) at the same time.

The Lone African-American Governor

In 1989 Virginia became the first state to elect an African-American governor: fifty-eight-year-old L. Douglas Wilder of Richmond. Four years earlier, Wilder, a Democrat, had been elected lieutenant governor, making him the first African-American since Reconstruction to gain a major statewide political office in the South.

Another black American, Pinckney B.S. Pinchback, had served as acting governor of Louisiana for about a month in 1872, but, unlike Wilder, he was not popularly elected.

Although African-Americans held only one gubernatorial chair in 1993, there were more than four hundred African-American elected state officials throughout the country, most of them serving in state legislatures.

Hispanic Governors

Hispanics have been somewhat more successful than African-Americans in winning governorships. The first two Hispanic governors were elected in 1974: Jerry Apodaca in New Mexico and Raul Castro in Arizona. Those elected after 1974 were Toney Anaya, New Mexico, 1982, and Robert Martinez, Florida, 1986. All were Democrats except Martinez, a Republican.

Brotherly Contest

Brothers Robert L. Taylor, a Democrat, and Alfred A. Taylor, a Republican, ran against each other for governor of Tennessee in 1886. Robert won by a comfortable margin, and Alfred had better luck thirty-four years later. He defeated another Democrat in 1920 and finally got to sit in the governor's chair. Both Taylors also served as members of Congress.

Problem Governors/Governors' Problems

In 1921 the voters of North Dakota ousted Gov. Lynn J. Frazier, a Republican, from office part way through his second term. No other governor has been removed by this method, known as popular recall. Frazier won election to the Senate the following year and served there until 1941.

Arizona governor Evan Mecham, also a Republican, was facing a recall election in April 1988 when he was forced out of office by impeachment and conviction. The state senate convicted him of trying to obstruct a death-threat investigation and lending state funds to his auto dealership.

In all, seventeen U.S. governors have been impeached and convicted.

Alabama governor Guy Hunt, a Republican, was removed from office on April 22, 1993, immediately after he was convicted of putting campaign funds to personal use.

■ State Legislatures

Like Congress, the lawmaking body of every state except one is bicameral—that is, it has a senate and a house. The one exception is Nebraska, which has a one-chamber (unicameral) legislature elected on a nonpartisan basis. In some states, the larger chamber is called the assembly rather than the house of representatives.

One of the smallest states, New Hampshire, has the biggest legislature, with twenty-four seats in the senate and four hundred in the house. Nebraska's single-unit legislature is the smallest, with forty-nine members called senators.

■ State Capitals and Other Places Named for Presidents

Four state capitals are named after presidents: Jackson, Mississippi; Jefferson City,

Missouri; Lincoln, Nebraska; and Madison, Wisconsin.

George Washington leads in the number of American places bearing presidents' names. Besides the nation's capital and Washington state, there are Washington counties in thirty-one states. Twenty-two cities and towns throughout the country are known to be named for the first president, as is Mount Washington in New Hampshire. Some additional towns called Washington may have been named in honor of other persons with that name.

Maryland boasts the first Washington monument, dedicated July 4, 1827, atop South Mountain in Washington County.

The more famous Washington Monument in the nation's capital was opened to the public October 9, 1888. Based on Robert Mills's design, the obelisk stands 555 feet, 5 ⅛ inches high. Many of its marble blocks are inscribed with the names of states and other donors.

Construction began in 1848 but halted at the 150-foot mark. Donations fell off after a block donated by the pope was stolen in 1854, and they remained short because of the Civil War. Work resumed with public funds in 1876.

Since 1959 flags representing the fifty states have ringed the monument base.

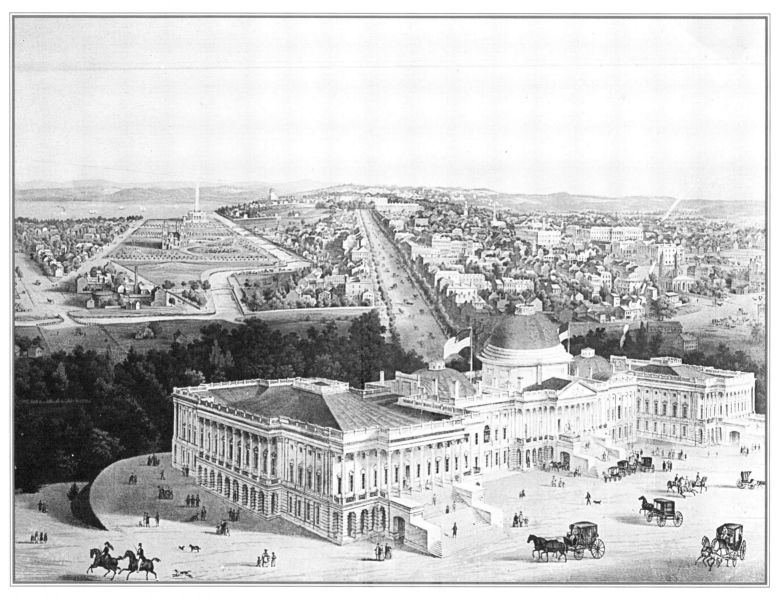

The seat of government as envisioned in this 1852 lithograph. Linked by Pennsylvania Avenue, the Capitol and the White House would be the focal points of central Washington, D.C.

GOVERNMENT, *Take a Seat*

With the birth of the United States of America, regions competed for the honor of having the capital in their area. Northerners wanted it in the North; southerners wanted it in the South. New York and Philadelphia wanted it, as did dozens of small towns.

But in the Residence Act of 1790, Congress said in effect, "None of the above." It decided on "a district or territory . . . on the river Potomac," touching off a contest among towns along the river in Maryland and Virginia. The area then, and still, known as Georgetown won the honor.

At first there was grumbling about the new location, especially about the subtropical climate. Some European countries classed Washington a "hardship post" and paid diplomats extra for serving there. Years later, however, Washington became known as one of the most beautiful capital cities in the world, and air conditioning made living there tolerable if not enjoyable.

■ Oh, Give Me a Home

The United States government sat in eight locations before it settled in Washington, D.C., in November 1800. The original seat under the Constitution was New York City in 1789–1790. Then it moved to Philadelphia for ten years.

Philadelphia was a popular location for the Continental Congress (1774–1781), which sometimes had to move to avoid the British army. Three Continental Congresses convened there, and others met in Baltimore, Lancaster, or York. While the country was governed under the Articles of Confederation from 1781 to 1789, its capitals were Philadelphia, Princeton, Annapolis, Trenton, and New York.

When Congress decreed in 1790 that the capital after 1800 would be somewhere along

NEW YORK · 1785

PHILADELPHIA · 1774

TRENTON · 1784

Shown here are three murals painted by Allyn Cox that grace the corridors of the U.S. Capitol. Created between 1973 and 1982, the murals feature twenty-four historical scenes, accompanied by paintings of the early meeting places of Congress and numerous portraits.

the Potomac River, George Washington, a former surveyor, selected the present site upriver from his Mount Vernon home.

The dozen disappointed would-be capitals included Williamsport, Maryland, which had widened its main artery to one hundred feet in anticipation. Bypassed by both the government and modern interstate freeways, Williamsport remains a remote town boasting an unusually wide street.

Easy Come, Easy Go

In 1788 and 1789 Maryland and Virginia each ceded land on which to locate the nation's new capital, and Congress, using President Washington's boundaries, accepted enough from each state to make up a ten-mile square (one hundred square miles). The states merely gave up jurisdiction.

Private owners were compensated for public building sites but not for street areas. In the case of the Capitol grounds, Congress paid twenty-five pounds (equal to $66.66) per acre to Daniel Carroll of Duddington, Maryland.

In 1846 Congress returned to Virginia the part of the District of Columbia that originally belonged to that state. The larger part on the Maryland side of the Potomac River, where most of the public buildings were, still makes up the District, an area of sixty-nine square miles.

My Capital or Yours?

In the years-long debate about where to place the seat of government, there was general agreement in Congress that it should be apart from any state capital to avoid jurisdictional disputes. The location finally chosen, at Georgetown on the Potomac, was thirty-five miles from Annapolis, the capital of Maryland. Today U.S. Route 50, linking Washington and Annapolis, is marked with signs designating it the "Capital Corridor."

L'Enfant Terrible?

Major Pierre Charles L'Enfant's grand-scheme plan for the capital city was largely carried out over many years, even though President Washington fired him in February 1792 because the work was behind schedule. Other reasons behind the firing were the planner's refusal to compromise and his frequent clashes with city commissioners.

There was little dissatisfaction with L'Enfant's plan, which called for a grid of streets intersected by broad avenues radiating from the Capitol, White House, and numerous circles. L'Enfant divided the city into quadrants with the center of the Capitol as point zero.

L'Enfant died in poverty in 1825, but though gone he was not forgotten. Congress belatedly honored him in 1909 by laying his remains in state in the Capitol Rotunda. In 1991 a computer-enhanced copy of the original map of the city went on display at the Library of Congress.

As L'Enfant envisioned, the Capitol and the White House became the focal points of the city, linked by a broad boulevard, Pennsylvania Avenue. But L'Enfant had in mind a much larger White House to counterbalance the Capitol in both size and political symbolism. Future architects discarded that idea. They estimate that L'Enfant's White House would have been 696 feet long and 206 feet deep—ten times larger than the mansion actually built.

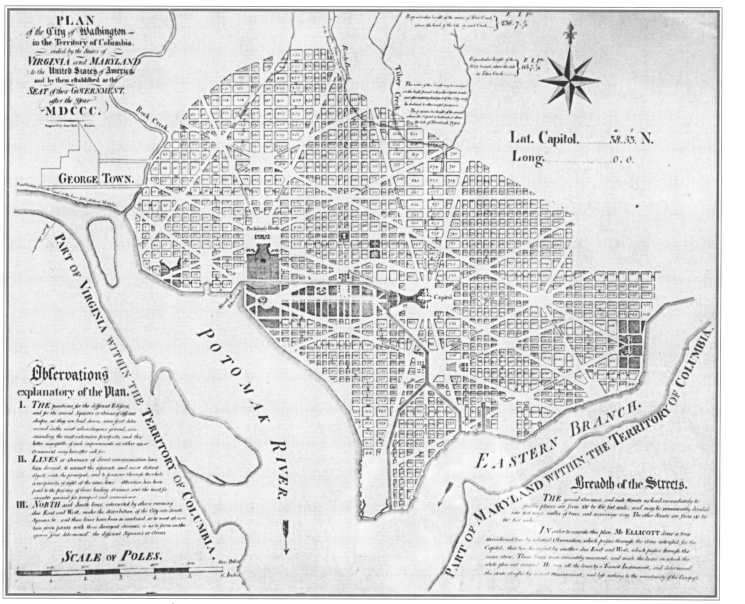

Andrew Ellicott, a surveyor who worked with L'Enfant, completed this plan for the city in 1792 after L'Enfant was dismissed by President Washington. Ellicott's drawing is very similar to the one promised by L'Enfant.

War of 1812: A Capital Loss

Fire and Rain

The United States government was still in its formative years when it suffered the humiliating sacking of its capital during the War of 1812, a war largely over British interference with American trade. Meeting weak resistance, a British expeditionary force penetrated Washington the night of August 24, 1814, and burned the Capitol, the White House, the Treasury, and other important structures.

One of the few public buildings spared was the Patent Office, and the man credited with saving it was the designer of the Capitol, Dr. William Thornton, a physician, inventor, and amateur architect. Thornton reportedly talked the troops out of torching the office, which he headed. But the building was heavily damaged that night anyway, by the same violent rainstorm that prevented the Capitol and White House from burning to the ground.

"The Taking of the City of Washington," an engraving published October 14, 1814.

Words and Deeds

The fighting in Washington and nearby Baltimore during the War of 1812, America's first declared war, inspired other memorable words and deeds. Dolley Madison, wife of President James Madison, refused to flee without Gilbert Stuart's full-length portrait of George Washington. Cut out of its frame, the rolled-up canvas accompanied the Madisons on their flight through the countryside. And lawyer Francis Scott Key began writing his poem, "The Star-Spangled Banner," while temporarily detained by the British during their bombardment of Baltimore's Fort McHenry on September 14, 1814. (Contrary to some accounts, he was not a prisoner.)

The War of 1812 ended with the signing of the Treaty of Ghent on December 24, 1814. Not knowing the war was over, however, Gen. Andrew Jackson attacked and defeated the British at New Orleans the following January 8. The victory made Jackson a hero who went on to political success as a senator and president.

The White House

While Under Construction . . .

The first president of the United States, George Washington, never lived or even slept in the White House—although judging by all the historical markers scattered around the country, he slept almost everywhere else.

When Washington became president in 1789, New York was the nation's capital. In New York, George and Martha Washington first lived in what is now lower Manhattan at the Walter Franklin House, located at Cherry Street and Franklin Square. In February 1790 the Washingtons moved nearby into the larger Macomb Mansion on Broadway. In August they left for the new capital of Philadelphia, where the Robert Morris House was made available to the president—and later to his successor in office, John Adams. Morris, then a U.S. senator, was a wealthy banker known as the financier of the American Revolution, but Washington insisted on paying the rent of $3,000 a year. Washington lived in the temporary capital of Philadelphia until his second term ended in March 1797. En route

George Washington

Martha Washington

home to Mount Vernon, he stopped by the White House, then being built, for the first and only time.

The capital moved to the city named after Washington in 1800, and the second president, John Adams, became the first occupant of the still-uncompleted executive mansion in November 1800, only four months before his single term ended.

Commuters and Renovators

All presidents since Adams have lived in the White House, although for a time

Historian John Zweifel and his wife Jan spent more than twenty-five years building this scale model of the White House. It is sixty feet long by twenty feet wide. From the lit chandeliers to the rugs on the floor, the detail is based on the actual mansion.

Grover Cleveland commuted from the suburbs (from a Washington community now known as Cleveland Park) and four presidents—James Madison, Theodore Roosevelt, Calvin Coolidge, and Harry S. Truman—had to move out to make way for reconstruction.

All returned after the repair work was done except James and Dolley Madison, who lived in rental houses until the end of his term.

What's in a Name?

The White House started out as the "President's Palace," the name preferred by capital planner Pierre Charles L'Enfant, or the "President's House," as George Washington called it. Officially, it became the "Executive Mansion." People began calling it the "white house" after a Baltimore reporter referred to it that way in print in 1810. By 1817 the name was in common use. Theodore Roosevelt made it official in 1901, and now the president's letterhead reads: The White House, Washington.

Stats

As mansions go, the White House is not huge—especially for one that doubles as the main office of the executive branch. The four-story house is 170 feet long, 85 feet wide, and sits on eighteen acres of landscaped grounds. The three-floor East and West wings give it a sprawling appear-

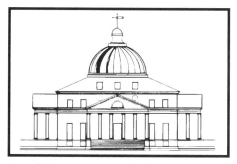

One of the many entrants in the White House design competition was a mysterious Mr. A.Z. For years the plan (above) was attributed to builder Abraham Faws. Then the truth came out. Believing a gentleman should sometimes remain anonymous, Thomas Jefferson had kept his authorship secret.

ance. There are 132 rooms in all, including 32 bathrooms. The presidential family living quarters are on the second floor of the main structure, with the president's Oval Office in the West Wing and the visitors' reception area in the East Wing.

Construction Phases

A self-taught Irish master builder named James Hoban designed the president's house after winning a competition for the honor. (Thomas Jefferson was the anonymous loser, "A. Z.") The cornerstone was laid on October 13, 1792, on a site chosen by Washington. A fourth floor was added in later years but otherwise the exterior and the layout of the first or "state" floor still appear much as Hoban designed them.

Winner in the government-sponsored competition for a presidential residence was this Georgian design by James Hoban, who later supervised the building's construction. Congress voted to give a prize award of either $500 or a gold medal for the design. Hoban, who had to feed his wife and ten children, chose the money.

The White House today.

An 1886 wood engraving shows gas light fixtures illuminating the portico during a holiday reception at the White House.

The interior has been entirely rebuilt twice, after the British destroyed it in 1814 and in 1949–1952 because of deterioration. Lesser renovations took place during the administrations of Theodore Roosevelt and Calvin Coolidge.

The West Wing of presidential offices, originally built as temporary space in 1902, was doubled in size in 1909 and rebuilt after a Christmas Eve fire destroyed it in 1929.

Heating, Lighting, Cooking

Martin Van Buren put in a furnace to supplement the twelve fireplaces architect Hoban had added when he built the White House the second time, after the 1814 fire.

Franklin Pierce installed a coal-burning central hot-air and water-heating system in 1853.

James K. Polk introduced gas lighting before the Millard Fillmores installed the first White House cookstove in the 1850s.

The Benjamin Harrisons were the first to have electric lighting (1891), but they were skittish about touching the switches for fear of getting a shock.

Where's the Kitchen?

The tradition of the first lady's giving a White House tour for the incoming president's wife began on March 2, 1909, when Edith Roosevelt showed Helen Taft around

the mansion. Two days later William Howard Taft succeeded Theodore Roosevelt in the first presidential transition of the twentieth century. (William McKinley had succeeded himself in 1901, and his assassination later that year elevated Roosevelt to the presidency.)

In 1933 Lou Hoover, the best-educated first lady until Hillary Clinton, declined to show Eleanor Roosevelt the kitchen. "I'm sorry, but the housekeeper will have to show you the kitchens," Mrs. Hoover reportedly said. "I never go into the kitchens."

On Exhibit

Caroline Harrison, the first wife of Benjamin Harrison, complained about people streaming past her sewing room on their way to the president's office. The place was "a circus . . . a show," she said. For more privacy she proposed a separate residence and a couple of remodeling plans, but Congress rejected all three of her schemes. She had to content herself with $35,000 for decoration, electrification, and rat extermination.

Just by making an issue of the privacy problem, however, Mrs. Harrison helped to bring about future changes, including construction of the East and West office wings in 1902.

Plumbing

The original White House had no plumbing and no indoor bathrooms. Water for the John Adamses had to be hauled from a half mile away. Thomas Jefferson improved things dramatically by installing wooden pipes connected to an attic cistern. Two water closets replaced the Adamses' outhouse. By 1833, in his second term, Andrew Jackson had true running water (hot and cold) through a system of iron pipes. He even had a bathing room with copper washtubs and a shower.

According to the White House Historical Association, no one knows just when modern plumbing came to the White House. But Jackson at least had a start with his hot and cold running water, and records show that by 1853 Franklin Pierce's family quarters had permanent bathtubs.

It is no myth, however, that 340-pound president William Howard Taft had a custom-made tub big enough for four grown men.

The Fillmore Bathtub Myth

In 1917 the New York *Evening Mail* published a detailed "history of the bath-tub" that credited Millard Fillmore with installing the first White House bathtub in 1851. From there, the Fillmore story found its way into countless articles and "books of fact." The trouble is, it's not true. Rascally writer H. L. Mencken confessed in 1926 that he had made it all up to entertain his war-weary readers. But even some serious histories still call Fillmore the father of the White House bathtub.

The Lincoln Bedroom Myth

Although one of the rooms in the White House family quarters is called the Lincoln Bedroom and contains an eight-foot bed, long enough for the tallest president, Abraham Lincoln never slept in the bed nor was the room his bedroom. It was the president's office and was open to job seekers until civil service ended the spoils system in 1883. Presidential offices were relocated to the West Wing in 1902.

The key to the Lincoln Bedroom myth was Harry Truman. He had the big bed moved into the room in which on New Year's Day 1863 Lincoln signed the Emancipation Proclamation.

Truman Reconstruction

For the second time in its history (the first was when the British burned it in 1814) the White House was reduced to a

The White House as it appeared on the twenty-dollar bill before and after the addition of the balcony by Harry S. Truman.

shell during the Truman administration and completely rebuilt inside. The need for wholesale repairs had long been suspected, but the last straw was when a leg of daughter Margaret Truman's piano went through the floor of her bedroom in 1948.

While the Trumans lived across Pennsylvania Avenue in the guest residence, Blair House, for twenty-seven months, the mansion received stronger foundations, a new steel frame, fireproofing, air conditioning, and the latest communications wiring. The interior appearance was faithfully restored. As part of the project Truman had a controversial balcony built under the South Portico as a place where the first family could sit and catch the evening breezes.

Change a Twenty?

A side effect of Truman's insistence on building a second-floor balcony was that millions of twenty-dollar bills then in circulation showed the South Portico with no "porch." The printing plates had to be changed. Two days after he visited the reconstructed White House on March 27, 1952, Truman announced that he would not seek reelection—and therefore would not be getting much use out of his balcony.

The White House Calling . . .

The first president to reach out and touch someone by phone was Rutherford B. Hayes. He saw the instrument demonstrated by its inventor, Alexander Graham Bell, and had one installed in the White House in 1877. Then there was one operator; during the Reagan and Bush administrations there were about twenty operators handling some ten thousand calls a day.

With the arrival of the Clinton administration and its emphasis on accessibility to the public, the volume of calls shot up to 65,000–

67,000 a day. Most were to a new "comment line" staffed by about twenty volunteers. By punching "1" on a push-button telephone after reaching the White House, callers could leave a recorded message for the president. The number of regular operators remained about the same.

Because Clinton staffers complained about the inadequacy of what they called "Jimmy Carter's telephone," a new state-of-the-art phone system was being planned. White House offices were also equipped with fax machines, but statistics on incoming calls were not being given out.

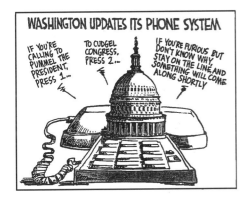

WASHINGTON UPDATES ITS PHONE SYSTEM

IF YOU'RE CALLING TO PUMMEL THE PRESIDENT, PRESS 1...

TO CUDGEL CONGRESS, PRESS 2...

IF YOU'RE FURIOUS BUT DON'T KNOW WHY, STAY ON THE LINE AND SOMETHING WILL COME ALONG SHORTLY

Dealing with 'Mayday'

The White House Situation Room under the Oval Office is in constant communication with military facilities around the world. It is run by a twenty-five-person duty staff of communications experts from the U.S. Army Signal Corps. Twenty-four hours a day they operate the Signal Board, which links the White House with the Pentagon, State Department, Central Intelligence Agency, and other military and intelligence facilities. It is said that the president is never more than thirty seconds away from the communications link to the White House command post.

In the early 1960s John F. Kennedy and Nikita Khrushchev installed a "hot line" between Washington and Moscow to avert nuclear emergencies. A popular misconception is that the president's end of the line is in the White House; it is in the Pentagon.

The Ultimate Home Office

Technology enthusiast Rutherford B. Hayes also brought the first typewriter into the White House. And later Woodrow Wilson typed his own correspondence.

Today, though, the personal computer is the thing. It has enabled many Americans to avoid commuting by working at home. But President George Bush already had a home office, the Oval Office, when he switched to a computer to produce his famous personally

typed memos and thank-you notes. He wanted to show that old presidents (he was sixty-seven) could learn new tricks. His White House was the first to make widespread use of computers, with an integrated system available to seventeen hundred Executive Office staffers. Bush himself was not hooked up to the system, but he praised telecommunicating as the way to save gasoline and work efficiently. "I know the advantages of working at home," he said in an understatement.

The Electronic Postman Cometh

Going the Bush administration one better, Bill Clinton opened the White House to computer technology in a big way. His administration signed up with the major on-line services—such as Prodigy and

which included a putting green during the Eisenhower adminstration. For years afterward the marks of presidential cleats were visible in the Oval Office floor.

Run, Bill, Run

Like Jimmy Carter and George Bush before him, Bill Clinton kept running after he won the election. The difference was,

CompuServe—so that the public could send electronic messages (E-mail) to the president. Within weeks he was receiving more than seven hundred messages a day.

Although he knew how to type, Clinton was not a computer user himself. Being a lawyer, he preferred to write out his messages on yellow legal pads.

No Corners

The president's Oval Office is just one of four oval-shaped rooms in the White House. The others are the diplomatic reception room on the ground floor, the Blue Room on the first floor, and the Yellow Oval Room on the second (family quarters) floor. Theodore Roosevelt, who was occupying the White House during the 1902 construction of the West Wing, copied the oval shape for his new office in that wing. He wanted his office to look more ceremo-

nial so he could greet visitors there instead of having to troop over to the reception area.

White House Grounds

The first Easter egg roll was held at the Capitol some time after the Civil War (exact date unknown), but in 1876 Congress chased the children and their Easter eggs off the Capitol grounds to save the grass. Hearing this, Rutherford B. Hayes opened the "President's Park" to the children, and First Lady Lucy Hayes presided over the first annual Easter egg roll on the White House lawn. Her son Scott Russell Hayes took part.

President William Howard Taft's cow, Pauline Wayne, helped to keep the grass short, as did grazing sheep as recently as the Wilson administration. The National Park Service now maintains the grounds,

Clinton had a track on the White House grounds for his jogging. In the first few months after his inauguration, Clinton caused quite a stir around the capital city when he often jogged during the morning rush hour. The track cost $30,000 in donated cash and materials, but the White House said it would save money because a large Secret Service contingent would not have to jog with the president.

Carter did most of his jogging at Camp David or on the South Lawn. Bush often ran at Hains Point, a park on the Potomac River.

That's Recreation

Without leaving the White House grounds, presidents can keep fit and have fun in a number of ways. Besides Clinton's jogging track, facilities on the South Lawn —and presidents who favored them—are a tennis court (Theodore Roosevelt and most later presidents), horseshoe pit (Truman, Bush), golf putting green (Harding, Eisenhower), and swimming pool (Ford). Jimmy Carter's personal scheduling of tennis court use became a symbol of the micromanagement style that helped to doom his presidency.

Franklin Roosevelt, his legs paralyzed by polio, made heavy use of the earlier indoor swimming pool. Harry Truman,

Harry Truman prepares for his turn to pitch horseshoes, and Gerald Ford swims a lap for the press.

John Kennedy, and Lyndon Johnson also swam often. But swimming unenthusiast Richard Nixon had other plans for the pool. He had it filled in and covered for a new press room. The outdoor pool was built during Gerald Ford's term.

For indoor entertainment at the White House there's a library, a movie theater, an exercise room, and a bowling alley.

Butt Out

Seeing the road to good health as more than daily exercise, Hillary Rodham Clinton snuffed out the White House's long-standing tolerance for tobacco products in 1993. Under her edict smoking was banned in the mansion's residence and nonoffice spaces, with the possibility of a complete ban later. Smoking already was prohibited in most of Washington's government and commercial buildings.

No one could say what would happen if a foreign dignitary happened to light up a cigarette at a White House state dinner.

A Peek at White House Pay

In 1992 a House subcommittee gave the public a rare glimpse at White House pay scales. Individual salaries traditionally had been confidential.

The published list for fiscal year 1991 showed salaries ranging from $125,100 for

WHITE HOUSE TIME CAPSULE

To mark the White House's two-hundredth anniversary, a thousand-pound steel and concrete time capsule was buried near the Rose Garden on October 13, 1992. The spot was believed close to the original cornerstone, dedicated October 13, 1792, but never found.

Unlike President George Washington, who was absent from the cornerstone ceremony, President George Bush presided at the capsule burial. Items placed inside for future generations to discover included:

✳ A signed copy of *Millie's Book,* written "by" the Bush's dog "with" Barbara Bush

✳ A souvenir watch of a Bush meeting with Soviet leader Mikhail Gorbachev

✳ A Bush pen

✳ A White House executive roster

✳ A 1992 White House Christmas tree ornament

✳ A copy of the Bushes' schedule for the day

✳ An American flag that flew over the White House

✳ Paint chips from the mansion's recent exterior restoration

✳ A White House commemorative stamp

✳ A White House grounds brochure

✳ A 1991 inventory of the White House

✳ A video, "Within these Walls"

✳ Seeds from a magnolia tree Andrew Jackson planted in memory of his wife, Rachel

✳ An engraving of the White House

✳ A photo of the Bush family

✳ Copies of *Life* magazine, the *Washington Post,* and *USA Today*

chief of staff John H. Sununu and other presidential assistants to $12,385 for student assistants. The salary paid to the top staffers was more than half the president's pay of $200,000.

Of the ninety-five persons listed as White House residence employees, head usher Gary Walters was the highest paid, $83,141. The salaries of the five White House chefs ranged from $44,129 to $67,806. Engineers made up the largest single bloc of residence workers, with ten earning from $27,729 to $54,037. The nine maids made $19,213 to $25,288. The highest-paid of five florists received $54,037; the lowest, $28,481.

William Kristol, chief of staff to the vice president, received $125,000. Other top vice-presidential aides earned $115,300.

◼ Finally, a Vice-Presidential Home

Although the president has had an official Washington residence since 1800, Congress did not provide one for the vice president until July 1974. It is located on the grounds of the Naval Observatory on Massachusetts Avenue, NW, and was known as the Admiral's House because the chief of naval operations had lived there since 1928.

The increasing costs of providing security for a series of private vice-presidential homes prompted the government to displace the admiral and renovate the white brick Queen Anne-style house for the vice president and his family.

Gerald R. Ford, the intended first resident, abruptly became president when Richard Nixon resigned, and his successor, Nelson A. Rockefeller, had his own home in Washington. The Rockefellers supervised the renovation until the Walter F. Mondales became the first full-time residents.

Congress appropriated money for extensive repairs and additions during the Bush, Quayle, and Gore vice presidencies.

■ Government-Issue Workplaces for Bureaucrats

About 12 percent of the nation's 3.1 million federal civilian employees work in Washington, D.C. Their workplaces, ranging from architectural treasures to nondescript rented offices, take up much of the downtown area. Besides the headquarters for each of the fourteen cabinet departments, there are more than five hundred executive branch buildings.

Block that View!

The oldest departmental headquarters, the Treasury building, is famous for spoil-

Old Executive Office Building

ing the grand vista that Pierre Charles L'Enfant envisioned for Pennsylvania Avenue between the Capitol and the White House. Legend has it that Andrew Jackson obstinately declared, "Right here is where I want the cornerstone!" Now inaugural parades have to detour around the Treasury to pass in front of the White House.

Wedding Cake Bliss

Mark Twain called it "the ugliest building in America." Indeed, its nine hundred columns make it look like a wedding cake. The Old Executive Office Building (OEOB) barely escaped the wrecking ball in 1960, but now, restored and still functioning, it is one of Washington's best known and most beloved structures.

Located just west of the White House, the French Second Empire building was completed in 1888. It originally housed the State, War, and Navy departments. Today almost one thousand staffers from the Executive Office of the President work there.

Foggy Bottom

The State Department gained its nickname, Foggy Bottom, from the low-lying drained swamp it moved to in 1947. Some say the title is appropriate because cloudy language often suits the purposes of diplomacy.

Five-Sided Wonder

Built in seventeen months in the early years of World War II, the Pentagon still

holds the title of the world's largest office building. Its 6.5 million square feet of floor space (three times more than that of the Empire State Building) make up a small city for the 32,000 Defense Department employees who work there. But as big as the Pentagon is, it's not big enough. More than 100,000 people work at twenty-five other Defense facilities in the Washington area.

Monument to Bureaucracy

One of Washington's most spectacular interiors—the Great Hall of what is now the National Building Museum—once swarmed with employees of the presently defunct Pension Bureau. Opened in 1885, the building features an enclosed courtyard measuring 316 feet by 116 feet, with towering Corinthian columns at either end. The Great Hall has been the site of numerous inaugural balls.

◼ The Capitol

Amateur Designer

Pierre Charles L'Enfant, the young French engineer who planned Washington, D.C., and chose a site for the legislative branch, did not design the Capitol itself. That honor went to an amateur architect, Dr. William Thornton, who won a design

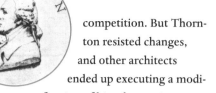

competition. But Thornton resisted changes, and other architects ended up executing a modification of his scheme. Among them was James Hoban, the designer of the White House.

Congress convened in the Capitol on November 21, 1800, but construction continued for many more years, including reconstruction after the British burned the city in 1814 during the War of 1812. The Capitol acquired its present-day look in 1863 with completion of a cast-iron dome replacing the original low wooden dome.

Work began on the Capitol dome in 1856. President Lincoln ordered construction to continue during the Civil War "as a sign we intend the Union shall go on."

West Front of the Capitol on January 20, 1993

Two-Faced Solution

People who accuse Congress of practicing "back-door politics" are wrong. The Capitol has no back door. In fact, it has no back. The building instead has two fronts—the East Front and the West Front. George Washington laid the cornerstone on September 18, 1783, but when the East Front was extended in 1958–1962, no one could find the historic stone.

Most presidential inaugural ceremonies since 1829 (Jackson) have taken place on the East Front steps. President Ronald Reagan changed the site in 1981 to the West Front overlooking the Mall. Bitterly cold weather forced the second Reagan inaugural, also planned for the West Front, into the Capitol Rotunda in 1985. The West Front also was used for the inaugurations of George Bush in 1989 and Bill Clinton in 1993.

Capitol Stats

From its East Front base to the top of the statue crowning its dome, the Capitol is 287 feet, 5.5 inches high. Its overall length is 751 feet, 4 inches. At its widest point it measures 350 feet. The interior height of the Rotunda is 180 feet, 3 inches.

The building has five levels totaling 16.5 acres of floor space. Besides the House and Senate chambers and central Rotunda, there are about 540 offices, restaurants, workshops, and other rooms.

In all, the building covers about four acres on a site, formerly called Jenkins Heights or Hill, eighty-eight feet above the Potomac River. The grounds, including other congressional buildings and the separate Supreme Court, cover about 181 acres.

Congress decreed in 1901 that the Capitol dome must remain the highest point in Washington. Consequently, the nation's capital has no "skyscrapers" taller than about thirteen stories.

Architect of the Capitol

The presidentially appointed architect of the Capitol has charge of not only the Capitol itself but also the Library of Congress and other congressional structures, the Supreme Court building, the Botanic Garden, and some two hundred acres of grounds.

Only nine persons have held the job in two hundred years. They are William Thornton (1793–1794), Benjamin Henry Latrobe (1803–1811, 1815–1817), Charles Bulfinch (1818–1829), Thomas Ustick Walter (1851–1865), Edward Clark (1865–1902), Elliott Woods (1902–1923), David Lynn (1923–1954), J. George Stewart (1954–1970), and George M. White (1971–   ). White was the first professional architect to win the appointment since Walter.

Name that Statue

As originally designed, the bronze "Statue of Freedom" atop the Capitol dome was called "Armed Liberty" by its sculptor, Thomas Crawford. But one of Crawford's critics prevailed, and the sculptor replaced her soft cap, like that worn by freed Roman slaves, with a feathered headdress to please Jefferson Davis, then secretary of war and

later president of the Confederacy. Davis feared the cap would inflame antislavery passions. The bronze figure is 19.5 feet tall and weighs 14,985 pounds.

In 1993 Capitol architect George White arranged for the statue to be lowered from its perch by helicopter for cleaning and repair. As tricky as it was, the operation was much simpler than the one used by workers, mostly slaves, to hoist the statue to its pedestal in 1863 with derricks, winches, and a steam engine.

Put Out More Flags

Many Americans can truthfully say they own a flag that flew over the United States Capitol. But the whole truth is that it likely flew there only a few seconds. Crews of workers spend hours raising and lowering flags for members of Congress to send to their constituents. The record was set on the nation's bicentennial birthday, July 4, 1976, when 10,471 Stars and Stripes were flown over the Capitol on eighteen temporary flagpoles.

Cloakrooms

Inside the Capitol, the Senate and House have two cloakrooms each, one for Democrats and one for Republicans. Narrow, L-shaped rooms along the sides and rear of the two chambers, the cloakrooms feature well-worn leather chairs, refrigerators stocked with soda and candy, and televisions. The cloakrooms are a favorite place for legislators to relax between floor votes—private, yet convenient to the chambers. A separate cloakroom for women was set up in 1927, but today women members frequently use the original cloakrooms.

On January 20, 1993, the Senate, bowing to the reality of its growing female membership, opened a new restroom for woman senators on the same floor as the Senate chamber. Before, those members had to resort to restrooms in private offices or on the floor below.

The Final Honor

The final honor of lying in state in the Capitol Rotunda is reserved for presidents, war heroes, and other respected dignitaries. Few members of Congress have received the tribute. One who did was Florida Democrat Claude D. Pepper, who died May 30, 1989. He was the first incumbent House member so honored since Pennsylvanian Thaddeus Stevens, in 1868. Stevens, though not the Speaker, won respect after the Civil War as the House leader and as a champion of equal rights. Former senator Pepper had spent the last of his eighty-eight years as a champion of the elderly.

Another incumbent honored earlier in the Rotunda was Hubert H. Humphrey of Minnesota, who returned to the Senate after serving as vice president in the Lyndon B. Johnson administration. Humphrey died in 1978.

Henry Clay, an illustrious former member of Congress and secretary of state, was the first to lie in state there, in 1852. Since then almost thirty men, but no women, have received the same tribute.

Empty Crypt

When George Washington died in 1799, Congress reserved a space for his tomb directly below the center of the Capitol. That part of the building was not completed until years later, however, and in 1832 the family refused permission to move his remains from Mount Vernon.

Meanwhile, in 1828 Congress closed the ten-foot hole in the Rotunda floor that would have permitted visitors to gaze down at a statue of Washington, which was to have stood in what is now known as the Crypt. The tomb itself was to be one floor below that in the Capitol basement. That space is now used to store the black-draped Lincoln catafalque, on which have rested the caskets of all the men who have lain in state in the Rotunda since 1865. The Crypt itself contains several pictorial exhibits about the history of the Capitol.

Shhh! Someone Might Hear!

An accident of architecture created the Capitol's famed "whispering spot" in Statuary Hall. Hushed words spoken here can be clearly heard across the room at a floor plaque marking the spot where John

The Unknown Serviceman of the Vietnam era lies in state in the Capitol Rotunda. "We may not know his name, but we know his courage," President Reagan said in his eulogy.

Quincy Adams suffered the stroke that killed him in 1848. Adams was the only former president elected to the House.

The strange acoustics were no joke in 1807–1857 when Statuary Hall was the House of Representatives' chamber. Legislators were annoyed that their oratory went unheard in some places, while their secrets could be overheard from the whispering spot.

The Real 'Year of the Woman'

American women gained the right to vote under the Nineteenth Amendment, ratified in 1920. In celebration, banner-waving women marched around the Crypt in 1921 to dedicate a memorial to three pioneer suffragettes: Susan B. Anthony, Lucretia Mott, and Elizabeth Cady Stanton. Sculptress Adelaide Johnson carved their likenesses from an eight-ton block of Car-rara marble. Generations of visitors have since given the impressive statue an irreverent nickname, "Ladies in a Bathtub." Johnson died in 1955 at age 108.

Doors to Nowhere

A giant pair of cast bronze doors are displayed near the Crypt. Designed by Louis Amateis for the Capitol's central west entrance, they were never used because the West Front was restored, not extended as anticipated.

The 'Big Tent'

During the Civil War some three thousand Union soldiers lived in the Capitol, which they called the "Big Tent." They cooked food in heating furnaces and turned brick-lined committee rooms into giant bread ovens. No sooner were the troops moved out in mid-1862 than the Capitol became a temporary hospital, with about fif-teen hundred cots set up for the wounded from the battles of Second Bull Run and Antietam.

Explosive Issues

Bombs apparently planted by political protesters have damaged the Capitol three times since 1915. No one has been hurt.

This mural shows wounded Civil War soldiers being attended to inside the Rotunda. The scaffold at right was part of the construction work then under way on the Capitol's unfinished dome. Nurses such as Dorothea Dix and Red Cross founder Clara Barton served here during this time, as did poet Walt Whitman. The mural was painted by Allyn Cox and decorates a ceiling in the U.S. Capitol.

Erich Muenter, formerly a Harvard German instructor, placed the first bomb in the Senate Reception Room. It went off July 2, 1915. Muenter was angered by U.S. companies' munitions sales to the Allies in World War I.

On March 1, 1971, another bomb caused extensive damage. The perpetrator was never caught, but it was believed the bombing was a protest against the Vietnam War.

A group called the Armed Resistance Unit claimed responsibility for the bomb that exploded November 7, 1983, about thirty feet from the Senate chamber. In 1990 three persons pleaded guilty to the bombing, and charges were dropped against four others.

Capitol security was tightened after the 1971 and 1983 incidents. Visitors must now pass through airport-type metal detectors, and the Capitol Police force was doubled to 1,265 by 1990.

The Greenbrier resort, location of Congress's secret emergency shelter.

Protective Luxury

If the bombs had ever become bigger and more dangerous, Congress was ready. The *Washington Post* disclosed in May 1992 that for thirty years an emergency "Capitol" existed deep underground at the luxurious Greenbrier resort in White Sulphur Springs, West Virginia. Begun in 1960 at the height of the Cold War with the former Soviet Union, the $14 million concrete bunker featured giant steel doors designed to withstand a nuclear blast.

Disclosure of the hardened hideaway triggered a controversy. With the secret out, the shelter was useless, congressional leaders complained. Some suggested shutting it down to save money. It had long been an open secret, however, that the White House had a similar shelter tunneled beneath Mount Weather near Bluemont, Virginia. Its existence made the news briefly in 1974 after a disastrous airliner crash on the rock mountain.

Capitol Offshoots

The rapid growth of congressional staff is reflected in the massive office buildings that ring the Capitol. Until 1908 members had little or no staff. Lawmakers came to Washington only part of the year and made do with a desk in the House or Senate chamber and a room in a boardinghouse. Files were kept in memory or in pockets.

Today, besides several annexes, both chambers have office buildings for members, committees, and their staffs. The House office buildings are named for former Speakers Joseph G. Cannon (building opened in 1908), Nicholas Longworth (1933), and Sam Rayburn (1965).

The Senate buildings honor the memory of distinguished senators Richard B. Russell (building opened in 1933), Everett McKinley Dirksen (1958), and Philip A. Hart (1982).

Congress's Choo-choo

Congress has its own little subway system to help members hustle over to the House or Senate floor for votes. Visitors can ride it too, for free, provided there are empty seats. But members have top priority, especially for the front seat.

The eighteen-passenger electric cars travel about twenty miles an hour between the three Senate office buildings and the Capitol. On the House side, the line goes only to the Rayburn building; pedestrian tunnels connect with the Cannon and Longworth buildings.

Some fitness-minded members prefer to walk or jog. Republican Strom Thurmond from South Carolina, at ninety the oldest senator in 1993, could often be seen trotting alongside the subway cars.

Books, Books, and More Books

The Library of Congress, an important arm of the legislative branch, outgrew its quarters in the Capitol and moved to its own building in 1897. Now named for Thomas Jefferson, who provided the library's basic collection of books, the main building stands opposite the East Front of the Capitol, across East Capitol Street from a relative newcomer, the Supreme Court building.

The massive Jefferson Building has since been joined by two large additions named for other early presidents, the John Adams Building (1939) and the James Madison Building (1980). The buildings attract some 2.5 million visitors a year, particularly the Jefferson Building with its spectacular Great Hall and towering, domed Main Reading Room. Both spaces were renovated in the early 1990s. The Reading Room holds 45,000 reference books and desks for 250 readers.

While it was still housed in the Capitol, the library suffered two devastating fires, the first in 1814 when the British burned the building and the second, an accidental blaze, in 1851. It was after the 1814 fire that former president Jefferson sold six thousand books to the library for $24,000. After the second fire, Congress helped to replenish the collection by enacting in 1865 a law that required persons seeking a copyright to give the library a copy of the completed work. A similar requirement is still in effect.

In all, the library covers 64.5 acres of floor space and contains 535 miles of bookshelves. Its annual budget is more than $322 million.

As early as 1880 it was clear that the Library of Congress's collection was overflowing its Capitol quarters.

The Great Hall of the Jefferson Building was reopened in January 1993 after a three-year renovation. During this time the painted murals were restored from dark, dull images to brilliant, subtly lit scenes in bold colors, with intricate details and textures once again evident.

THE NATION'S OTHER ATTIC

Like its neighbor across the Mall, the Library of Congress is a repository of American culture. Unlike the Smithsonian, the library's collection is best known for its books and periodicals. Still the 100 million items in the Library of Congress collections include a surprising variety of materials, ranging from a film reel of *Star Wars* to a stringed instrument made by Stradivari. In addition to books, magazines, and periodicals, the library's collections contain historical and contemporary examples of the following items. A comprehensive list would go on—and on.

* Books in Braille
* Drawings, etchings, and prints
* Globes and maps
* Incunabula (books published before 1500)
* Manuscripts in scrolls, sheets, notebooks, and codex form
* Motion pictures, silent and sound
* Music in written and printed notations
* Musical instruments
* Photographic negatives, prints, and slides
* Posters and broadsides
* Speeches, recitations, narratives, poetry, and dramatic performances on film, phonograph records, or tape

Thirty-five hundred images of American Indians, including this one of tribal leader Geronimo, are part of the library's collection. The earliest image in the American Indian collection is dated 1863, although most of the photographs were taken between 1890 and 1920. Images depict ceremonies, dances, games, domestic tasks, and homes.

"Contemplation of Justice," one of two marble figures by James Earle Fraser flanking the main entrance to the Court.

Among the library's treasures are Jefferson's handwritten rough draft of the Declaration of Independence and Abraham Lincoln's first two drafts of the Gettysburg Address—written not on the back of an envelope (as legend has it) but on ruled paper.

Housing the Supreme Court

The Supreme Court was the last of the three branches of the federal government to build a permanent home. Its Greek classical-style structure opened in 1935, a relatively short time ago compared with the Capitol and the White House.

Earlier Quarters

For its first 145 years, the Court bounced around as a tenant in about a dozen other buildings intended for other purposes. It first met in 1790 in the Royal Exchange Building in New York City, then the temporary U.S. capital. But the Court had no cases to decide, and it busied itself with appointing a crier, now the Court clerk, and admitting lawyers to the bar.

In 1791 the Court moved with the rest of the federal government to another temporary capital, Philadelphia. Still having no cases to attend to, the Court met only one day in Independence Hall and then moved to the new City Hall, also being

The Royal Exchange, New York City

Old City Hall, Philadelphia, Pennsylvania

The old Supreme Court chamber in the U.S. Capitol

used by Congress, other courts, and the state legislature. There the justices began wearing robes over their street clothes.

When the government moved to the permanent capital, Washington, in 1801, the White House and Capitol were partly completed, but the Supreme Court had no place to go. Congress then made available a small room on the first floor of the Capitol, and the Court met there on February 2, 1801. Displaced by renovation in 1808, the Court met elsewhere until 1810, including one year in Long's Tavern, where the Library of Congress now stands.

From 1810 to 1814, when the British burned the Capitol, the Court had its own specially designed courtroom in the building. After the fire, the Court and Congress moved to temporary locations, including the Brick Capitol where the Supreme Court building now stands. The Court returned in 1817 to the Capitol, where it occupied the former Senate chamber from 1860 until it moved to its own building in 1935. The last major decision announced at the Capitol, in 1934, struck down President Franklin Roosevelt's National Industrial Recovery Act. Recently restored, the old Senate chamber remains unused except as a visitors' attraction.

Justices Louis D. Brandeis, Willis Van Devanter, Chief Justice William Howard Taft, Justices Oliver Wendell Holmes, Pierce Butler, George Sutherland, and Harlan Fiske Stone observe the model of the soon-to-be-built Supreme Court building.

Supreme Court Building

The Court's home, opposite the East Front of the Capitol at One First Street, NE, has no name. It is simply the "Supreme Court building." If it were named for someone, an appropriate choice would be President William Howard Taft, who began pushing for a Court building in 1912. When he became chief justice in 1921—the only former president to do so—he continued the campaign, finally winning congressional authorization in 1929. He died the following year, and Chief Justice Charles Evans Hughes saw the completion of Taft's dream.

Building Features

Instead of memorializing an individual, the Supreme Court building is a monument to the principle carved in stone over its front pillars: "Equal Justice Under Law."

The first-floor chamber where the Court hears oral arguments measures eighty-two by ninety-one feet and has a forty-foot ceiling. Visitors are not apt to see any Court members, except when they are hearing arguments or announcing opinions. Architect Cass Gilbert designed the building so that the justices could freely move about their offices and corridors in private.

In 1992 the first renovation of the Court building was completed at a cost of

$264,000, most of which came from fees to belong to the Court bar. The other $69,000 came from Congress.

Hearing Oral Arguments

When important cases are being heard, the Supreme Court chamber is too small to accommodate all the people who want to get in. It has only 150 seats for visitors. Seating is first-come, first-served, and, once seated, spectators are not allowed to come and go until the justices recess. A "three-minute line" is available to people just wanting a glimpse of the hearing.

The Court is open for oral arguments during two-week periods from the first Monday in October to May 1. Arguments are heard on Monday, Tuesday, and Wednesday of those weeks.

◼ Washington Today

Two centuries after the nation's founding, its seat of government was a city of contrasts. While tourists flocked to see the District of Columbia's fabled cherry blossoms, or the Smithsonian museums, or the stately government buildings, not far away in the poorer neighborhoods nightly gunfire symbolized an entirely different community. Washington was known in the 1980s as the "murder capital" because its

homicide rate was higher than that of any other U.S. city. In some areas drug wars imperiled innocent people in their homes and on the streets. Infant mortality was higher than in many Third World countries. Schools struggled against a pathetic dropout rate.

Yet as a new millennium approached, there were signs of hope. District voters elected a new government to replace one headed by a mayor who had gone to jail for drug use (and who on his return won a seat on the city council). Some old inner-city schools gleamed physically and in spirit. Residents reported fewer potholes and other signs of more efficient government. And, for a time at least, the murder rate dipped slightly.

Status of Statehood

The District of Columbia gained self-government in 1974, with an elected mayor and city council. But the District has voted in favor of becoming the fifty-first state, which Congress has yet to approve.

If D.C. eventually does become the state of "New Columbia," there is one problem: North Carolina already has the postal designation of NC.

Beltway Mentality

Issues thought to be of little interest outside Washington are said to be "inside the Beltway" issues. Capital Beltway is another name for Interstate 495, the sixty-mile highway that encircles Washington in Maryland and Virginia. Consulting firms that make their money off the federal government are sometimes called "Beltway bandits."

D.C. Stats

It takes more than a Capital Beltway to define the Washington area. In 1992 the federal government lumped the capital and its neighbor to the north into one giant Washington-Baltimore CMSA (Combined Metropolitan Statistical Area), stretching from Shepherdstown, West Virginia, on the west to Centreville on Maryland's Eastern Shore. It became the nation's fourth largest metropolitan area, with over 6 million people.

Even under the old configuration, the Washington metropolitan area ranked as the nation's eighth largest, with a population of 3.9 million, according to the 1990 census.

In several categories Washington ranked at the top: people with advanced college degrees, 16.6 percent; women in the labor force, 68.8 percent; median household income, $47,254; workers in executive and management positions, 20.0 percent.

Washington had the dubious honor of ranking second in commuting time to work: 29.5 minutes one-way, just under New York's 30.6 minutes.

Only in the percentage of people living below the poverty line did Washington rank at the bottom: 6.2 percent.

The "toughest job in the world"—President Kennedy in the oval office.

The Toughest Job in the World
The Presidency

When it was created by the Founders in 1787, the United States presidency was like no other institution. Today it has many imitators around the world—but no equal. No other chief executive of a free country has the powers, the responsibilities, or the prestige to match the American president's.

Yet, for all its originality, the Constitution placed few specific requirements on the president, other than to take the oath of office before starting the job. One of the other requirements is that the president "take Care that the Laws be faithfully executed." But, far from making the chief executive a mere caretaker, the "take care" provision gives the president much of the authority needed to provide leadership in good times and bad.

The presidency has been called "the toughest job in the world." Certainly it carries many headaches—and some presidents have visibly aged under the strain—but

most seem to relish the power and prestige, and they work hard to get the job and stay there. As Sen. Robert Dole once said when asked why he was running, "It's inside work with no heavy lifting."

◼ How Many Presidents: Forty-One or Forty-Two?

Although Bill Clinton is officially the forty-second president of the United States, he is only the forty-first person to hold the job. The difference is attributable to Grover Cleveland, whose terms in office (1884–1889 and 1893–1897) were nonconsecutive. Cleveland is therefore counted twice in the official tabulation of presidencies.

◼ Qualifications for the Top Jobs

To be president, a person must be at least thirty-five years old, a native-born citizen (or a citizen when the Constitution was adopted), and a resident of the United

States for fourteen years. Other than that, who gets the job is up to the voters.

The Constitution originally said nothing specific about the qualifications for being vice president of the United States. But the

Sub-zero temperatures forced the second inauguration of Ronald Reagan inside. The indoor ceremonies marked the first presidential inauguration held in the Capitol Rotunda.

Harry Truman's vice president, Alben W. Barkley, who was seventy-one when he was inaugurated in 1949 and seventy-five when he left office.

■ The Veep: Standby President?
Vice-Presidential Duties

Under the Constitution's separation-of-powers doctrine, the vice president is one of the few officials with a foot in both the legislative and executive branches. In Congress, the vice president presides over the Senate but may vote only to break a tie. In the executive branch, the vice president serves as a standby president. As historian Arthur M. Schlesinger, Jr., bluntly put it: "It is a doomed office. The Vice President has only one serious thing to do: that is, to wait around for the president to die."

In practice, modern presidents have found work for their vice presidents. Lyndon B. Johnson used Hubert H. Humphrey as a goodwill ambassador on Capitol Hill, and Jimmy Carter sent Walter F. Mondale abroad on substantive missions. Bill Clinton put Al Gore in charge of government revitalization.

But going to the funerals of foreign dignitaries remains a steady chore for vice presidents. As vice president, George Bush went to so many he coined a slogan: "You die, I fly."

Twelfth Amendment (1804), besides changing the method of electing the vice president, made it clear that the vice president had to meet the same few requirements as the president.

Separating the Men from the 'Boys'

Theodore Roosevelt was the youngest president—forty-two when he succeeded the assassinated William McKinley. John F. Kennedy was the youngest when elected—forty-three in 1960.

Ronald Reagan was the oldest president—sixty-nine when he took office in 1981 and seventy-seven when his second term ended. The next oldest, Dwight D. Eisenhower, was seventy when he left the White House.

The youngest vice president, at thirty-six, was John C. Breckinridge, who served with James Buchanan. The oldest was

Because the job is so unappealing, the vice presidency has attracted some laughable candidates—and indeed no other office has been the butt of so many jokes. At the same time, the vice presidency has supplied fourteen presidents, some of them among the "greats," and two winners of the Nobel Peace Prize, one who won as vice president (Charles G. Dawes) and the other who won after he became president (Theodore Roosevelt).

■ Taking Office

Date and Time

The Twentieth Amendment to the Constitution, ratified in 1933, was called the "lame-duck" amendment because it gave newly elected presidents and Congresses less time to wait until they replaced the outgoing lame ducks. It specified that congressional terms would expire at noon on January 3 after elections and that the four-year terms of the president and vice president would expire at noon on January 20. Before 1933 presidential inaugurations were held on March 4 as called for by a 1792 act of Congress.

Because in 1957 and 1985 inauguration days fell on a Sunday, Dwight Eisenhower and Ronald Reagan took the oath privately on the twentieth and again the next day in public.

Swearing-in Locales

George Washington first took the oath of office at Federal Hall on Wall Street in New York City. His second inauguration in 1793 and John Adams's in 1797 were held at Congress Hall in Philadelphia.

With one exception, later inaugurations took place at the Capitol in Washington, D.C., most often outdoors at the East Front portico.

Because of wartime austerity, Franklin D. Roosevelt's fourth swearing-in, held in 1945, took place at the South Portico of the White House.

Vice presidents assuming the presidency because of death have been sworn in at various locations, including an airport. Lyndon Johnson took the oath aboard *Air Force One* in Dallas following the assassination of John Kennedy in 1963. Johnson was the only president sworn in by a woman, federal district judge Sarah Tilghman Hughes.

'I do solemnly swear . . .'

Article II, section 1, of the Constitution requires the president to take the following oath of office:

I do solemnly swear (or affirm) that I will faithfully execute the Office of President of the

George Washington traveled from Mount Vernon to New York City to take the oath of office on April 30, 1789. He was greeted by cheering crowds at every stop throughout his journey.

United States, and will to the best of my Ability, preserve, protect and defend the Constitution of the United States.

George Washington added "so help me God" after reciting the oath, and all other presidents have done the same.

Only Franklin Pierce in 1853 chose to affirm the oath rather than swear it. He and his wife, Jane, had recently survived a train wreck that killed their eleven-year-old son, Benjamin. Believing that the tragedy was

Vice President Lyndon Johnson is flanked by his wife and Jacqueline Kennedy as he is sworn in as president following the assassination of President Kennedy in Dallas in 1963.

Vice President Calvin Coolidge was summering in Vermont when word arrived that President Warren Harding had died unexpectedly. Coolidge's father, a notary public, administered the presidential oath.

God's punishment for his sins, Pierce declined to place his hand on a Bible, which traditionally is opened to a passage the incoming president has chosen.

The chief justice of the United States usually administers the oath. In one of the rare exceptions, Calvin Coolidge was sworn in by his father, a notary public. Just to be sure, Coolidge repeated the oath before a judge a few days later.

Vice-Presidential Oath

On inauguration day, the vice president recites the following oath when taking office:

I, [name], do solemnly swear (or affirm) that I will support and defend the Constitution of the United States against all enemies, foreign and domestic, that I will bear true faith and allegiance to the same; that I take this obligation freely, without any mental reservation or purpose of evasion; and that I will well and faithfully discharge the duties of the office on which I am about to enter. So help me God.

The oath, the same one taken by all other federal officers except the president, is prescribed by Congress in the *United States Code.*

An associate justice of the Supreme Court usually swears in the vice president. The first vice president sworn in by a woman was Dan Quayle, who took the oath in

1989 from the first female justice, Sandra Day O'Connor.

He Talked Himself to Death

The longest inaugural address (8,445 words) may have led indirectly to the shortest presidential time in office (31 days). William Henry Harrison caught cold and developed pneumonia after speaking almost two hours in a driving rain. He died April 4, 1841. Ironically, he pledged in the speech to serve only one term.

George Washington gave the shortest inaugural speech, 135 words, the second time he was sworn in.

Memorable Inaugural Words

Transitions from one presidency to another in American history have often come at difficult times, calling for words of healing, encouragement, or inspiration. Here are excerpts from some of the finest examples of such speeches.

WITH MALICE TOWARD none, with charity for all, with firmness in the right as God gives us to see the right, let us strive on to finish the work we are in, to bind up the nation's wounds, to care for him who shall have borne the battle and for his widow and his orphan, to do all which may achieve and cherish a just and lasting peace among ourselves and with all nations.

—conclusion of Abraham Lincoln's second inaugural address, March 4, 1865

SO FIRST OF ALL LET ME assert my firm belief that the only thing we have to fear is fear itself—nameless, unreasoning, unjustified, terror which paralyzes needed efforts to convert retreat into advance. . . .

—Franklin D. Roosevelt's first inaugural address, March 4, 1933

LET THE WORD GO FORTH from this time and place, to friend and foe alike, that the torch has been passed to a new generation of Americans—born in this century, tempered by war, disciplined by a hard and bitter peace, proud of our ancient heritage—and unwilling to witness or permit the slow un-doing of those human rights to which this nation has always been committed, and to which we are committed today at home and around the world.

Let every nation know, whether it wishes us well or ill, that we shall pay any price, bear any burden, meet any hardship, support any friend, oppose any foe to assure the survival and the success of liberty. . . .

And so, my fellow Americans: ask not what your country can do for you—ask what you can do for your country. . . .

—John F. Kennedy's inaugural address, January 20, 1961

MY FELLOW AMERICANS, our long national nightmare is over. Our Constitution works; our great Republic is a Government of laws and not of men. . . .

As we bind up the internal wounds of Watergate, more painful and more poisonous than those of foreign wars, let us restore the golden rule to our political process, and let brotherly love purge our hearts of suspicion and of hate. . . .

—Gerald R. Ford's remarks on becoming president, August 9, 1974

Calvin Coolidge escorts Herbert Hoover to the Capitol for Hoover's presidential inauguration.

Having a Ball, Maybe

The inauguration of a new president is a time of great celebration, with parades, balls, and general merriment. But sometimes the excitement is marred by weather, bitterness, or bad timing, among other things. Here is a potpourri of inaugural firsts, good and bad.

✳ John Adams snubbed Thomas Jefferson's inauguration in 1801, John Quincy Adams boycotted Andrew Jackson's in 1829, and Andrew Johnson ignored Ulysses S. Grant's in 1869.

✳ The first inauguration captured on sound film was Herbert Hoover's in 1929.

✳ The first organized inaugural parade was for James Madison in 1809.

✳ Lyndon B. Johnson was the first president to review his inaugural parade from behind bulletproof glass, in 1965.

✳ Three inaugural parades were cancelled: by president-elect Warren Harding in 1921 out of concern for Woodrow Wilson's poor health; in 1945 because of World War II austerity; and in 1985 because of extremely cold weather that drove Ronald Reagan's second swearing-in inside the Capitol.

✳ Martha Washington was late arriving in New York from Virginia and missed the first inaugural ball, in 1789. But George had a ball, leading two cotillions and a minuet.

✳ Dwight Eisenhower set the precedent for multiple inaugural balls, with two in 1953. John Kennedy had five in 1961, George Bush had eleven in 1989, and Bill Clinton had ten in 1993.

✳ The old Pension Building, now the National Building Museum, fell into disuse for inaugural balls between 1909 and 1973, when one of Richard Nixon's parties was held there.

Contrasting Inaugurations

Except that they were both held by Democrats, the inaugurations of Andrew Jackson and John Kennedy could not have been more different. Jackson, disdaining the pomp of a parade, walked to the Capitol to be sworn in. Afterward, he threw open the White House to anyone who wanted to come. Thousands did and, as someone might say today, they trashed the place. They destroyed furniture, china, and glassware. It was a mess, but it was a great party for ordinary men and women who until then had never savored the rewards of political victory.

Jackson's election and inauguration symbolized the great change that had taken place in presidential politics. The two-party system and popular elections were finally in full vogue, enabling the rural, back-woods majority of the country to take power for the first time from the aristocratic elite that had held sway since the beginning of the Republic.

Kennedy's inauguration, while it also marked the passing of the torch to a new generation of Americans, was a model of decorum and good taste, from the poetry reading by Robert Frost to the dignified balls that closed out the day of celebration. Dress for the men in the ceremony was formal—top hats and tails. And on the in-

Jubilant throngs celebrated the inauguration of Andrew Jackson at the White House; the Kennedys ushered in the Camelot era with their formal inauguration ceremonies.

President Jimmy Carter and his family surprised the nation (and the Secret Service) when they emerged from their limousines to walk the parade route during Carter's inaugural parade in 1977. In 1993, the Clintons also walked part of the way to the White House.

augural platform were many of the 155 noted scholars, artists, and writers who had received special engraved invitations from Kennedy, including Nobel Prize novelist John Steinbeck. But the just plain folks were not left out of the celebration. Through the magic of television they enjoyed it in a way that Jackson's revelers never could have imagined.

Strolling Down the Avenue

Woodrow Wilson was the last president to ride to his inaugural in a horse-drawn carriage, in 1913. Jimmy Carter walked from Capitol Hill to the White House after his 1977 swearing-in, and George Bush walked part of the way in 1989, as did Bill Clinton in 1993.

■ The Long and Short of It

Grover Cleveland, the only president to serve nonconsecutive terms, made a comeback after being defeated for reelection in 1888. He won the popular vote by 100,000 votes that year against Republican Benjamin Harrison but lost in the electoral college, 233–168, largely because he had not carried his own state of New York with its 36 electoral votes. Four years later, Cleveland defeated Harrison and gained another term.

Presents and Vice Presidents Who Served Incomplete Terms

Some presidents served partial terms:

- *Died during first term:* William Henry Harrison, Zachary Taylor, James Garfield, Warren G. Harding, John F. Kennedy
- *Died during second term:* Abraham Lincoln, William McKinley
- *Died during fourth term:* Franklin D. Roosevelt
- *Resigned during second term:* Richard Nixon
- *Succeeded to office at midterm:* John Tyler, Millard Fillmore, Andrew Johnson, Chester A. Arthur, Theodore Roosevelt, Calvin Coolidge, Harry S. Truman, Lyndon B. Johnson, Gerald R. Ford

These vice presidents also served partial terms:

- *Died during first term:* Elbridge Gerry, William R. King, Henry Wilson, Thomas A. Hendricks, Garret A. Hobart, James S. Sherman
- *Died during second term:* George Clinton
- *Succeeded to presidency during first term:* Tyler, Fillmore, Andrew Johnson, Arthur, Theodore Roosevelt, Coolidge, Truman, Lyndon Johnson, Ford
- *Resigned during second term:* John C. Calhoun, Spiro T. Agnew
- *Appointed at midterm:* Ford, Nelson Rockefeller

IN MEMORY OF

PRESIDENT WM. H. HARRISON, WHO DEPARTED THIS LIFE, APRIL 4, 1841, AGED 68,

---

One-Day President?

His name is best known from Judy Garland's movie song "Atchison, Topeka, and the Santa Fe," but David Rice Atchison has another claim to fame: he may have been acting president for a day.

Atchison, a Missouri Whig, was president pro tempore of the Senate on March 4, 1849, when the terms of the president and vice president expired. Because it was a Sunday, the swearing-in of Zachary Taylor and Millard Fillmore was put off until the next day. Under law existing at the time, the president pro tem took over if the vice presidency was vacant, and in this case both of the top jobs were empty—leading Missourians to boast that Atchison became the interim president.

But most historians don't take the claim seriously. They list Taylor as becoming president at noon on March 4, Sunday or no Sunday. At any rate, the system has been changed since Atchison's day. The Twenty-fifth Amendment, ratified in 1967, provides for the appointment of a vice president if the office becomes vacant.

William Henry Harrison is acknowledged to have served the shortest time as president: thirty-one days from March 4 to April 4, 1841.

Two-Term Limit

Franklin Roosevelt served longer than any other president—twelve years and thirty-nine days. He was elected four times and would have served sixteen years had he not died on April 12, 1945.

No other president had sought more than two four-year terms. George Washington retired after eight years mostly for personal reasons; John Adams was denied reelection after one term; and Thomas Jefferson set a precedent by refusing a third term on philosophical grounds. He had argued for a term limit in the Constitution to prevent a president

'MR. GERGEN, THERE'S A GROWN-UP TO SEE YOU. SAYS HE'S TANNED, RESTED AND READY. SAYS YOU'D KNOW WHAT THAT MEANS... MR. GERGEN, LIKE AM I MISSING SOMETHING...?'

from gaining unchecked power for life.

The Twenty-second Amendment to the Constitution, ratified in 1951, fulfilled Jefferson's wish. It limited future presidents to two terms. Ironically, the limit has hurt only Republican presidents, even though the GOP pushed for it to avoid another FDR. Through 1992, no Democratic president since FDR had been elected more than once.

'He's Tanned, Rested, and Ready'

Richard Nixon is the only person elected twice as vice president (1952 and 1956) and twice as president (1968 and 1972). He left office August 9, 1974, because of the Watergate scandal, the first president to resign.

Could Nixon run again? Many Republicans wondered that aloud in 1992, when a poor economy endangered the Bush presidency. Since Nixon did not complete his second term, some argued that the two-term limit would not bar him, even though the amendment states, "No person shall be elected to the office of President more than twice. . . ."

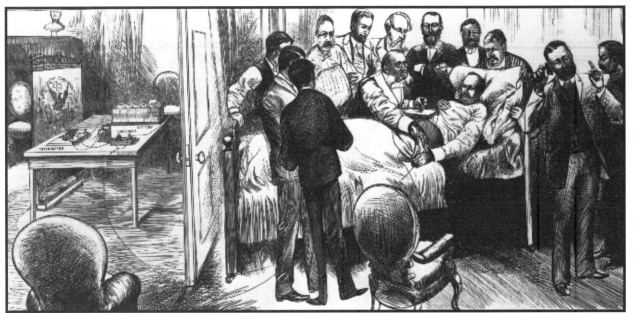

President Garfield struggles to recover from a wound inflicted by an assassin on July 2, 1881. Alexander Graham Bell, hoping to locate the bullet, listens with the telephone-like receiver of an electrical device he invented for detecting metal; steel springs in the mattress interfered.

■ Succession

Under the Presidential Succession Act of 1947, the line of succession to the presidency is vice president, Speaker of the House of Representatives, president pro tempore of the Senate, and then cabinet secretaries in the chronological order the departments were created: state, Treasury, defense, justice (the attorney general), interior, agriculture, commerce, labor, health and human services, housing and urban development, transportation, energy, education, and veterans affairs.

Congress amended the 1947 act as each new department was added.

Who's in Charge Here?

In the pandemonium after Ronald Reagan was shot in 1981, Secretary of State Alexander M. Haig, Jr., briefed the press in the absence of Vice President George Bush, who was out of town. Asked who was in charge, Haig erroneously replied that he was. "Constitutionally, gentlemen," he said, "you have the president, the vice president, and the secretary of state, in that order. . . ."

In fact, the Constitution leaves it to Congress to decide the line of succession after the vice president. Haig confused the current line, spelled out in 1947, with an earlier law that did have the secretary of state third in line.

Tyler's Precedent

One uncertainty facing early lawmakers was the extent of the vice president's powers in case of the president's death or "inability" to serve (as the Constitution originally put it). The first test came in 1841 when William Henry Harrison died after only a month in office and John Tyler became president. Tyler set precedent by assuming the office and title of president and serving out the rest of Harrison's term instead of calling a special election.

Presidential Disability

John Tyler's assumption of the title and powers of the presidency after the death of William Henry Harrison resolved most doubts about the vice president's rights in that situation, but questions still remained about what happened if the president were impaired but not dead. For example, Chester A. Arthur waited helplessly during the seventy-nine days that James Garfield lay in a coma before dying of an assassin's bullet. More recently, the health problems of President Dwight Eisenhower created periods when it was unclear whether Vice President Richard Nixon should have taken over some responsibilities. Eisenhower did authorize Nixon to act in case of nuclear attack.

The Twenty-fifth Amendment, ratified in 1967, empowered presidents to declare themselves disabled and put the vice president in charge. If a president is unwilling or unable to do so, the vice president and a majority of the cabinet may make that determination.

Twice during his presidency Ronald Reagan was temporarily incapacitated—when he was shot on March 30, 1981, and when he underwent cancer surgery on July 13, 1985. He did not invoke the Twenty-fifth Amendment either time, although he did make George Bush acting president

While president, Eisenhower suffered a heart attack, underwent surgery for ileitis, and had a stroke. His illnesses fueled efforts to develop a procedure for transferring power to the vice president when the president is incapacitated.

during the cancer operation. Bush spent the eight hours quietly at home.

Cleveland's Secret Operation

President Grover Cleveland went to great lengths in 1893 to hide his grim disability from the public and his detractors—he had cancer of the jaw, probably the result of his love for cigars. Surgery was needed, but an economic crisis loomed and Cleveland's advisers feared a panic if the story got out. They arranged to have the operation performed, supposedly while Cleveland was vacationing aboard a friend's yacht, the *Oneida,* anchored in New York's East River. From inside his mouth, much of Cleveland's upper left jaw was removed, distorting his face and speech until a rubber device restored a near-normal appearance and diction. While the press soon obtained a sketchy outline of the incident, it was twenty years—long after Cleveland's death from heart disease in 1908—before the full story emerged.

Appointed Vice Presidents

Gerald Ford and Nelson Rockefeller were appointed under the Twenty-fifth Amendment, which calls for the president to fill vice-presidential vacancies subject to approval of both houses of Congress. Richard Nixon appointed Ford to succeed Spiro T. Agnew, who resigned. Ford, who became president when Nixon resigned in 1974, then selected Rockefeller. Thus, Ford became the only nonelected vice president and president.

■ What Presidents Do

The U.S. president has a more difficult job than some other world leaders partly because of the American system of checks and balances. The president's power to govern is limited because it is shared with Congress and the Supreme Court, and each branch serves as a check on the other.

Hail to the Chief Executive

The president is first and foremost the chief executive. As head of the executive branch, the presidents acts as the main administrator, legislative leader, law enforcer, diplomat, military commander, head of state, party leader, and maker of economic policy.

Along with the vice president, the president is the only executive branch member directly elected by the people. The Constitution says simply: "The executive Power shall be vested in the President of the United States of America."

Within the executive branch, there is little democracy. The president is the boss. As Abraham Lincoln once put it in a disagreement with his cabinet, "Seven nays, one aye; the ayes have it."

Executive Office of the President

Together with the White House Office, which includes the chief of staff and other members of the president's inner circle, the supporting organizations of the presidency make up the Executive Office of the President (EOP). Since Franklin Roosevelt created it in 1939, the EOP has undergone many changes, with agencies coming and going, gaining or losing stature, and in general reflecting the dynamic nature of the U.S. presidency.

Throughout the lineup changes, two units have remained at the core of the EOP—the White House Office and the Office of Management and Budget (OMB), formerly the Bureau of the Budget. Under most recent presidents, the EOP also included the Vice President's Office, Office of Policy Development, National Security Council, National Space Council, National Economic Council, Council of Economic Advisers, Office of Science and Technology Policy, Council on Environmental Quality (CEQ), Office of Administration, and Office of the U.S. Trade Representative.

The president appoints the directors of EOP offices, subject to confirmation by the Senate.

Bush Administration's Budget for the Executive Office of the President

Office	No. of Employees	Amount
Office of National Drug Control Policy	130	$103,348,000
Office of Management and Budget	572	52,981,000
White House Office	414	35,385,000
Office of Administration	234	24,486,000
Office of the U.S. Trade Representative	162	21,697,000
Executive Residence of the White House	97	7,598,000
National Security Council	65	6,118,000
Office of Science and Technology Policy	43	4,446,000
Office of Policy Development	51	3,772,000
Council of Economic Advisers	41	3,428,000
Special Assistance to the President	26	3,150,000
Council on Environmental Quality	40	2,763,000
National Space Council	7	1,598,000
National Critical Materials Council	3	235,000

Billion-Dollar White House?

What it costs today to operate the Executive Office of the President (EOP), including the White House, is hard to pin down. Much of the expense is charged to other agencies, such as an estimated $185 million a year for *Air Force One* and other military transportation.

The Bush administration's final budget requested $281 million for the EOP, but a congressional subcommittee estimated the actual cost at closer to $1 billion. Besides the president's travel, the EOP budget did not include $140 million for the Secret Service, $90.6 million for White House communications operated by the Defense Department, $27 million for maintenance of presidential buildings other than the White House by the General Services Administration, $2.8 million for the upkeep of the White House grounds by the National Park Service, and $330,000 from the State Department for state dinners. Nor did it include numerous other hidden costs, such as the operation of Camp David, the pay of sixty-seven army drivers, or the Naval Imaging Command, which videotapes presidential activity.

Shortly after he took office in 1993 President Bill Clinton ordered cutbacks that affected the White House budget, including a staff reduction and restrictions on the use of military aircraft. He also proposed abolishing the Council on Environmental Quality and making the independent Environmental Protection Agency a cabinet department.

■ The President and the Executive Branch

The president's official cabinet is made up of the men and women who head the various departments of the executive branch. In 1992, there were fourteen such departments, and they formed the core of the executive branch. The attorney general heads the Justice Department. The other department heads are called secretaries.

For the first half of the country's existence, there were only five departments. In the second half, the number exploded, with nine more departments being added, including seven since the end of World War II in 1945.

The President's Cabinet

Establishment of the president's cabinet came about through practice rather than by law. George Washington began the tradition of meeting regularly with his department heads to get their advice on policy matters, and all other presidents have done the same.

In addition to the attorney general and the thirteen departmental secretaries who make up the basic cabinet, the vice presi-

Washington often made policy decisions after listening to his two most important and eloquent advisers, Secretary of State Thomas Jefferson and Secretary of the Treasury Alexander Hamilton, debate an issue. Secretary of War Henry Knox, Attorney General Edmund Randolph, and Postmaster General Samuel Osgood (not pictured) completed the cabinet.

with longtime officials and lobbyists that they begin to put the department's interests ahead of the president's. But the president can deal with this problem in ways not possible against unmovable bureaucrats who have civil service protection.

Presidents can and do fire cabinet officers who displease them. In 1983, for example, Gerald Ford sacked Agriculture Secretary Earl Butz for telling an off-color, racist joke. And in 1979 Jimmy Carter fired three cabinet members for disloyalty as part of a broader team shakeup. Usually, dismissals are handled more quietly, with firings masked as voluntary resignations, particularly if the president wins a second term and wants to bring in fresh players.

White House Interference

The reverse side of the "going native" coin has been a problem for some recent administrations. In such cases White House operatives called the shots in certain departments, leaving the affected department heads little more than figureheads. For example, before it was brought down by the Watergate scandal, the Nixon administration centralized power in the president and a few close aides such as H. R. Haldeman and John Ehrlichman. With few exceptions, cabinet members had little authority. National Security Adviser Henry A.

dent usually sits in on the meetings. Modern presidents also have given cabinet status to other top officials, such as the director of the Office of Management and Budget, the White House chief of staff, and the U.S. trade representative.

Kitchen Cabinet

The so-called kitchen cabinet is a group of friends and advisers whose opinions the president seeks. The term originated during the presidency of Andrew Jackson, who was said to have met sometimes with close associates in the White House kitchen.

'Marrying the Natives'

After they have been on the job awhile, cabinet secretaries have a tendency to "go native"—that is, they spend so much time

(left to right) **Henry Kissinger, John Ehrlichman, Richard Nixon, and Bob Haldeman meet in the Oval Office. Several officials in the Nixon administration, including Haldeman and Ehrlichman, were indicted in the aftermath of the Watergate investigation.**

Kissinger in effect ran the State Department before he replaced Secretary William P. Rogers in that office in 1973, during Nixon's second term.

■ Presidential Hiring and Firing

Presidents have the authority, subject to Senate approval, to appoint their own cabinet members, Supreme Court justices, federal judges, ambassadors, and other top government officials. Justices and judges have lifetime appointments, but most of the others serve at the pleasure of the president and can be fired for no cause.

Although they are overshadowed by the more glamorous cabinet and Supreme Court nominations, many thousands of appointments go to the Senate every year for confirmation under the "advice and consent" clause of the Constitution. The number of presidential nominations has declined since the peak of 186,264 reached in 1981–1982, the first year of the Reagan administration. In the 101st Congress (1989–1991), the Senate received 93,368 nominations from President George Bush, and it confirmed (approved) 88,078 of them, 48 were withdrawn, and 5,241 did not reach the Senate floor. Only one nomination—President Bush's appointment of former senator John G. Tower to be secretary of defense—was rejected outright by the Senate in 1989. Ironically, the Senate rejected him on the recommendation of a committee he formerly headed—Armed Services.

The Nays Have It

John Tyler had the poorest record of any president in obtaining Senate approval of his cabinet choices. In 1843–1844 the Senate rejected four of his nominees—

Roger Taney was the first cabinet nominee to be rejected by the Senate. Andrew Jackson had appointed him secretary of the Treasury after firing his predecessor during the national bank crisis. Taney served in the post for nine months before the Senate formally rejected him. He would later serve as the first Roman Catholic on the Supreme Court.

three times in the case of Caleb Cushing, whom Tyler wanted as secretary of the Treasury. Cushing and James S. Green, nominated for the same post, never served in Tyler's cabinet, but two other rejectees, David Henshaw for secretary of the navy and James M. Porter for secretary of war, eventually won confirmation.

Twice in 1925 the Senate rejected Calvin Coolidge's nomination of Charles B. Warren as attorney general. Four other presidents have had one cabinet choice rejected: Andrew Jackson's of Roger B. Taney for Treasury secretary, 1834; Andrew Johnson's of Henry Stanbery for attorney general, 1868; Dwight Eisenhower's of Lewis L. Strauss for secretary of commerce, 1959; and George Bush's of John Tower for secretary of defense, 1989. All the rejections except one—John Tower—came in the president's midterm.

Cushing and Taney also were rejected for the Supreme Court. Cushing never made it to the Court, but he served as attorney general in Franklin Pierce's cabinet. Eventually Taney was approved for the Court and became chief justice of the United States.

Janet Reno became the first woman appointed attorney general. Previous nominees had withdrawn their names after news surfaced that they failed to pay Social Security taxes for domestic help.

Cabinet Fixtures

Elliot L. Richardson holds the record for cabinet posts—four under two presidents. Under Nixon, he was secretary of health, education, and welfare, 1970–1973; secretary of defense, 1973; and attorney general, 1973. Under Ford, he served as secretary of commerce, 1976–1977.

Henry L. Stimson was in the cabinet of five presidents: as secretary of war, 1911–1913 (Taft and Wilson) and 1940–1945 (Franklin Roosevelt and Truman), and as secretary of state, 1929–1933 (Hoover).

Cabinet Holdovers

It is common for incoming presidents, especially of the same party, to keep some members of their predecessors' cabinets. In such cases the holdovers do not need to be reconfirmed by the Senate. The Constitution does not specify when a cabinet secretary's term ends.

In 1989 George Bush retained three of Ronald Reagan's cabinet members. Not counting cases in which the president died and the vice president took over, Bush's holdovers were the most since 1929 when Herbert Hoover succeeded Calvin Coolidge in a similar friendly takeover.

Firsts for Women in the Executive Branch

At the cabinet level, Frances Perkins was the first woman to serve; she became secretary of labor in 1933. The first female head of a new executive department was Oveta Culp Hobby, appointed secretary of health, education, and welfare in 1953.

Patricia Roberts Harris was the first African-American woman to serve in a president's cabinet. She served as secretary of housing and urban development, 1977–1979; health, education, and welfare, 1979–1980; and health and human services, 1980–1981.

Other women who have headed cabinet departments include Carla Anderson Hills, secretary of housing and urban development, 1975–1977; Juanita M. Kreps, secretary of commerce, 1977–1980; Shirley M. Hufstedler, secretary of education, 1979–1981; M. Margaret Heckler, secretary of health and human services, 1983–1985; Ann McLaughlin, secretary of labor, 1987–1989; Elizabeth H. Dole, secretary of transportation, 1983–1987, and secretary of labor, 1989–1990; Lynn M. Martin, secretary of labor, 1990–1993; Hazel R. O'Leary, secretary of energy, 1993–; Janet Reno, attorney general, 1993–; and Donna E. Shalala, secretary of health and human services, 1993–.

The first woman to head an independent agency was Virginia Mae Brown, who was designated chair of the Interstate Commerce Commission in 1969.

'Nannygate'

Bill Clinton's original nominee to head the Justice Department in 1993 was Zoë Baird, a Connecticut corporate lawyer. Her Senate confirmation seemed assured until she disclosed that she had illegally hired undocumented aliens as a babysitter and driver and had not paid Social Security taxes on their wages. After a few days of "Nannygate" commotion, Baird withdrew her name. Another leading contender, also a woman, dropped out for similar reasons. Clinton then nominated Janet Reno, an unmarried Miami prosecutor with no children. Reno quickly won confirmation as the first woman attorney general of the United States. Women's rights advocates said the episode pointed up a double standard: no one thought to ask male nominees about their child care arrangements.

Secretary of French Fries

Why french fries? "Because I wasn't good at hamburgers," explained Lynn M.

Lynn Martin donned the McDonald's uniform and worked the counter to show her concern for the American worker.

General Colin Powell, chairman of the Joint Chiefs of Staff, became a household name during the Persian Gulf crisis in 1990.

head the then-new Department of Housing and Urban Development (HUD). Weaver served two years as HUD secretary.

Since then at least one African-American has been in the cabinet of every president except Richard Nixon. They were William T. Coleman, Jr., secretary of transportation, 1975–1977; Patricia Roberts Harris, HUD secretary, 1977–1979, secretary of health, education, and welfare, 1979–1980, and secretary of health and human services (HHS), 1980–1981; Samuel R. Pierce, Jr., HUD secretary, 1981–1989; Louis W. Sullivan, HHS secretary, 1989–1993; Ron Brown, secretary of commerce, 1993–; Jesse Brown, secretary of veterans affairs, 1993–; Mike Espy, secretary of agriculture, 1993–; and Hazel R. O'Leary, secretary of energy, 1993–.

In 1989 President George Bush appointed an African-American army officer, Gen. Colin L. Powell, Jr., to the nation's highest military post—chairman of the Joint Chiefs of Staff.

'Mayor' Pierce

Samuel R. Pierce, Jr., kept a low profile as the lone African-American member of President Ronald Reagan's cabinet—so low that early in his presidency Reagan did not recognize his own secretary of housing and urban development. At a gathering of the

Martin, who as secretary of labor could be found working at McDonald's restaurants and other unlikely places. During her two years in the Bush cabinet, Martin tried her hand at hosting a TV show and getting behind the camera, operating a forklift, packing computer disks, grinding lenses, bookkeeping, cutting sugar cane, selling clothes, making egg rolls, and, of course, cooking french fries ("I was good at that").

She said the experience helped her to

understand the pride and problems of ordinary American workers. Her own background included teaching school and serving ten years as a Republican member of Congress from Illinois.

African-Americans in the Executive Branch

The first African-American cabinet member was Robert C. Weaver, appointed by President Lyndon Johnson in 1966 to nation's mayors in the Rose Garden, Reagan addressed Pierce as "Mr. Mayor" when he came through the receiving line.

The widely publicized gaffe was quickly forgotten, but Pierce's management of the Department of Housing and Urban Development proved to be an even greater embarrassment to the Reagan administration. After Reagan left office, investigators uncovered widespread corruption at HUD under Pierce. The secretary pleaded the Fifth Amendment to avoid self-incrimination when congressional committees tried to question him about the allegations.

Before going to HUD, Pierce had a distinguished career in New York where he was the first African-American to become a partner in a major law firm and the first African-American board member of two large corporations. He was also the first African-American to hold a subcabinet position at the Treasury Department, where he was general counsel in the Nixon administration.

Hispanics in the Cabinet

The first Hispanic member of a president's cabinet was Lauro S. Cavazos, appointed by Ronald Reagan in 1988 as secretary of education. Cavazos also held the post in the Bush administration until he resigned December 12, 1990.

Other Hispanics who have been cabinet secretaries are: Manuel Lujan, Jr., secretary of the interior, 1989–1993; Henry G. Cisneros, secretary of housing and urban development, 1993–; and Federico F. Peña, secretary of transportation, 1993–.

'I Refuse to Answer'

Three cabinet members have invoked the Fifth Amendment to avoid self-incrimination during congressional investigations. They are Secretary of the Interior Albert B. Fall and Secretary of the Navy Edwin Denby, both in connection with the Teapot Dome scandal of the 1920s, and Samuel R. Pierce, Jr., while testifying about corruption in the Department of Housing and Urban Development during his tenure as secretary under President Ronald Reagan.

■ Executive Branch Scandals

Considering its huge size (almost three million employees in 1993), scandals in the executive branch are comparatively rare. But they tend to make bigger headlines than those in the legislative branch, especially if they involve the White House. A case in point is Watergate, the most publicized American scandal of all time and the only one serious enough to drive a president from office.

Because of the government's system of checks and balances, it's Congress's job to act as a watchdog over the executive branch. And when it sniffs a juicy scandal it goes after the facts with vigorous investigations and no-holds-barred televised hearings. The spacious Senate Caucus Room has provided some of the most-watched dramas in TV history.

Conversely, the Justice Department keeps a watchful eye on Congress, and FBI sting operations have exposed Capitol Hill corruption and sent more than a few lawmakers to jail.

Both branches naturally would rather find dirt in the other's camp than in their own. Recognizing this reluctance to investigate one's own boss or close associates, Congress since 1978 has requested special counsels (formerly called special prosecutors) independent of the attorney general to investigate major executive scandals and, if warranted, to bring charges.

The Media and Scandals

Changes in journalistic ethics and public tastes have contributed to the impression that government is more scandal-ridden than in the past. For example, reporters and photographers used to hide or at least downplay such things as President Franklin Roosevelt's paralysis and the rumored mar-

A Watergate Pop Quiz

What started it? A break-in on June 17, 1972, at Democratic National Headquarters in the Watergate office/hotel complex in Washington, D.C.

Who discovered the break-in A security guard, Frank Wills, who noticed that a piece of tape on a door lock had been replaced after he removed it. He called the D.C. police (and later played himself in a movie about the scandal, *All the President's Men*).

Who was arrested inside? Four anti-Castro Cubans from Miami—Bernard L. Barker, Virgilio R. Gonzalez, Eugenio R. Martinez, and Frank Sturgis—and James W. McCord, Jr., security director for CREEP, the Committee for the Reelection of the President (Richard Nixon).

Who was arrested elsewhere? G. Gordon Liddy and E. Howard Hunt, Jr., the burglary's directors.

What did they steal? Nothing. They were caught in the act and probably were not there to steal but to bug the office of DNC chairman Lawrence F. O'Brien.

Who at first denied any White House complicity? Nixon, his campaign manager and former attorney general John N. Mitchell, and White House press secretary Ronald L. Ziegler, who dismissed the break-in as a "third-rate burglary."

Who exposed White House involvement? Washington Post reporters Bob Woodward and Carl Bernstein, who pursued the story after Nixon won reelection in 1972 and later wrote *All the President's Men*.

Who was Woodward's secret informant? The still-secret "Deep Throat."

Who tried the Watergate burglars? Federal judge John J. Sirica.

Who was chairman of Senate Watergate Committee? Sam J. Ervin, Jr., Democrat from North Carolina.

Who disclosed the Oval Office taping system? Alexander P. Butterfield, a former White House aide, to a Senate investigator on July 13, 1973. Three days later he discussed the bugging system in public testimony.

What was the "Saturday Night Massacre"? Chain reaction on October 20, 1973, after Nixon ordered removal of special prosecutor Archibald Cox, who was fired by Acting Attorney General Robert Bork after Attorney General Elliot Richardson and his deputy, William D. Ruckelshaus, refused the order and resigned.

Who was Cox's successor? Leon Jaworski.

What were the consequences for President Nixon? The House Judiciary Committee approved three articles of impeachment July 27–30, 1974, charging obstruction of justice, abuse of powers, and contempt of Congress.

What was the "smoking gun"? Tape of June 23, 1972, on which Nixon is heard ordering a halt to the FBI's investigation of the burglary. Nixon released the tape August 5, 1974, to comply with a July 24 Supreme Court ruling.

Who Won? Who Lost? On August 9, 1974, Richard Nixon became the first president in history to resign. The new president, Gerald Ford, pardoned Nixon on September 8 for any crimes he may have committed as president. Jailed for the burglary or coverup were the seven Watergate burglars plus at least seven others, including Nixon's first attorney general and campaign manager John N. Mitchell and former Nixon aides H. R. Haldeman, John D. Ehrlichman, John W. Dean III, Charles W. Colson, Jeb Stuart Magruder, and Egil Krogh, Jr.

Nashville lawyer Fred D. Thompson, minority counsel on the Watergate committee, went on to a successful career as a Hollywood character actor.

✍ ✍ ✍ ✍ ✍ ✍ ✍ ✍ ✍ ✍ ✍ ✍ ✍ ✍ ✍ ✍ ✍ ✍ ✍ ✍

ital infidelities of FDR and John Kennedy. Today, in an era of supermarket tabloids and gossip TV, sleaze seems to win out if it's there, and the public appears eager to read and hear about it.

'Petticoat Wars'

One of the earliest and most bizarre executive branch scandals centered on Peggy Eaton, the wife of President Andrew Jackson's secretary of war, John Eaton. The other cabinet wives refused to accept Mrs. Eaton into Washington society because of her allegedly promiscuous past. Although Jackson sided with the Eatons, the so-called petticoat wars escalated, disrupting cabinet affairs for two years. In 1831 Secretary of State Martin Van Buren resigned along with Eaton, permitting Jackson to shake up his cabinet. Jackson rewarded Van Buren in 1832 by dumping Vice President John C. Calhoun and replacing him with Van Buren, who won the presidency four years later.

Greed under Grant

Ulysses S. Grant, the victorious Civil War general, was less successful in politics than on the battlefield. He was honest but many of his appointees were not, and his administration was scarred by scandals. Both of his vice presidents, Schuyler Colfax and Henry Wilson, were implicated in the Crédit Mobilier scandal of the transcontinental railroad project. Other political associates were linked to the 1870s Whiskey Ring plot to avoid liquor taxes through bribery. And Grant's secretary of war, William Belknap, resigned to escape impeachment for bribery.

Teapot Dome

The first cabinet officer to go to jail was Albert B. Fall, secretary of the interior in the corruption-riddled administration of Warren G. Harding (1921–1923). After

managing to have naval oil reserves at Teapot Dome, Wyoming, and Elk Hills, California, transferred to his control, Fall opened the reserves to drilling without competitive bidding. The sure-thing leases enriched his cronies, including oil pioneer Harry Sinclair, and Fall was convicted of accepting a bribe in return. Sinclair also went to prison.

Sherman Adams

President Dwight Eisenhower's chief of staff, Sherman Adams, was forced to resign in 1958 amid accusations that he interceded with federal regulatory agencies in behalf of Bernard Goldfine, a Boston industrialist who had given Adams an oriental rug, a vicuña coat, and other gifts. Adams, a former governor of New Hampshire, already was unpopular with his fellow Republicans for tightly restricting access to the president. When questioned by a House committee about Goldfine, Adams refused to answer and was convicted later of contempt of Congress, contempt of court, and tax evasion.

Iran-Contra

In 1986 the Reagan administration was shaken by revelations of a high-level secret operation that sold arms to Iran and used the proceeds to help antigovernment guerrillas ("contras") fighting in Nicaragua. Congress had barred both aid to the contras and arms sales to Iran, where American embassy personnel had been held hostage for 444 days during the Carter administration.

At a dramatic news conference on November 13, President Ronald Reagan and Attorney General Edwin Meese III confirmed the illegal arms sales, which had been reported abroad. Reagan announced the resignation of his national security adviser, Vice Adm. John M. Poindexter, and the firing of Poindexter's aide, Marine Lt. Col. Oliver L. North. The president said he had authorized some arms sales to Iran to help gain the release of hostages held in Lebanon by Iran sympathizers but that he had been deceived about the scope and implications of North's operation.

Details of the Iran-contra affair emerged over the next five years in congressional hearings and prosecutions brought by special counsel Lawrence E. Walsh. Both North and Poindexter were found guilty, but in 1991 North's conviction was set aside as tainted by the publicity of his congressional testimony under partial immunity. Poindexter's charges were dismissed.

On Christmas Eve 1992, after he had

been defeated for reelection, President George Bush pardoned six former officials linked to the Iran-contra affair, including former national security adviser Robert C. McFarlane, who had been convicted, and former defense secretary Caspar Weinberger, who had recently been indicted.

◼ The President and Congress

Legislative Leader

The average American probably overestimates the president's power. Whenever things go wrong, or right, with the country, the man or woman in the street tends to blame, or credit, the president. But by the same token people tend to underestimate the president's role in lawmaking. If a law is unpopular, Congress takes the heat. Often overlooked is the fact that no bill passed by Congress becomes law unless the president signs it or, under special circumstances, allows it to become law without a signature.

The Power of Suggestion

Modern presidents do not sit back and wait for Congress to send them something to sign or veto. They generally take the lead in suggesting laws and programs, and a suggestion from the president carries a lot of weight. The bill may not pass, but Congress is forced to react by holding hear-

The state of Wisconsin celebrated its Diamond Jubilee Cheese Week in April 1939. In honor of the event, a bust of Vice President John Nance Garner was sculpted in cheddar cheese and presented to his wife in the nation's capital.

ings and giving the proposal serious consideration.

OMB: Legislative Traffic Cop

Over the years, the Executive Office of the President has become a powerful instrument in the drafting and promotion of presidential legislation. The authority of the Office of Management and Budget, one organization within EOP, goes far beyond the budget. No proposal from the executive branch goes to Congress without

OMB's approval. And no act of Congress goes to the president until OMB reviews it and recommends whether it should be signed or vetoed. OMB even has the final say on the content of the many blank forms used by federal agencies.

Presidential Arm-Twisting

Early presidents carried the separation of powers to extremes and stayed out of the legislative process. But that began to change early in the twentieth century.

Woodrow Wilson addresses a joint session of Congress on the afternoon of February 26, 1917.

Woodrow Wilson met weekly with Texas Democrat John Nance Garner, who would slip through a White House side door to brief the president on what the House Ways and Means Committee was up to.

Garner, later Speaker of the House, was the first vice president to serve under Franklin Roosevelt, who bombarded Congress with proposed legislation during his first hundred days in office in 1933.

Dwight Eisenhower was the first president to formalize White House lobbying.

He created the Office of Congressional Relations, headed by experienced Capitol Hill hand Bryce Harlow.

State of the Union

The Constitution says that the president "shall from time to time give to the Congress Information of the State of the Union," but it does not say that it has to be delivered personally. Presidents George Washington and John Adams did appear personally, but Thomas Jefferson began a long tradition of submitting the report in writing.

Not until 1913 did Woodrow Wilson revive the State of the Union address, which presidents since have used with varied success. Former actor Ronald Reagan was the acknowledged master of the televised occasion. In 1988 he dramatically plopped down a 3,296-page bill to illustrate that the budget process had gotten out of hand.

A little-known fact is that one cabinet member is always designated to be absent during the State of the Union address. Otherwise, with the entire line of succession in one room, a disaster could leave the nation without a president.

Head for the Hill

Next to the inaugural address, the annual State of the Union address is the most publicized of any president's routine speeches. It brings together in the House of Representatives chamber a joint meeting of Congress, the cabinet, the Supreme Court, the Joint Chiefs of Staff, and a prestigious list of guests headed by the first lady.

Because it usually takes place in January or early February, some new presidents are reluctant to give the State of the Union so soon after the January 20 swearing-in. Dwight Eisenhower felt that way, but he delivered it anyway on February 2, 1953.

Today, State of the Union addresses are a prime-time television event.

His successor, John Kennedy, did it twice —ten days after taking office and again in May 1961.

Richard Nixon held off for a year, until January 22, 1970, before giving his first State of the Union speech. Every other president since World War II who has taken office in a change of party has given a major address to Congress shortly after taking office. Bill Clinton was no exception. He spoke to Congress in his first month as president.

By Another Name

The saying "if it swims like a duck and quacks like a duck, it must be a duck" does not always apply to the State of the Union address. It may sound like it and be given at the customary time, but the president may have another name for it.

For example, Jimmy Carter's premier address to Congress in April 1977 was on energy, not on the overall state of the Union. Ronald Reagan's speech in February 1981 was on the economy. After he recovered from being shot, Reagan gave another speech in April and again focused on economic matters.

Taking his cue from Reagan, Bill Clinton gave an economic speech in his first formal Hill appearance, February 17, 1993, following up a televised speech to the nation two days earlier.

Of the new, change-of-party presidents since 1945, only Eisenhower and Kennedy called their first speeches to Congress State of the Union addresses. Actually, the formal title is not that old anyway. It began with Harry Truman in 1947, although Woodrow Wilson in 1913 had revived the custom of annual presidential speeches to Congress.

More Presidential Speechifying

Modern television audiences are accustomed to those grand spectacles of the president speaking to Congress in the House chamber, with the Speaker and vice president seated on the dais behind him. But such occasions are a fairly recent development in the history of presidential-congressional relations.

From George Washington to Bill Clinton, only fifteen of the forty-one presidents personally appeared before Congress to push their programs. And all but two of those were twentieth-century presidents.

Washington made ten appearances and

his successor, John Adams, made six. After that the custom fell into disuse until the administration of Woodrow Wilson, who still holds the record: twenty-six appearances between 1913 and 1919. Others who frequently spoke to Congress were Franklin Roosevelt, sixteen times; Harry Truman, seventeen times; and Ronald Reagan, eleven times. True to his nickname, Calvin "Silent Cal" Coolidge spoke only twice on Capitol Hill.

■ Presidents, Congress, and Foreign Affairs

Divided Authority

What little diplomatic power the president has under the Constitution is shared with Congress. Presidents can make treaties, if two-thirds of the Senate approves, and they can appoint ambassadors and other ministers, subject to Senate confirmation. That's about it.

Mostly, presidents have made themselves important in foreign affairs through leadership and adroit use of their other powers, such as the veto and command of the military. In what has been called "an invitation to struggle" with Congress, modern presidents have gained the upper hand in foreign policy.

A Little Diplomacy, Please

Theodore Roosevelt's adage "Speak softly and carry a big stick" has served presidents well in foreign affairs. No matter how softly presidents speak as the nation's chief diplomat, the world listens because they are also the commander in chief of a powerful military force.

TR's own sallies into diplomacy made possible the building of the Panama Canal and helped to end the Russo-Japanese War in 1905, a feat that earned him the Nobel Peace Prize. Other presidents, even some with lackluster records at home, have made history in their dealings with foreign

countries. Jimmy Carter, for example, achieved the Camp David peace accords between Egypt and Israel, among other notable acts. Yet he is also remembered for the embarrassing Iran hostage crisis.

Treaty Maker

Presidents make deals with other countries in two ways: with treaties and with executive agreements. A treaty is the more formal of the two and requires approval by two-thirds of the Senate. It may be with one country or more than one country (multilateral).

In 1825 the Senate killed its first treaty, one with Colombia on African slave trade. Since then, most recently in 1983, nineteen other treaties have failed to win Senate approval, including in 1920 the famous Treaty of Versailles after World War I.

The president decides whether to go for a treaty or an executive agreement, and the latter usually wins. In the history of the country there have been only 1,523 treaties (through 1990), compared with 13,612 executive agreements.

Many executive agreements carry out the terms of treaties or acts of Congress. An example is President Harry Truman's agreement establishing the United Nations headquarters in New York, after Congress okayed the idea.

Theodore Roosevelt's most famous act during his first term as president was acquiring the land for the Panama Canal. Colombia owned Panama and refused to give the United States rights to a canal zone. A determined Roosevelt supported a Panamanian revolution to overthrow Colombian rule. The new Panamanian government, of course, agreed to lease the zone to the United States. Here, Theodore Roosevelt runs an American steam shovel at Culebra Cut, Panama Canal, in 1906.

Panama Canal Brawl

The fact that only twenty U.S. treaties have died in the Senate does not tell the full story. One that survived barely got out alive after some of the most ferocious fighting ever witnessed on Capitol Hill. It was President Jimmy Carter's proposal to turn over the Panama Canal to Panama by the year 2000.

Panamanians had resented U.S. ownership of the canal on their soil. For years every president had supported the transfer, but none until Carter had tried to make it happen. Emotions ran high after the treaty was signed, and opponents tried hard to block it in the Senate. Former California governor Ronald Reagan, who would unseat Carter in 1980, was among the most outspoken. "We built it, we paid for it, we own it," he said of the canal.

In spring 1978 the Senate approved the treaty by just one vote more than the two-thirds necessary. In all, the debate had taken thirty-eight days, the longest since the Treaty of Versailles. In 1992 Panama's Gen. Manuel Noriega became the first foreign head of state convicted in U.S. courts. He was tried for drug trafficking.

We'll Hold the Coats

Although later presidents sometimes got into hot water by involving the United States in foreign disputes, such as Vietnam, George Washington set an important precedent by keeping the country out of one. In 1793, without congressional approval, he declared U.S. neutrality in the war between Britain and France. By doing so, he showed that presidents don't need to wait until Congress tells them what to do.

Buying Louisiana

Thomas Jefferson pioneered in the use of executive agreements to take major action in foreign affairs without waiting for Senate approval. In 1803 he doubled the size of the United States by agreeing to buy the Louisiana Territory from France for $15 million, or about four cents an acre. Fearing that Napoleon might change his mind, Jefferson delivered payment before asking the Senate to approve the deal—which it eventually did.

Monroe's Doctrine

James Monroe did not consult Congress in 1823 when he warned European powers to keep their hands off the Western Hemisphere. At the time, Spain and Russia were eyeing territory in South America and Alaska. The so-called Monroe Doctrine gave a

Thomas Jefferson originally set out to buy only the port of New Orleans, but the French offered to sell the entire Louisiana Territory, which stretched from New Orleans to present-day Montana.

new dimension to presidential diplomacy. It paved the way for future presidents to lay down broad policies that they expected other countries to respect.

Theodore Roosevelt went further, declaring that the United States would police "chronic wrongdoing or impotence" in the hemisphere. Under the Roosevelt Corollary, U.S. troops have since intervened in several countries, including the Dominican Republic, Cuba, Nicaragua, Grenada, and Panama.

President vs. Congress

Congressional backlash against presidential assertiveness in diplomacy killed Woodrow Wilson's proposal for a strong League of Nations after World War I. The Senate defeated the peace treaty that Wilson helped to negotiate at Versailles, France, in 1919. By keeping the United States out of the League, the defeat ensur-ed that the League would never be effective.

The power pendulum swung back to

After World War I, uneasiness about surrendering national sovereignty to the League of Nations was widespread. In this cartoon President Wilson offers the peace dove an olive branch while it asks, "Isn't this a stick?"

the presidency when the United States entered World War II in 1941, and it has remained poised there ever since. In 1945 Harry Truman was instrumental in forming the United Nations, an even stronger world body than Wilson's League of Nations.

War Powers

Under the Constitution, only Congress can declare war, but the president is the commander in chief. In that capacity presidents have committed U.S. military forces to almost two hundred overseas conflicts large and small, only five of which were wars formally declared by Congress.

Undeclared Wars

Undeclared conflicts fought by the United States have included relatively minor actions, such as the invasion of Grenada in 1983 and the capture of Panamanian dictator Manuel Noriega in 1989, as well as some of the longest and costliest wars in U.S. history, such as the Korean War in the 1950s and the Vietnam War in the 1960s and 1970s. Official reasons for the actions usually fell into two classes: to protect American lives, as in Grenada after a Marxist coup and in Panama after Noriega was indicted for drug trafficking; or to help democratic allies such as South Korea and

The Five 'Official' Wars

• War of 1812 against Britain, declared by Congress in June 1812 and ended by the Treaty of Ghent in 1814. The dispute arose from British seizures of American merchant ships and arms shipments to hostile Indians.

• War with Mexico, declared by Congress in 1846 and ended by the Treaty of Guadalupe Hidalgo in 1848. This dispute arose when Texas, which had been annexed by the United States, claimed land occupied by Mexico. The Treaty of Guadalupe Hidalgo gained California for the United States and set the Rio Grande as the border between Mexico and Texas. Land occupied by Mexico but claimed by Texas, which had been annexed by the United States, was the war's justification.

• War with Spain, declared by Congress in 1898 with public support for rescuing Cuba from tyranny. The war ended the same year when Spain agreed to free Cuba and cede Puerto Rico to the United States. After the war in 1899, Spain agreed in the Treaty of Paris to grant the Philippines to the United States for $20 million.

• World War I, declared by Congress in 1917 to halt Germany's aggression in Europe and submarine attacks on American vessels. An armistice stopped the fighting in 1918 and the Treaty of Versailles ended the war in 1919.

• World War II, declared by Congress against Japan, Germany, and Italy after Japan attacked Pearl Harbor on December 7, 1941. Their surrender ended the war in 1945.

First Lady Barbara Bush accompanied her husband to Saudi Arabia over the Thanksgiving holiday during Operation Desert Shield. They celebrated Thanksgiving Day in a desert encampment with the troops.

South Vietnam resist Communist invaders.

Although Congress has not declared war since World War II, it has supported some presidential use of force, including U.S. participation in the United Nations effort that ousted Iraqi forces from Kuwait in 1991.

War Satchel

Speaking of war, no matter where they go, modern presidents are accompanied by the "football," the presidential emergency satchel containing the secret codes needed to deal with threats to national security.

War Powers Act

Frustrated by its lack of a say in U.S. war policy, Congress in 1973 passed the War Powers Resolution (sometimes called the War Powers Act), which requires the president to notify Congress within forty-eight hours after sending U.S. troops into combat situations. Any such commitment would have to end in sixty days unless Congress authorizes the troops to stay.

President Richard Nixon's veto of the resolution was overridden by Congress.

Between 1975 and late 1992, four presidents—Gerald Ford, Jimmy Carter, Ronald Reagan, and George Bush—sent twenty-five such notifications to Congress. They included Carter's 1980 attempt to rescue U.S. embassy hostages in Iran, Reagan's 1986 bombing strikes against Libya, and Bush's 1990 deployment of U.S. forces to Saudi Arabia after Iraq invaded Kuwait.

■ Executive Orders

Most of the president's powers are *implied.* They have evolved over time from a reading between the lines of the Constitution rather than from what the document actually says (which is very little on this point). One of the major implied powers is that of issuing executive orders. These directives usually affect only government agencies or officials, but sometimes their impact is almost as widespread as a law of Congress.

By the Numbers

Beginning with George Washington (who issued a mere eight), presidents have issued between fifteen thousand and fifty thousand executive orders. No one knows just how many orders most presidents signed because numbering didn't begin until 1907 and went back only to Abraham Lincoln. Records before that were too spotty for accurate counting.

One of Bill Clinton's first actions as president was to order a cutback of 100,000 federal jobs by 1995. That was Executive Order 12839, signed February 10, 1993.

The president who served the longest, Franklin Roosevelt, holds the record for executive orders—3,522 for an annual average of 285.64 in 12.33 years. Among FDR's successors, George Bush had the lowest average—about forty-one a year over four years.

By law all executive orders are noted in the daily *Federal Register*. But those dealing with secret national security matters are listed by number only, with no text.

It's the Law

Executive orders carry the force of law, even though Congress has no part in them. Presidents in fact have used them in sensitive areas, such as discrimination, where an action might have little chance of getting through Congress. For example, Harry Truman integrated the armed services in 1948 by Executive Order 9981. In 1993 gay rights advocates cited Truman's action to support President Clinton's pledge to lift the military ban on homosexuals.

Veto Vital Statistics

- Total bills vetoed from 1789 to 1992: 2,513, of which Congress overrode 104
- Most bills vetoed: Franklin Roosevelt, 635, and Grover Cleveland, 584. Cleveland's average of 73 a year over eight years exceeded Roosevelt's average of 53 over twelve years
- Most vetoes overridden: Andrew Johnson, 15 of 29
- First president since Harry Truman to have vetoes overridden by Congress controlled by his own party: Jimmy Carter, 2 of 31

- Presidents who used vetoes heavily with few overrides: Ulysses S. Grant, 4 of 93; Franklin Roosevelt, 9 of 635; Harry Truman, 12 of 250; Cleveland, 7 of 584; McKinley, 0 of 42; Theodore Roosevelt, 1 of 82; Dwight Eisenhower, 2 of 181; John Kennedy, 0 of 21; Lyndon Johnson, 0 of 30; Ronald Reagan, 9 of 78; and George Bush, 1 of 44
- Most bills "pocket vetoed" (not signed within ten days after Congress adjourned): Franklin Roosevelt, 263

■ The Ultimate Firepower: The Veto

The veto is the president's ultimate weapon in fighting for or against congressional legislation. A bill cannot become a law unless the president signs it, or unless Congress overrides the veto by a two-thirds majority of each house.

Not in the Constitution

The word *veto* (Latin for "I forbid") does not appear in the Constitution. But the presidential veto power is set forth in Article I, section 7, which gives the president ten days (excluding Sundays) to sign a bill or return it to Congress with objections. A bill not signed within ten days becomes

A popular and forceful president, Andrew Jackson was caricatured by his opponents as a despotic monarch because he expanded the powers of the president at the expense of the legislature. This caricature charges that Jackson exceeded his authority by vetoing the 1832 bill to recharter the National Bank.

law without the president's signature unless Congress has adjourned, in which case the bill is said to be "pocket vetoed" (or, as the Constitution actually says, "[I]t shall not be a Law").

Early presidents used the veto sparingly, thinking its purpose was to block defective legislation. Three of the first six presidents (John Adams, Thomas Jefferson, and John Quincy Adams) vetoed no bills. Andrew Jackson began the practice of rejecting legislation he didn't like. He vetoed twelve bills and had none overridden by Congress.

Item Veto

Unlike the governors of most states, the president cannot pick and choose among items in an appropriations bill, crossing out items thought to be wasteful. It's all or nothing. A president either signs the whole bill or vetoes it, even if only one item out of hundreds is distasteful.

Since the 1870s many presidents, especially former governors with item veto experience, have sought that power from Congress. One ex-governor, Franklin Roosevelt, gained House approval for an item veto in 1938, but the Senate killed it. Ronald Reagan and Bill Clinton, both former governors, sought the item veto, as did George Bush.

Most item veto campaigns have called for a constitutional amendment, but in the late 1980s almost half the Senate proposed a two-year trial run. It went nowhere.

■ Pardon *You?*

The Constitution (Article II, section 2) empowers the president to grant pardons or reprieves for federal offenses, except in impeachment cases. A pardon wipes out guilt and punishment, as if the offense had never been committed. A reprieve reduces the offender's punishment.

A pardon may be individual or blanket, applying to groups of people. Blanket pardons are called *amnesties*. A pardon may be unconditional or it may have strings attached. Congress has no say in the matter.

Presidents Abraham Lincoln and Andrew Johnson signed amnesties for Confederate soldiers and political leaders. Presidents Gerald Ford and Jimmy Carter did the same for Vietnam War draft evaders.

Labor leader Jimmy Hoffa received a conditional pardon. President Richard Nixon pardoned Hoffa on the condition that he never return to union activities.

Ford's Pardon of Nixon

The first president ever to resign from office, Richard Nixon, is also the only former president granted a presidential pardon. Nixon received a "full, free, and absolute pardon" from his successor, Gerald Ford, on September 8, 1974. Following protocol, Nixon had submitted his resignation to Secretary of State Henry Kissinger on August 9. Ford's pardon protected Nixon from prosecution in connection with his role in the scandal that ended his presidency—the coverup of the 1972 burglary at Democratic National Headquarters in Washington's Watergate office/hotel complex.

By resigning, Nixon ended the impeachment proceedings he faced in the House. Because it was no longer an impeachment case, Ford was free to grant the pardon.

Bush's Pardon of Weinberger

On Christmas Eve 1992, President George Bush put the final touches on his holiday gift for former secretary of defense Caspar Weinberger and five others who had been indicted or convicted in the Iran-contra scandal of the Reagan administration. It was a "full, complete, and unconditional" pardon. All had been charged with lying to or withholding information from Congress.

Besides Weinberger, those pardoned were former national security adviser Robert C. McFarlane; former CIA officials Clair E. George, Alan D. Fiers, Jr., and Duane R. Clarridge; and former State Department official Elliott Abrams. All except Weinberger and Clarridge already had been convicted or had pleaded guilty. Weinberger had been facing trial on charges that he withheld diary notes from Congress, including some that indicated that Bush, as vice president, had endorsed the plan to sell arms to

Iran and use the money to help the rebels (contras) in Nicaragua.

At the same time, Bush pardoned eighteen other persons sentenced in unrelated cases, including a postal worker given probation in 1971 for stealing three letters.

■ Executive Privilege

When from time to time presidents have had Congress breathing down their necks demanding records or testimony, some have claimed *executive privilege,* thereby rejecting congressional demands. This means that as a separate but equal branch of government, the executive has the right to withhold information from the legislative branch. Although the right is not spelled out in the Constitution, presidents since George Washington have used it. Congresses, however, have disputed the notion, and it remains a continuing subject of litigation.

Watergate Ruling

A clash over executive privilege was at the heart of the Watergate scandal that brought down the presidency of Richard Nixon in 1974. Nixon tried to withhold tapes and documents showing whether he had helped to conceal White House involvement in the 1972 break-in at Democratic headquarters in the Watergate of-

fice/hotel complex in Washington, D.C. The Supreme Court ruled that executive privilege is not absolute, and that in this case Nixon had to give up the tapes. He complied but then resigned on August 9, 1974, ending congressional efforts to impeach him for defying committee demands for the tapes.

Post-Executive Privilege?

Even after they have left office, some presidents have claimed executive privilege in refusing to testify before congressional committees. In the nineteenth century, John Tyler was the only former president to appear before a committee, in 1846. He had been subpoenaed to answer questions about allegations made against his former secretary of state, Daniel Webster.

In the twentieth century, several former presidents testified voluntarily on various matters. In 1953 Harry Truman became the first former president since Tyler to be subpoenaed to testify (about an alleged communist). He refused, claiming executive privilege, and the committee backed down. Another committee also backed down in 1977 when Richard Nixon refused to testify, using the Truman case as a precedent. In 1978 Gerald Ford, who had served on the Warren Commission, charged with determining the truth about the 1963 assassination of John Kennedy, testified before a House committee that was reexamining the slaying.

Court Testimony

Ronald Reagan was the first former president compelled to testify in a criminal trial. Complying with a court order, he gave videotaped testimony February 9, 1990, in the Iran-contra trial of former national security adviser Vice Adm. John Poindexter. Poindexter and Marine Corps aide Lt. Col. Oliver North were convicted for their roles in a scheme to sell arms to Iran and use the profits to help guerrilla fighters (contras) in Nicaragua, in violation of congressional bans on such aid. Charges against North were dismissed in 1991 because he had been promised immunity from prosecution in exchange for his congressional testimony in the scandal.

Other former presidents had testified in court cases, but they did so voluntarily, not under court order.

Presidents and Their Publics

The Presidency as Bully Pulpit

Bully pulpit, a term bantered about often in the 1992 presidential campaign, especially by independent candidate Ross Perot, was first applied to the presidency by Theodore Roosevelt. The term refers to a president's power to use words, images, and actions to set the tone for American public policy.

In TR's time, *bully* meant "great" or "fantastic." The term did not have the modern meanings of "intimidate" or "shove people around."

Going Public

Some presidents have been better than others at using their bully pulpits to sell their programs to the American people, but all presidents use public appearances, statements, interviews, TV and radio broadcasts, and other means of communication to get their ideas across.

During the Great Depression of the 1930s, millions of people gathered by their radios to hear Franklin Roosevelt's reassuring "fireside chats." In the 1960s John Kennedy used his smile and wit to master the first live televised news conferences. In the 1980s Ronald Reagan's acting and broadcasting skills won him the title the "Great Communicator."

Often the president's target audience is not the one sitting in the same room but Congress. Even when addressing a joint session of Congress, as in the State of the Union address, the president may actually be going over the members' heads, hoping the public will bring pressure on the House and Senate to enact the administration's program.

Early in his presidency, with only the Senate controlled by his own party, Reagan used this strategy to win passage of his hands-off economic program. Twelve years later Bill Clinton openly borrowed the technique in an effort to have Congress reverse those policies and increase government's role in creating jobs.

The Talk Explosion

Early presidents were less talkative than those of today. The twenty-four presidents who served between 1789 and 1900 gave

Theodore Roosevelt

Franklin D. Roosevelt

only one thousand or so speeches. By comparison one recent president alone, Gerald Ford, spoke at 1,236 public appearances during his two-and-a-half years in office.

Most of the early presidents' speeches were brief greetings or other ceremonial remarks. Of the three wars that occurred between 1789 and 1900, only the Civil War was mentioned by a president, Abraham Lincoln. A mere three presidents—Martin Van Buren, Andrew Johnson, and Grover Cleveland—gave partisan political speeches.

Millard Fillmore was the first president

since Washington to discuss policy in public. But Fillmore was not trying to sway the public with his speeches about the Compromise of 1850. That policy, which was designed to save the Union by permitting some slavery, already had been set.

After World War II presidential speechmaking increased almost 500 percent. In his only full term (1949–1952), Harry Truman made 53 U.S. appearances outside Washington, D.C. In his first term (1981–1985), Ronald Reagan made 260 such appearances.

Media Bypass

Technology has enabled modern-day presidents to bypass the news media and present their unfiltered views to the people. Jimmy Carter pioneered in holding televised "town meetings" around the country, taking questions from the audiences. Ronald Reagan began giving regular Saturday morning radio talks, a practice continued by George Bush and Bill Clinton.

In the 1992 election campaign, presidential candidates of both parties took advantage of a new opportunity, appearing and

The "Great Communicator," Ronald Reagan

sometimes debating on radio and TV call-in shows such as "Donahue" and "Larry King Live." After he became president, Clinton continued to use the talk-show format. He held a question-and-answer session with children and appeared on MTV, cable TV's rock-music channel, to tout his national service program for college students.

"WE CAN WATCH CLINTON ON MTV, BUSH ON LETTERMAN, PEROT ON 'ARSENIO'.....OR MADONNA ON 'MEET THE PRESS'...."

White House Life

Good Help Is Hard to Find . . .

Being president was largely a do-it-yourself operation in the early years. James Buchanan managed to wrangle money from Congress for a secretary, but he was the first to do so. His successor, Abraham Lincoln, needed two secretaries because of the Civil War, and both men became famous in their own right: John Nicolay feuded with newspaper editors on Lincoln's behalf, and John Hay became a novelist and served as secretary of state under two presidents. Nicolay and Hay began the now-standard practice of aides writing briefing summaries for busy presidents.

Picking Up the Check

It was not until the twentieth century that Congress began paying most of the expenses that went with the office. Taft was the first president to have government-paid servants, and Warren G. Harding obtained money for official entertaining.

Special Guests

Ulysses S. Grant threw a state dinner in 1874 for the first ruling monarch to visit the White House: King David Kalakaua of the Sandwich Islands, now Hawaii. The king took no chances on the food; escorts in-

Educator Booker T. Washington and President Theodore Roosevelt

spected each plate before he accepted it.

Theodore Roosevelt entertained black educator Booker T. Washington at the White House in 1901, causing some controversy on both sides of the race issue. At one time the visit of a pope also would have been protested, but the first such visit, by John Paul II to the Carter White House, drew little attention.

Presidential Pay and Perks

Most Americans—especially corporate executives—have received several cost-of-living pay increases since the president last got a raise. As of 1993, the president's salary was $200,000—the same as it was in 1969.

Sequoia, the former presidential yacht used by President Herbert Hoover through President Gerald Ford, was sold at the request of President Jimmy Carter.

Camp David

The president also receives a taxable expense account of $50,000 and a travel allowance of $75,000, most of which is not needed because the president generally travels free on *Air Force One* or other government aircraft. The White House operates a dozen limousines and cars, including a bullet-proof one for the president.

The first family must pay for its own food and other incidentals, but most major expenses such as official entertaining are paid for by the government. Congress appropriated $8.4 million in 1992 to operate the 132-room mansion, with its ninety-seven-person staff including five florists and five calligraphers.

Not Exactly Roughing It

A popular presidential retreat is Camp David in the Catoctin Mountains of Maryland. Originally called Shangri-La by Franklin Roosevelt, it later was renamed for Dwight Eisenhower's grandson Dwight David Eisenhower II.

Presidents have used Camp David for serious matters of state as well as for relaxation. During World War II, FDR mapped out the Normandy invasion there, and Eisenhower welcomed Soviet premier Nikita Khrushchev to the retreat in 1959. In 1978 Jimmy Carter brought Israel's Menachem Begin and Egypt's Anwar Sadat to Camp David and helped to negotiate a historic Middle East peace treaty.

Jacqueline Kennedy and Ronald Reagan—both avid horseback riders— made frequent use of the camp's riding trails. George Bush's divorced daughter, Dorothy Bush LeBlond, remarried in 1992 in the camp's chapel.

For recreation, Camp David outdoes even the White House. Besides the pool, bowling alley, and tennis court, there's a trout stream, a one-hole par-three golf course, and ranges for archery and skeet shooting. Gregarious, workaholic president Bill Clinton reportedly found Camp David too quiet. In his first months in office he rarely went there and for his first vacation he chose Martha's Vineyard off Cape Cod, Massachusetts.

WHITE HOUSE *Personae*

The story is told that Calvin "Silent Cal" Coolidge and a friend were walking near the White House one evening when his companion looked at the Executive Mansion and asked jokingly, "I wonder who lives there?" "Nobody," the president replied. "They just come and go."

And so they do. Presidents and their families are just temporary residents of 1600 Pennsylvania Avenue. But so long as they occupy that famous address, they are far from being "nobodies." They are the closest thing to royalty that the American democracy has to offer, and there is intense public interest in every aspect of their lives.

Not far away in a less famous mansion dwells the vice-presidential family. Its members too are on the top rungs of Washington's political and social ladder.

■ President *** Was Born Here

Births and Birthplaces

Virginia claims eight presidents—more than any other state. Born there were George Washington, Thomas Jefferson, James Madison, James Monroe, William Henry Harrison, John Tyler, Zachary Taylor, and Woodrow Wilson. Ohio is second with seven: Ulysses S. Grant, Rutherford B. Hayes, James A. Gar-field, Benjamin Harrison, William McKin-ley, William Howard Taft, and Warren G. Harding.

New York and Massachusetts are tied for third place with four each: New York— Martin Van Buren, Millard Fillmore, and

both Roosevelts; Massachusetts—John and John Quincy Adams, John F. Kennedy, and George Bush.

The first president born outside the original thirteen states was Abraham Lincoln (1809, Kentucky). The last president born in a log cabin was Garfield (1831, Ohio). Jimmy Carter was the first president born in a hospital (1924, Georgia).

Breeders of Presidents

Several families have produced two presidents. John Adams, the second president, was the father of John Quincy Adams, the sixth. William Henry Harrison, the ninth president, was the grandfather of Benjamin Harrison, the twenty-third. And twenty-sixth president Theodore Roosevelt was a distant cousin of thirty-second presi-

PUCK.

Cartoonist Joseph Keppler portrays President Benjamin Harrison as too small to wear the hat of his grandfather, President William Henry Harrison.

dent Franklin D. Roosevelt and also an uncle of Franklin's wife, Eleanor. His brother Elliott was Eleanor's father.

Characterizing Presidents

All presidents, including Bill Clinton, have been of north European ancestry, mostly from the British Isles. The only ones of other descent were Van Buren and both Roosevelts (Dutch), Hoover (Swiss), and Eisenhower (German).

Most but not all presidents went to college, and more than half have been lawyers (twenty-five counting Clinton). Twenty-four of the men who have been president also served in Congress, and fourteen have been vice presidents. Finally, most presidents have served in the military (including career generals Taylor, Grant, and Eisenhower).

All but one (Kennedy) of the presidents were Protestant, and all but one were married (Buchanan remained a bachelor)

Presidential Book Learning

Woodrow Wilson was the only president to earn a Ph.D.—from Johns Hopkins in 1886. His first book, *Congressional Government,* published the previous year, served as his dissertation. Prevented by the Civil War from attending school until he was nine, Wilson was eleven before he learned to read and write. He is believed to have suffered from the learning disability now known as dyslexia.

Several other presidents also overcame educational handicaps to achieve the nation's highest office. In fact, nine had no college at all: Washington, Jackson, Van Buren, Taylor, Fillmore, Lincoln, Andrew Johnson, Cleveland, and Truman.

Bill Clinton is the first Rhodes scholar to become president. In 1967–1968, he studied at Oxford University under the scholarship program that Englishman Cecil Rhodes established for foreign students in 1902.

Wilson's Lighter Side

For all his scholarship and professorial demeanor, Woodrow Wilson could poke fun at himself. He was particularly fond of a limerick written by Anthony Euwer and published in 1917. The poem, which Wilson often recited, reads:

As a beauty I'm not a great star
Others are handsomer by far;
But my face I don't mind it
Because I'm behind it;
It's the folks in front that I jar.

President Woodrow Wilson with his bride, Edith, in 1915.

state New York. While teaching, he studied law and was admitted to the bar at age twenty-three. Johnson, who was thirteen when apprenticed, ran away after two years. His family later moved with him from North Carolina to Greeneville, Tennessee, where he opened a tailor shop and began his political career.

Hold that Pose

Gerald Ford and Ronald Reagan worked as professional models before they got into politics. Ford modeled menswear while going to Yale Law School, and Reagan, in

■ Religion

Episcopalian, Presbyterian, and Unitarian have predominated among the presidents' religious affiliations. Thomas Jefferson, Abraham Lincoln, and Andrew Johnson belonged to no specific denomination.

The first Catholic presidential nominee of a major party was Gov. Alfred E. Smith of New York in 1928. But he was no match for his Republican opponent, Herbert Hoover, who refused to play on anti-Catholic fears. Another Democrat, Sen. John F. Kennedy of Massachu-

setts, met the issue head-on in 1960, vowing his independence from the pope. He became the first Catholic president.

■ Pre-Presidential Careers

Up from Servitude

Two presidents, Millard Fillmore and Andrew Johnson, were apprenticed as boys under terms that almost made them prisoners. Both managed to escape the contracts that in effect indentured them to their "owners"—a clothmaker in Fillmore's case and a tailor in Johnson's.

Fillmore bought his freedom for $30 and began teaching at a nearby school in up-

John Quincy Adams died soon after posing for this daguerrotype in early 1848.

conjunction with his movie career, appeared in ads for cigarettes and other products.

Speaking of poses, the first photographed president was John Quincy Adams, who was captured on a daguerrotype shortly before his death in 1848, nineteen years after he left the presidency.

Military Service

Twenty-nine of the forty-one men who have been president have served in the military, mostly as volunteers or draftees. All had been soldiers until 1960 when John Kennedy was elected. After that, all were

General Ulysses S. Grant

navy veterans except Ronald Reagan, who served in the army air force, and Bill Clinton, who did not serve.

Soldiering for Their Country

Twelve presidents were generals: George Washington, Andrew Jackson, William Henry Harrison, Zachary Taylor, Andrew Johnson, Ulysses S. Grant, Rutherford B. Hayes, James A. Garfield, Franklin

General Dwight D. Eisenhower

Pierce, Chester A. Arthur, Benjamin Harrison, and Dwight D. Eisenhower. Washington (three stars), Grant (four stars), and Eisenhower (five stars) each reached the highest rank attainable at the time. Only Washington and Eisenhower commanded Allied forces, not just Americans.

As for injuries, James Monroe, hit in the shoulder during the Battle of Trenton, and Hayes, wounded four times in the Civil

General George Washington

Soon after the United States declared war with Spain over its supression of an independence movement in Cuba, Roosevelt resigned as assistant secretary of the navy to fight in Cuba. He secured the rank of lieutenant colonel and organized the Rough Riders, a cavalry regiment. TR's exploits in Cuba made him a celebrity at home.

Milwaukee. Folded papers in his pocket slowed the bullet, and TR finished the speech before going to a hospital.

World War I Vets

During World War I, professional soldier Eisenhower wanted desperately to see combat in France, but he was kept at home as a training officer. The other president who served in the war, Harry S. Truman, saw extensive action, and his artillery unit may have fired the last shots before the armistice.

On the High Seas

John Kennedy, the first navy veteran elected president, was the fourth president hurt in combat. During World War II, he was injured when the Japanese sank his patrol torpedo boat, PT-109, on August 2, 1943, and he is credited with saving a sailor's life. The crew was rescued from an island after carving an SOS on a coconut shell, which natives carried to U.S. forces. Kennedy received the Navy and Marine Corps medal for valor and the Purple Heart for his injuries, which included back damage that plagued him the rest of his life.

Presidents Lyndon B. Johnson, Richard Nixon, and Gerald R. Ford also saw navy service during World War II. Jimmy

War, were the only presidents struck by enemy bullets. (Jackson was shot in duels but not in battle.) Pierce injured a knee when his horse threw him in the Mexican War.

TR's Rough Riders or Rough Walkers?

Theodore Roosevelt's cavalry unit lost almost seven times as many men as the enemy in a famous but misnamed battle of the Spanish-American War. Cuba's San Juan Hills were a range, not a single peak. The hill that TR and the Rough Riders took—on foot—from the entrenched Spaniards was Kettle Hill.

In 1912, after he left the presidency, Roosevelt was shot while giving a speech in

Carter spent the war years at the U.S. Naval Academy and was its first graduate to become president.

In the Wild Blue Yonder

George Bush, the navy's youngest pilot when he got his wings at eighteen, escaped death when his torpedo bomber was shot down in the Pacific on September 22, 1944, near the Japanese-held island of Chichi Jima. A submarine came to his rescue. Bush later received the Distinguished Flying Cross. He was the first combat pilot to become president, although Eisenhower knew how to fly and received a pilot's license in 1939.

Rough, Ready, and Away

Zachary Taylor, a career soldier nicknamed "Old Rough and Ready," was ready for everything except voting. His military travels prevented him from qualifying as a voter until late in life. He voted for the first time when he was sixty-two.

Easy Target

Abraham Lincoln was the only president exposed to enemy fire while in office. He visited Fort Stevens on the northern outskirts of Washington while Confederate forces under Gen. Jubal Early were making the Civil War's only direct raid on the Union capital in July 1864. At six feet, four inches, Lincoln made an easy target on July 11 as he mounted a parapet to see the action. The president is said to have obeyed when a young captain, allegedly future Supreme Court justice Oliver Wendell Holmes, Jr., shouted: "Get down, you damned fool, before you get shot!"

Southern Unionist

Andrew Johnson was the only U.S. senator from a seceded state (Tennessee) who did not resign his seat during the Civil War. Appointed by President Lincoln as the state's military governor late in the war, Johnson helped to lead Tennessee back into the Union. He was rewarded with nomination and election as Lincoln's second vice president—the one who succeeded the assassinated president six weeks into his new term.

Soldier, No; Hangman, Yes

As permitted by law at the time, future president Grover Cleveland hired a substitute for $300 to avoid the Civil War draft and stay home to care for his mother and younger siblings. Yet after the war Cleveland proved that he was capable of distasteful duties. In two years as sheriff of Buffalo,

President Abraham Lincoln towers above Union officers in this Mathew Brady photograph.

New York (1871–1873), Cleveland personally hanged two murderers rather than delegate the task to a subordinate. In his first successful race for the presidency, in 1884, Cleveland drew criticism for not serving in the Civil War and for fathering an illegitimate child, but his brief career as a sheriff did not hurt his campaign.

Last WWII Vet?

The year 1992 marked the passing of an era. George Bush was likely to be the last World War II veteran to appear on the presidential ticket of a major party. Every president for forty years, beginning with Eisenhower and ending with Bush, had been in uniform during that war. Neither Franklin Roosevelt nor Bill Clinton had served in the military. Roosevelt's successor, Harry Truman, was in the army in World War I.

Hypothetically, the youngest veteran of World War II (someone who turned eighteen in 1945 and joined the military just before the war ended) would be sixty-nine years old in 1996. Although Reagan was that age when he ran in 1980, the odds were against anyone doing that again. Nevertheless, Senate minority leader Robert Dole, a wounded World War II veteran, was not ruling out a try in 1996. If elected, the Kansas Republican would be seventy-three when inaugurated in 1997.

Capitalizing on a Capitol Experience

Although two ex-presidents—John Quincy Adams and Andrew Johnson—returned to Congress after holding the nation's highest office, it has been far more common for members of Congress to go to the White House. From James Madison through George Bush, twenty-four presidents had served in the House, Senate, or both.

The only Speaker of the House to become president was James K. Polk. James A. Garfield was the only sitting House member elected to the presidency. The only two senators who went directly from Congress to the White House were Republican Warren G. Harding and Democrat John F. Kennedy.

As for the two ex-presidents who returned to the Hill, Adams had been a senator before he became president in 1825. He became a member of the House in 1831 and died while in office after serving there seventeen years. Johnson had served in both the House and Senate before he succeeded to the presidency upon the death of Abraham Lincoln. Johnson died of a stroke in July 1875 only five months after returning to the Senate, which had come within one vote of removing him from office after the House impeached him in 1867.

Former president John Tyler, a Virginian, was elected to the Confederate Congress in November 1861, but he died in January before he could take his seat.

Governors in Waiting

Being the current governor of a large state might seem to be the best qualification for becoming president—but the political kingmakers and voters have not usually seen it that way. Until Massachusetts governor Michael Dukakis won the Democratic nomination in 1988, no sitting governor had been a major party standard bearer since Illinois Democrat Adlai E. Stevenson in 1952. Before that, the most recent nominee was Thomas E. Dewey, Republican from New York, in 1948.

With the Democrats making it two in a row by nominating Arkansas governor Bill Clinton in 1992, the trend may be changing. On the whole, statehouse experience has helped, not hurt. From Thomas Jefferson to Ronald Reagan, eighteen presidents have been state or territorial governors.

■ Presidential Honors

Two presidents have received the coveted Nobel Peace Prize: Theodore Roosevelt in 1906 for helping to end the Russo-Japanese War, and Woodrow Wilson in 1919 for his efforts to establish the League of Nations after World War I.

Jimmy Carter was instrumental in negotiating the Middle East peace treaty that won the 1978 Nobel Peace Prize for Egyptian president Anwar Sadat and Israeli prime minister Menachem Begin.

John Kennedy won the Pulitzer Prize for biography in 1957 for his *Profiles in Courage,* written while he was recuperating from back surgery.

Theodore Roosevelt with Russian and Japanese officials after the Russo-Japanese War.

■ Presidential Pastimes

Inventing, Among Other Things

Thomas Jefferson was known for his gadgetry, but Abraham Lincoln actually received a patent for one of his inventions—a device to help vessels navigate dangerous waters. Jefferson disdained patents. He wanted people to make free use of his contraptions, which included a walking stick chair, a pedometer, and a penholder that duplicated letters as he wrote them.

Architect, farmer, lawyer, musician, scientist, and more, Jefferson was the most talented of U.S. presidents. John Kennedy once told a gathering of Nobel medalists that they were "the most extraordinary collection of talents that has ever gathered at the White House, with

Thomas Jefferson designed his home, Monticello, which is located on a mountainside in Charlottesville, Virginia. Visitors can tour the home and grounds, see Jefferson's inventions, and visit the family cemetery.

Pantograph

an exhibition game with the semi-pro New York Metropolitans. After that the stretch became standard at the college's home games. The museum also has reports of the stretch at pro baseball games in New York as early as 1889. Everybody stood—and they've been standing ever since.

Another president, Ronald Reagan, got his start covering baseball and other sports on radio in Davenport, Iowa. As president, Reagan liked to entertain audiences by showing how he simulated "live" coverage of baseball games while actually reading from a news tickertape. George Bush, a southpaw, pitched at Yale.

the possible exception of when Thomas Jefferson dined alone."

'Take Me Out to the Ballgame . . .'

On April 14, 1910, William Howard Taft began the tradition of presidents throwing out the first baseball of the season. That's not in dispute. On shakier ground is the legend that Taft also originated the seventh-inning stretch, when he stood to ease his three-hundred-pound frame from the long discomfort of a stadium chair. According to the Baseball Museum at Cooperstown, New York, Brother Jasper of Manhattan College beat Taft by almost thirty years. Coach Jasper gave his team a seventh-inning break in June 1882 during

President Taft tosses the first ball in Washington, D.C., in 1910.

Boxing

Theodore Roosevelt boxed as part of an exercise regimen that turned him from a sickly youth into an athletic young man. Gerald Ford coached boxing as well as football at Yale.

Coaching/Playing Football

Not surprisingly, some presidents took to coaching. Woodrow Wilson coached at Wesleyan University, and Dwight Eisenhower played at West Point and coached at Fort Meade, Maryland. Gerald Ford played on two University of Michigan championship teams and was voted the team's most valuable player in 1934. But he passed up offers from professional teams and became an assistant coach at Yale, where he continued to coach after he was admitted to the law school in 1935.

Fore!

Dwight Eisenhower was among the most avid of several golfing presidents. He set up a putting green outside the Oval Office and hit a hole-in-one on February 6, 1968, after he left the presidency.

Swimming

Franklin Roosevelt, stricken with polio in 1921, regained partial use of his legs by swimming in the White House pool and

President Dwight D. Eisenhower on the links at the Newport Country Club in Rhode Island.

Bill Clinton played the sax during the presidential campaign on the Arsenio Hall show.

the naturally heated waters of Warm Springs, Georgia, where he visited frequently and died in 1945. John Kennedy swam on Harvard's varsity team, an experience that served him well in 1943 after the Japanese sank his patrol torpedo boat. He led the survivors on a four-hour swim to land, towing one of the injured.

Musical Execs

For the most part, U.S. presidents have not been musicians. Only three could play a wind instrument: Warren G. Harding (alto horn and cornet), Calvin Coolidge (harmonica), and Bill Clinton (saxophone). Thomas Jefferson and John Tyler played the violin, and Harry Truman and Richard Nixon were pianists.

The White House East Room boasts a grand piano with gilded American eagle legs. The Steinway Co. donated it in 1938.

Incidentally, another famous American—Benjamin Franklin—invented the harmonica.

■ Away They Go

Presidents have always traveled a lot. Even George Washington did his share—albeit using limited horsepower. Washington also got a taste of what future travel might entail. In Philadelphia, then the U.S. capital, on January 9, 1793, he watched a hydrogen balloon take

During the balloon flight witnessed by George Washington, Frenchman Jean Pierre Blanchard and his only passenger, a small black dog, reached an altitude of 5,813 feet. In forty-six minutes the balloon crossed the Delaware River and traveled fifteen miles.

off. With that, he became the first president to witness manned flight.

Adventurous Theodore Roosevelt was the first to ride in a car (1902), submerge in a submarine (1905), travel abroad while in office (Panama, 1906), and fly in an airplane

During Nixon's trip to China, he and his wife Pat visited the Great Wall—and stopped along the way for a photo opportunity.

(1910, after leaving office). Woodrow Wilson was the first president to cross the Atlantic Ocean as president, after World War I.

As air travel became more common, Franklin Roosevelt was the first chief executive to visit South America and Hawaii and have an assigned airplane (a special C-54). Dwight Eisenhower bettered that by having a jet aircraft assigned to him and using helicopters regularly.

It was not until 1964 that a president, Lyndon Johnson, flew around the world. A few years later (February 1971), Richard Nixon was the first president to visit China after the Communist government was installed in 1949.

In his many travels George Bush flew in style—in the first jumbo jet (a Boeing 747) to be assigned as *Air Force One.*

Presidential Summitry

Presidential travel abroad was rare until Franklin Roosevelt began a series of overseas meetings with Allied leaders during World War II. During the Cold War of 1945–1991, U.S. presidents held twenty summit meetings with leaders of the Soviet Union, from Joseph Stalin to Mikhail Gorbachev.

■ Names and Nicknames

Most presidents have had nicknames—some of them unflattering—but Jimmy Carter was the first to make his official. As president he seldom used his full name of James Earl Carter, Jr. He signed official documents as

Jimmy Carter

Bill Clinton took a two-tier approach. He preferred to be called Bill but signed documents as

[signature: William J. Clinton]

Some nicknames of earlier presidents require explanation. For example, John Adams was called "His Rotundity" because of his shape and his fondness for the titles of royalty. William Henry Harrison was known as "Tippecanoe" for his success at Tippecanoe Creek in defeating the Indian confederacy led by Shawnee chief Tecumseh. In 1840, the Whigs used the slogan "Tippecanoe and Tyler, Too," to push for the Harrison-John Tyler ticket.

Zachary Taylor became "Old Rough and Ready" for his dashing military exploits against the British, Indians, and Mexicans.

Vice presidents who succeeded to the presidency have been dubbed "His Accidency" or the "Accidental President."

Middle Names and Initials

Because Harry Truman's middle initial, S, stood for nothing, editors have debated for years whether to put a period after it. Asked about it in 1985, Truman's daughter, Margaret, told advice columnist Abigail Van Buren ("Dear Abby"), "My father always put a dot after the letter 'S'; that's why it appears on the cover of the biography I wrote about him."

[signature: Harry Truman]

(Maybe so, but the period is not visible in the signature reproduced with his official photograph.)

Richard Milhous Nixon took the opposite route; he dropped his middle name and signed simply, "Richard Nixon." Others who skipped their middle names were Ronald Wilson Reagan and George Herbert Walker Bush.

Three presidents—Grover Cleveland, Woodrow Wilson, and Calvin Coolidge—dropped their given names, Stephen, Thomas, and John, respectively.

The Names Have Been Changed . . .

Ulysses Simpson Grant originally was Hiram Ulysses Grant. Another famous West Pointer, David Dwight Eisenhower, became Dwight David Eisenhower, affectionately known as "Ike."

Presidents—All Shapes and Sizes

Like Americans in general, most presidents do not stand out physically, one way or the other. But some presidents did stand out . . . up . . . down in ways that exceeded the norm.

- Tallest—Abraham Lincoln, six feet, four inches
- Shortest—James Madison, five feet, four inches
- Heaviest—William Howard Taft, 300–340 pounds

Some other presidents came close:

- Over six feet—Lyndon Johnson, six feet, three inches; Thomas Jefferson and Bill Clinton, six feet, two and a half inches; George Washington, Chester A. Arthur, Franklin Roosevelt, and George Bush, all six feet, two inches; Andrew Jackson and Ronald Reagan, both six feet, one inch
- Under five feet, eight inches—Benjamin Harrison and Martin Van Buren, both five feet, six inches; John Adams, John Quincy Adams, and William McKinley, all five feet, seven inches
- Over 250 pounds—Grover Cleveland, 260 pounds

Although Julia Tyler was President John Tyler's second wife she had a few "firsts" of her own: she was the first first lady to have her own press agent and she initiated the custom of playing "Hail to the Chief" for the president.

Gerald R. Ford took the name of his adoptive father. His original name was Leslie Lynch King, allowing trivia buffs to pronounce Ford "the only president born a King."

Bill Clinton was named after his father, William Jefferson Blythe III, who was killed in an automobile accident three months before Bill was born on August 19, 1946. Young Bill was given the name Clinton after his mother married Roger Clinton in 1950.

First Families

Hitched

Some presidents entered the White House single but left as married men. Only one, James Buchanan (1857–1861), remained a lifelong bachelor.

John Tyler was the first president to marry while in office. His first wife, Letitia, died in the White House in 1842 after a long illness. Several months later Tyler fell head over heels in love with a young New York socialite, Julia Gardiner. They were married in New York after a year of courtship.

Grover Cleveland was the first and only one to marry in the White House itself. Cleveland, a bachelor when he became president, married twenty-one-year-old Frances Folsom, daughter of his former law partner, on June 2, 1886.

Although Grover Cleveland had the distinction of being the first president to marry in the White House, the actual first White House wedding took place in 1812 between Dolley Madison's widowed sister, Lucy Payne Washington, and Supreme Court Justice Thomas Todd.

Frances Cleveland's charm and beauty was a contrast to her husband, Grover, who could be rude and boorish. She was widely admired and held public receptions on evenings and Saturdays so that working women could attend. At one such reception, nine thousand people went through the receiving line and Frances's arms had to be massaged afterward.

Marrying the Once Hitched

Andrew Jackson was the first president married to a divorcée—Rachel Donelson Robards. Other divorced first ladies were Florence Kling De Wolfe Harding and Betty Bloomer Warren Ford.

In 1956 divorcé Adlai E. Stevenson was the Democratic presidential nominee, but not until 1980 did Ronald Reagan prove that a divorced man could be elected president. He had been married to a divorcée, actress Jane Wyman.

'Mrs. President'

The first presidential wife to be called "first lady" was Julia Grant. But it was the high visibility of her successor, Lucy Hayes, that raised the term to its current status. She was the first president's wife with a college degree, from Wesleyan Women's College, Cincinnati, in 1850.

Before the Civil War, the country experimented with other titles for the president's wife. Among the rejects were Lady Washington, Mrs. President, presidentress, and Republican (or Democratic) queen.

First Lady Aliases

The press dubbed Lucy Hayes "Lemonade Lucy" because she banned alcohol from White House functions.

The real name of Mrs. Lyndon Johnson

Beyond the ban of alcohol from the White House, "Lemonade" Lucy Hayes displayed no other political leanings while first lady. A popular, national figure, she initiated the custom of the children's Easter egg roll on the White House lawn that continues to this day.

was Claudia Alta (Taylor) Johnson. But a nurse had called her "Lady Bird" while she was a baby and the nickname stuck.

More Than a Desk and a Chair . . .

Theodore Roosevelt's wife, Edith, was the first first lady to hire an aide, in 1901. Since then, the first lady's staff has grown to almost thirty.

First Lady Lawyer

Hillary Rodham Clinton, a lawyer and childrens' rights activist, is regarded as the

Hillary Rodham Clinton is one of the most active first ladies the White House has seen in recent years. Her leadership role on the Clinton administration's health care task force has her traveling around the country, meeting with the press, and visiting leaders on Capitol Hill.

first president's wife to have had a successful professional career before she entered the White House. She is the first first lady with a professional degree (Yale law, 1973). Hillary Clinton also has the heaviest official responsibility of any first lady in history. In one of his first acts, President Clinton appointed his wife as head of his task force on health care reform, charged with proposing a massive overhaul of the nation's trillion-dollar-a-year health care industry.

A strong believer in voluntarism, Barbara Bush donated much of her own time to helping the less fortunate. As first lady, she was actively involved in programs to improve literacy in the United States. When her book about the Bush family—told from the point of view of their cocker spaniel—became a success, she donated the profits to major literacy organizations.

Some First Ladies of Accomplishment

Many first ladies have had reputations for accomplishments independent of their spouses. For example, Woodrow Wilson's second wife, Edith, practically became "acting president" for several months after her husband suffered a stroke in 1919. She controlled access to him and screened all his papers while he recovered.

Eleanor Roosevelt earned $100,000 in 1938 from speaking and writing, which was more than her husband's salary. Her prede-cessor, Lou Hoover, was a geologist who spoke five languages (she and Herbert chatted in Mandarin when they wanted privacy).

Lady Bird Johnson, who held two bachelor's degrees from the University of Texas (liberal arts in 1933 and journalism in 1934), led the replanting of Washington's public flower beds and championed a highway beautification bill that her husband signed into law.

Rosalynn Carter, who was often compared to Eleanor Roosevelt, frequently sat in on cabinet meetings and gave 258 speeches in her first two years as first lady. Her major cause was mental health.

Jacqueline Kennedy was a news reporter and photographer, and Betty Ford and Nancy Reagan were in show business. As first ladies, they were known for their special interests: Mrs. Kennedy for redecorating the White House; Mrs. Ford for her fight against alcoholism (after leaving the White House she opened the Betty Ford center for treatment of addiction); and Mrs. Reagan for urging children to "just say no" to drugs. Barbara Bush drew acclaim for her campaign against illiteracy.

White House Hostesses

Not every president had a wife to act as first lady. Four presidents (Thomas Jeffer-

Lady Bird Johnson traveled 200,000 miles to make speeches on behalf of her national beautification project, which she envisioned as contributing to the quality of life in both urban and rural areas. She personally lobbied Congress for passage of the Highway Beautification Act of 1965.

First Ladies: How They Rated

A poll of history professors in 1982 ranked Eleanor Roosevelt highest among forty-two first ladies or White House hostesses. Others who scored among the top ten were, in order, Abigail Adams, Lady Bird Johnson, Dolley Madison, Rosalynn Carter, Betty Ford, Edith Wilson, Jacqueline Kennedy, Martha Washington, and Edith Roosevelt. The eccentric Mary Lincoln rated lowest. Nancy Reagan ranked thirty-ninth, but she might have scored higher or lower if the poll had not been taken during her husband's administration.

son, Andrew Jackson, Martin Van Buren, and Chester A. Arthur) entered the White House as widowers. James Buchanan never married but the other bachelor president, Grover Cleveland, married while in the White House. All had friends or relatives serve as official hostesses. Similarly, other women were hostesses for presidents whose wives were in poor health. Presidents in this category were William Henry Harrison, John Tyler (until he remarried in 1839), Zachary Taylor, Millard Fillmore, Franklin Pierce (whose wife, Jane, ultimately assumed her duties), and Andrew Johnson.

Wives Who Were Not First Ladies

The wives of four presidents died before their husbands reached the White House. They were Martha Jefferson, who died September 6, 1782, at age thirty-three; Rachel Jackson, December 28, 1828 (after Jackson was elected but before his inauguration), at age sixty-one; Hannah Van Buren, February 5, 1819, at age thirty-five; and Ellen Arthur, January 12, 1880, at age fifty-two. None of their husbands remarried.

Alice Lee Roosevelt, wife of Theodore Roosevelt, died in 1884 at the age of twenty-two, but Roosevelt married again before he became president, to Edith Kermit Carow in 1886.

Deaths of First Ladies

Three presidents' wives died while their husbands occupied the White House: Letitia Tyler, age fifty-one, September 10, 1842; Caroline Harrison, age sixty, October 25, 1892; and Ellen Wilson, age fifty-four, August 6, 1914. John Tyler and Woodrow Wilson remarried during their presidencies, Tyler in 1844 to Julia Gardiner, and Wilson in 1915 to Edith Bolling Galt. Benjamin Harrison, who was defeated for reelection two weeks after Caroline died, married Mary Scott Lord Dimmick in 1896.

Offspring

The first White House baby was James Madison Randolph, Thomas Jefferson's grandson. James was born January 17, 1806, while his mother was staying with her father. Martha Randolph frequently acted as hostess for Jefferson, a widower.

Grover and Frances Cleveland's second daughter, Esther, was the first president's child born in the White House (1893). Their first child, Ruth, had a candy bar named after her—the Baby Ruth. Two other Cleveland children were born during his second term and the fifth was born after he left office in 1897.

William Henry Harrison had the most children, ten, before he took office. His grandson president, Benjamin Harrison,

John Tyler had more children than any other president: fifteen—eight by Letitia, who died in 1842, and seven by his second wife, Julia.

remarried three years after leaving the White House in 1893 and had a daughter the next year, when he was sixty-three years old.

Cleveland's Baby

During his first run for the presidency in 1884, Grover Cleveland admitted paternity when political opponents revealed that he was a bachelor father—who, by the way, had continued to support the child. He went on to win the race, despite the taunts

of a chant that went: "Ma! Ma! Where's my Pa?" After the election, his supporters added the words: "Gone to the White House. Ha! Ha! Ha!"

Acid-tongued Alice

One of the most outspoken presidential daughters was Alice Roosevelt Longworth, the only child of Theodore Roosevelt and Alice Hathaway Lee, who died at twenty-two. Even as a teenager, "Princess Alice" was known for her independence. "I can do one of two things," her father once said. "I can be president of the United States or I can control Alice. I cannot possibly do both."

Alice Roosevelt Longworth

Alice's marriage in 1906 to Nicholas Longworth, later Speaker of the House, enhanced her fame but did not dampen her personality. As the grande dame of Wash-

ington society for many years, Alice was known for her barbed wit. "If you have nothing good to say about anybody," she remarked, "come sit by me." In the 1948 presidential campaign she likened Harry Truman's opponent, Thomas E. Dewey, to the groom figure on a wedding cake.

Harding's Affairs

One of President Warren G. Harding's personal scandals was, like Teapot Dome, not exposed until after he died of a heart attack in 1923. Nan Britton, a reporter he had known since his newspaper editor days in Ohio, disclosed in a 1927 book that she had given birth to Harding's child, a girl, in 1919 before he entered the White House. She called the book *The President's Daughter*.

Harding, whose wife, Florence, was in poor health, also carried on a long-running affair with Carrie Phillips, the wife of a close friend. Their relationship came to light in 1964 with the discovery of 105 love letters from Harding to Mrs. Phillips. By court order, the letters were sealed until 2014.

Musical Team: Truman & Truman

After singing along with her piano-playing father for fun, Margaret Truman tried being a concert singer. Reviewers who criticized her voice did so at their peril, as Paul

Actress Lauren Bacall hams it up as a lounge singer while President Harry Truman accompanies her on the piano.

Tricia Nixon and her new husband Ed Cox leave the Rose Garden after their wedding.

Hume of the *Washington Post* soon found out. After criticizing Margaret's performance in December 1950, Hume received an angry letter from the president, who warned the critic that he would need "a new nose and plenty of beefsteak" if he ever encountered the singer's proud father.

In later years, literary critics were kinder to Miss Truman. Writing under her married name, Margaret Truman Daniel, she found success with several mystery novels set in the White House and other Washington locales.

White House Weddings

The only president's son married in the White House was John Adams. His father, John Quincy Adams, had met his future wife, Louisa Catherine Johnson, in Nantes, France, when she was four and he was twelve. Louisa Adams was the only first lady born abroad, in London.

The first presidential daughter to marry in the White House was Maria Hester Monroe, in 1820. Others who had White House weddings were Ellen Grant, Alice Roosevelt, Jessie and Eleanor Wilson, Lynda Johnson, and Tricia Nixon. Ellen Grant lost her U.S. citizenship by marrying a British diplomat, but Congress restored it after her husband died. She later remarried.

The first outdoor wedding at the White House was held in 1971 for Tricia Nixon and Edward F. Cox.

The first wedding at Camp David, the presidential retreat in Maryland, took place on June 27, 1992, between Dorothy Bush LeBlond and Bobby Koch. It was the second marriage for the daughter of George and Barbara Bush.

In Dad's Footsteps

Three sons of presidents who had been in Congress also served on Capitol Hill: Charles Francis Adams, son of John Quincy Adams; John Scott Harrison, son of William Henry Harrison; and David Gardiner Tyler, son of John Tyler. All served in the House of Representatives.

In the lone father-son team of presidents, John Adams and John Quincy Adams, only the son had congressional service. He was in the Senate before he became president and in the House afterward.

The only other presidential son elected to the Senate was Robert A. Taft, son of William Howard Taft, who was president and chief justice of the United States but who never served in Congress.

Two sons of Franklin Roosevelt—Franklin, Jr., and James—were elected to the House. FDR himself bypassed Capitol Hill in going directly from the New York governorship to the White House.

Benjamin Harrison and George Bush were the only presidents preceded in Congress by their fathers. Harrison, a former senator, was the son of John Scott Harrison—the only person who was both the son and father of a president. Bush served two terms in the House from Texas; his father, Prescott Bush, was a senator from Connecticut.

Deaths of White House Children

William "Willie" Lincoln was the only president's child to die in the White House, of pneumonia in 1863. But four children of other presidents died while their fathers were in office: Charles Adams, son of John Adams, died at age thirty in 1800; Mary Jefferson, twenty-five, died in 1804; Calvin Coolidge, Jr., sixteen, died of blood poisoning from an infected toe in 1924; and Patrick Bouvier Kennedy died two days after he was born in 1963.

■ White House Animals: A to Z

All kinds of animals—from alligators to zebras—have lived at the White House, sometimes briefly as gifts that wound up in a zoo (or an oven) and sometimes for long periods as pets of the first family.

Who Elected This Turkey?

Every year for Thanksgiving the Turkey Growers Association donates a live turkey to the White House, which passes it on to a charity. Usually the turkey cooperates, but occasionally one acts up at the Rose Garden presentation, providing some hilarious news footage.

More fortunate are the exotic gift animals such as the giant pandas, Ling-Ling and Hsing-Hsing, that Richard Nixon re-

Grace Coolidge and her pet raccoon, Rebecca.

ceived from the People's Republic of China after his trip there in 1972. Like other species before them, the pandas were turned over to the Smithsonian's National Zoological Park in Washington.

Animal lover Theodore Roosevelt sent the zoo numerous specimens he brought back from his expeditions to Africa and South America.

"Baby McKee" and his pet goat, His Whiskers.

Theodore Roosevelt, Jr., and his pet macaw, Eli.

Top Dogs, Cats, and Other Pets

Tad Lincoln made a pet of a turkey (given the name Jack) that relatives gave his family for Christmas dinner. When the time came for preparation of the dinner, Tad's tears saved Jack—President Lincoln stayed the execution.

Other White House pets were equally bizarre. They included a trained mocking-bird (Jefferson), an alligator and silkworms (John Quincy Adams), white mice (Andrew Johnson), a Mexican parrot (McKinley), Pauline Wayne the cow and Enoch the gander (Taft), a raccoon (Coolidge), and sheep (Wilson).

A goat, His Whiskers, pulled Benjamin Harrison's grandson Benjamin, "Baby Mc-Kee," around in a cart. One day the cart escaped onto busy Pennsylvania Avenue, chased by the stout president wearing a top hat and frock coat.

Even the conventional dog and cat pets sometimes made news. Lyndon Johnson shocked dog lovers (and delighted cartoon-ists) by lifting his beagles, Him and Her, by the ears. The Bush family dog, Millie, re-portedly "earned" more than her president-owner's $200,000 salary in royalties on an as-told-to book by Barbara Bush. The pro-ceeds went to a charity. The Clintons kept a cat, Socks, despite a presidential allergy to cat dander.

The Roosevelt Menagerie

The Theodore Roosevelt White House was a veritable menagerie that included bear cubs, a young lion, a macaw, a don-key, raccoons, snakes, cats, dogs, rats, and guinea pigs.

When Archie Roosevelt, one of TR's sons, was sick, his brothers entertained him by bringing their pony, Algonquin, up the White House elevator to Archie's second-floor bedroom. Many years later, Caroline Kennedy also had a pony. She called it Mac-aroni.

FDR's Fala Fracas

In a 1944 speech to the Teamsters Union, Franklin Roosevelt accused his opponents of concocting a story that he had sent a navy destroyer to bring his Scottie, Fala, back from the Aleutian Islands. "These Republican leaders have not been content with attacks—on me, or my wife, or on my sons," FDR said. "No, not content with that, they now include my little dog, Fala. Well, of course, I don't resent attacks, and my family doesn't resent attacks, but Fala DOES resent them!" The audience roared with laughter.

RN's Checkers Speech

In 1952 Richard Nixon saved himself from being dumped as Dwight Eisenhower's running mate after it was disclosed that wealthy Californians had been supplementing Nixon's Senate pay. In what came to be known as the "Checkers speech," Nixon gave an emotional defense of his actions. "We did get something, a gift, after the nomination," he told the television audience. He went on to explain that

a man down in Texas heard Pat on the radio mention the fact that our two youngsters would like to have a dog and, believe it or not, the day before we left on this campaign trip we got a message from Union Station in Washington that they had a package for us. We went down to get it. You know what it was? It was a little cocker spaniel in a crate that had been sent all the way from Texas—black and white, spotted, and our little girl Tricia, the six-year-old, named it Checkers. And you know, the kids, like all kids, loved the dog, and I just want to say this, right now, that regardless of what they say about it, we are going to keep it. . . .

The appeal worked. Thousands of viewers telegraphed their support, and Eisenhower kept Nixon on the ticket.

By coincidence, both the Fala and Checkers speeches were given on September 23, eight years apart.

■ Presidents and Violence
Duel to the Death

Andrew Jackson, nicknamed "Old Hickory" for his toughness in war, killed a man in a duel. The victim, Charles Dickinson, had insulted Jackson about his marriage to divorcée Rachel Robards. They dueled in 1806 and Jackson, though injured himself, mortally wounded Dickinson in the abdomen.

The rest of his life Jackson suffered fits of pain from Dickinson's bullet, which lodged too near the heart for removal. Jackson received two more bullet wounds in 1813 in a shootout with Thomas Hart Benton and his brother Jesse. One of the bullets nearly cost Jackson his left arm.

Thomas Benton later served thirty years as a U.S. senator from Missouri. Jackson, who served in the Senate both before and after his fight with the Bentons, was elected president in 1828. During the campaign, Jackson's opponents renewed their attacks on his marriage, causing Rachel Jackson severe distress. Jackson blamed the criticism for contributing to her death of a heart attack shortly after the election.

Assaults

Aging gunfighter Andrew Jackson was the target of the first attempted assassination of a U.S. president. As he was leaving a congressman's funeral service at the Capitol on January 30, 1835, Jackson was con-fronted by a young man who pointed a pistol at him and pulled the trigger.

After a Capitol funeral service for Rep. Warren R. Davis, a "supposed maniac" tried to shoot President Andrew Jackson. The gun misfired.

Nothing happened. The man, Richard Lawrence, then drew another loaded pistol from his cloak, and it too misfired.

Jackson, by then sixty-two and infirm, brandished his cane at Lawrence as stunned onlookers seized him. Lawrence, deluded that he was the king of England, was later committed to an insane asylum.

The phrase "wrestled him to the ground" has since become a cliché associated with the Treasury Department's Secret Service, which has had the job of protecting presidents since 1901. Presidential families have had Secret Service protection since 1917.

Other Attacks

Franklin Roosevelt, Harry Truman, Gerald Ford, and Ronald Reagan were also targets of failed assassinations. Reagan was the only president actually injured (1981) in these attempts, but bullets intended for Roosevelt killed Chicago Mayor Anton J. Cermak in 1933. FDR was the president-elect when anarchist Joseph Zangara shot at him in Miami on February 15.

Truman was temporarily living in Blair House on November 1, 1950, when Puerto Rican nationalists Oscar Collazo and Griselio Torresola tried to shoot their way in. Griselio and a guard were killed; Collazo was wounded and later convicted of killing the guard.

Two women attacked Ford in separate California incidents in 1975. Lynette Alice "Squeaky" Fromme, a follower of mass murderer Charles Manson, was disarmed in a Sacramento crowd September 5 before she could fire a loaded handgun at the president. On September 22, Sara Jane Moore shot at but missed Ford as he was leaving a San Francisco hotel. Both women received life sentences.

John W. Hinckley, Jr., shot Reagan on March 30, 1981, less than three months after Reagan became president. Press secretary James Brady, a Secret Service agent, and a policeman were also hit by Hinckley's bullets outside a Washington, D.C., hotel. Brady, who suffered brain damage, and his wife, Sarah, became leading advocates of handgun control. Hinckley, found not guilty by reason of insanity, was placed in a mental institution.

◼ Deaths

The Short and Long of It

James K. Polk lived the shortest time after leaving office (three months) and Herbert Hoover lived the longest (thirty-one years).

The Twenty-Year Jinx

Seven of the eight presidents who died in office had one thing in common: they

had been elected or reelected at the opening of each even-numbered decade, beginning with 1840. The seven and their dates of death are William Henry Harrison, April 4, 1841; Abraham Lincoln, April 15, 1865 (assassinated); James A. Garfield, September 19, 1881 (assassinated); William McKinley, September 14, 1901 (assassinated); Warren G. Harding, August 2, 1923; Franklin D. Roosevelt, April 12, 1945; John F. Kennedy, November 22, 1963 (assassinated).

The only other president who died in office was Zachary Taylor, who had been elected in 1848. He died July 9, 1850. He and William Henry Harrison were the only two Whig presidents.

Ronald Reagan narrowly escaped being the eighth victim of the so-called twenty-year jinx. Elected in 1980, he was shot in an assassination attempt on March 30, 1981. Reagan recovered and survived both terms in office.

Assassinations

Of the four presidents who were assassinated while in office, two—William McKinley and John Kennedy—were shot after Secret Service protection was instituted in 1901. All were killed by handguns except Kennedy, whose assassin used a rifle.

Abraham Lincoln was shot in the head

John Wilkes Booth

England vacation. The assailant, Charles J. Guiteau, claimed that a divine vision told him to kill the president. Garfield died September 19 in Elberon, New Jersey, where he had asked to be moved as doctors continued to probe for the bullet lodged near his spine. They used a device invented by Alexander Graham Bell, but it failed to find the bullet because of interference from the metal bedspring. Guiteau was found guilty and hanged on June 30, 1882.

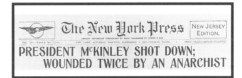

William McKinley was shot in the chest and stomach September 6, 1901, as he greeted visitors to the Pan-American Exposition at Buffalo, New York. The assailant, anarchist Leon Czolgosz, was quickly tried and executed. McKinley died September 14 of gangrene and other complications.

John F. Kennedy was shot in the head and neck on November 22, 1963, as he rode in an open car in a Dallas motorcade. Texas governor John B. Connally, seated in front of Kennedy, was wounded by one of the same bullets. Lee Harvey Oswald, arrested for the shooting, was himself killed on national television by Jack Ruby, a night-club

Lee Harvey Oswald and Jack Ruby (firing gun).

owner. The Warren Commission determined that Oswald had fired the fatal shots from the Texas Schoolbook Depository, but doubts remained that accurate shots could have been fired so rapidly with a bolt-action rifle. A 1991 movie, *JFK,* revived speculation that Oswald was part of a conspiracy.

Funerals and Burials

The only president who did not lie in state in the White House East Room after

April 14, 1865, as he sat in a box at Ford's Theater in Washington while watching a play, *Our American Cousin.* The assassin, actor John Wilkes Booth, broke a leg as he leapt to the stage and escaped. Lincoln died the following morning in a house across the street from the theater. Pursuing police killed Booth, a Confederate sympathizer, in Maryland.

James A. Garfield was shot in the back and arm at a railroad depot as he was leaving Washington on July 2, 1881, for a New

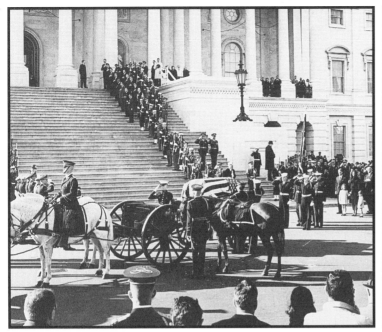

Jacqueline Kennedy and her children, Caroline and John, watch at the Capitol as President Kennedy's casket is readied for the funeral procession.

From left to right: Gerald Ford, Richard Nixon, George Bush, Ronald Reagan, and Jimmy Carter in the Oval Office.

dying in office was James Garfield. His body was taken by train from Long Branch, New Jersey, directly to the Capitol Rotunda, where the casket was placed on the same catafalque used to display Lincoln's coffin. All presidents who died in office, as well as some former presidents, have received the same honor.

Most deceased presidents are buried in their home states. Exceptions include Woodrow Wilson, the only president buried in Washington, D.C., and William Howard Taft and John Kennedy, the two presidents buried at Arlington National Cemetery in Virginia. Taft's widow, Nellie, is the only first lady buried at Arlington.

The remains of Zachary Taylor were exhumed in 1991 from a Louisville, Kentucky, national cemetery named for him. Tests confirmed that Taylor had died of natural causes, disproving a historian's theory that someone had poisoned him with arsenic.

John Tyler is the only former president buried under what was then a foreign flag—that of the Confederacy. He was buried in Richmond, where he died in 1862 as he prepared to become a member of the Confederate House.

◼ Remembering Presidents

Rating Greatness

Harvard's Arthur M. Schlesinger polled fellow historians in 1948 and came up with this list of the seven greatest presidents: Abraham Lincoln, George Washington, Franklin Roosevelt, Woodrow Wilson, Thomas Jefferson, Andrew Jackson, and Theodore Roosevelt.

Harry Truman was not eligible for consideration because he was president at the time, but in similar polls since then historians have rated him among the greatest or near-greatest presidents.

Five, Count 'em, Five

When George Bush left the presidency on January 20, 1993, the United States for the second time in history had five living former presidents: Richard Nixon, Gerald Ford, Jimmy Carter, Ronald Reagan, and Bush. The first time was in early January 1862, when ex-presidents Martin Van Buren, John Tyler, Millard Fillmore, Franklin Pierce, and James Buchanan were still living. Tyler died on January 18 of that year.

What to Do with All Those Papers?

Presidential libraries have been established or begun for eleven of the forty former presidents, through George Bush. The libraries and locations are: Hoover, West Branch, Iowa; Franklin Roosevelt, Hyde Park, New York; Truman, Independence, Missouri; Eisenhower, Abilene, Kansas; Kennedy, Dorchester, Massachusetts; Lyndon Johnson, Austin, Texas; Nixon, Yorba Linda, California; Ford, Ann Arbor, Michigan; Carter, Atlanta, Georgia; Reagan, Simi Valley, California; and Bush, College Station, Texas.

In visitors (310,000 in 1991) and square

feet (96,981) the LBJ Library on the University of Texas campus is the largest. In items held (46.1 million) the Nixon Library is largest, followed closely by Reagan's (45.5 million).

Mount Rushmore

How do you carve a giant statue of George Washington, Thomas Jefferson, Abraham Lincoln, and Theodore Roosevelt? You find a giant chunk of granite and blast away everything that doesn't look like Washington, Jefferson, Lincoln, or Teddy Roosevelt.

That, in effect, is what Gutzon Borglum did beginning in 1927 when he carved the spectacular memorial on South Dakota's Mount Rushmore. In fourteen years, he removed 450,000 tons of rock to create the sixty-foot likenesses. He died in 1941 before he was quite done, but his son Lincoln finished the work.

Why those particular presidents? Borglum chose them to represent, respectively, the nation's founding, political philosophy, unity, and expansion and conservation.

Before he died, Borglum also helped to plan the Stone Mountain, Georgia, memorial to Confederate heroes Jefferson Davis, Robert E. Lee, and Stonewall Jackson. Completed over the period 1963–1972, the sculpture surpassed Rushmore as the world's largest.

If the sculpting Ziolkowski family has its way, however, Mount Rushmore may someday be only the world's third largest sculpture. The Ziolkowskis are carving a monument to Crazy Horse, the Ogala Sioux war chief who helped to defeat Gen. George A. Custer at the Battle of Little Big Horn in 1876, on Thunderhead Mountain in South Dakota.

'Now Here's MY Version . . .'

Most former presidents write their memoirs or other retrospectives, perhaps more for vanity than for money. Few are bestsellers. An exception was the memoir by Ulysses S. Grant, who finished it four days before he died broke in 1885. The book sold 300,000 copies and earned $400,000 in royalties for his widow.

Right on the Money

Four of the most common U.S. currency bills have presidents' pictures on them: Washington, $1; Lincoln, $5; Jackson, $20; and Grant, $50. Jefferson is on the unpopular, rarely circu-

lated $2 bill. Nonpresidents Alexander Hamilton and Benjamin Franklin are on $10 and $100 bills, respectively.

Presidents on the big bills are McKinley, $500; Cleveland, $1,000; Madison, $5,000; and Wilson, $100,000.

Groupies for Chester and Millard

Some unlikely ex-presidents have fan clubs in unlikely places. One of the least likely is the Chester A. Arthur Society in, of all places, Australia. The hundred-or-so members gather occasionally to hear what any new book has to say about "Old Muttonchops," who became the twenty-first president when James Garfield was assass-

"Old Muttonchops," Chester A. Arthur

inated in 1881. The society members also try to stump each other with trivia questions about Arthur and other American politicians, such as: What one person was present at the assassinations of Lincoln, Garfield, and McKinley? (Answer: Robert Todd Lincoln)

Another relatively obscure president, Millard Fillmore, is honored annually at a gathering in Baltimore.

■ The Veep

Harry Truman's vice president, Alben W. Barkley, was affectionately known as the "Veep." His grandson called him that, and it has been the informal title of vice presidents ever since.

They Became President

Fourteen vice presidents have become president through succession or election: John Adams, Thomas Jefferson, Martin Van Buren, John Tyler, Millard Fillmore, Andrew Johnson, Chester A. Arthur, Theodore Roosevelt, Calvin Coolidge, Harry Truman, Richard Nixon, Lyndon Johnson, Gerald Ford, and George Bush. Nine of these fourteen reached the White House when their predecessors died or resigned. Adams, Jefferson, Van Buren, and Bush finished a term as vice president and were then elected president. Only Nixon finished his vice-presidential term and was elected president some years later; he lost to John Kennedy in 1960 but defeated Hubert Humphrey in 1968.

They Didn't Make It

Six incumbent vice presidents ran for president and lost. Four failed to win their party's nomination: Thomas R. Marshall in 1920, Charles G. Dawes in 1928 and 1932, John Nance Garner in 1940, and Alben W. Barkley in 1952. Two won the nomination but lost in the general election: Richard Nixon in 1960 and Hubert Humphrey in 1968 (who lost to Nixon).

Henry A. Wallace, Franklin Roosevelt's vice president from 1941 to 1945, ran unsuccessfully as the Progressive party nominee in 1948. Walter F. Mondale, vice president under Jimmy Carter from 1977 to 1981, was the Democratic nominee in 1984.

Two Bosses

Only two vice presidents served under two presidents: George Clinton (Thomas Jefferson and James Madison) and John C. Calhoun (John Quincy Adams and Andrew Jackson).

Vice-Presidential Tidbits

The youngest vice president was John C. Breckinridge, thirty-six. The oldest was Alben W. Barkley, seventy-one when he took office in 1949.

The only woman nominated for vice president by a major party was Geraldine A. Ferraro of New York, the Democratic nominee in 1984.

Quotable Veeps

The first vice president, John Adams, complained, "My country has in its wisdom contrived for me the most insignificant office that the intention of man contrived or his imagination conceived."

The witty Thomas R. Marshall, vice president to Woodrow Wilson, used his humor to puncture windbags and even the vice presidency itself. After listening to one long Senate speech about the country's needs, Marshall proclaimed loudly, "What this country needs is a really good five-cent cigar."

Years later, John Nance "Cactus Jack" Garner, FDR's first vice president, described the office as "not worth a bucket of warm spit."

A future vice president, Charles Dawes, became a folk hero after World War I when he deflected a congressional inquiry about his multimillion-dollar supply purchases

Vice President Thomas R. Marshall frequently told a story about two brothers: "One ran away to sea; the other was elected vice president. And nothing was ever heard of either of them again."

for the troops by saying, "Hell and Maria, we weren't trying to keep a set of books, we were trying to win the war!"

Richard Nixon's first vice president, Spiro T. Agnew, often used alliteration in his role as verbal hit man for the administration. For example, he called Nixon's media critics "nattering nabobs of negativism."

Former vice president Walter Mondale scored points in a debate with Sen. Gary

Hart in 1984 with words from a hamburger chain television commercial that featured a gruff-voiced little old lady. Borrowing Clara Peller's line, Mondale asked, "Where's the beef?" to make his point that Hart's proposals lacked substance. Mondale went on to win the Democratic presidential nomination but lost the general election to Ronald Reagan.

Vice-Presidential Bloopers

All vice presidents take a ribbing from comedians, as well as from themselves. They may not put their foot in their mouths more than any other politicians, but it seems that way because of all the publicity their gaffes get.

No one knows this better than Dan Quayle. During his four years as vice president, Quayle committed some classic bloopers. In 1989 he garbled the United Negro College Fund motto by saying: "What a waste it is to lose one's mind—or not have

a mind, that is." (The actual motto is "A mind is a terrible thing to waste.")

In 1992 Quayle told a California audience: "I love California. I grew up in Phoenix." And on June 15, 1992, reading from a cue card, he incorrectly advised a New Jersey spelling bee contestant to add an "e" to the end of "potato."

Quayle's successor, Al Gore, when running for president in 1988, accused a student of shouting the "ultimate heckle." And what was that? The heckler said Gore would make a good vice president.

Other Talents

Charles Dawes, Calvin Coolidge's vice president, was an amateur composer. His "Melody in A Major," published in 1911, became a hit song in 1951 after it was given lyrics and retitled "It's All in the Game."

Dawes's more substantive accomplishments included development of the Dawes Plan to help Germany recover after World War I. For that he was awarded the Nobel Peace Prize in 1925.

Spiro Agnew became a novelist to help pay his debts after he left the vice presidency in disgrace. His 1976 book *The Canfield Decision* told the fictitious story of a U.S. vice president who became involved with Iranian militants.

The Bizarre Burr: Hamilton's Killer

Aaron Burr, the third vice president and the first who didn't later become president, killed Alexander Hamilton in a duel at Weehawken, New Jersey, on July 11, 1804. Burr felt that Hamilton had slurred him during his failed race for governor of New York.

To escape arrest for murder, Burr returned to Washington and resumed his duties as vice president as if nothing had happened. Federal law at that time did not provide for extradition of criminals from the capital.

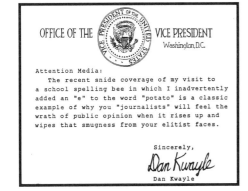

OFFICE OF THE **VICE PRESIDENT**
Washington, D.C.

Attention Media:
    The recent snide coverage of my visit to a school spelling bee in which I inadvertently added an "e" to the word "potato" is a classic example of why you "journalists" will feel the wrath of public opinion when it rises up and wipes that smugness from your elitist faces.

Sincerely,

Dan Kwayle

Dan Kwayle

In another bizarre episode for the most bizarre of vice presidents, Burr was tried for treason in 1807 after apparently hatching a plot to conquer Mexico and establish his own western empire. Although he had assembled a small force, he was acquitted because the plot was exposed before he could commit an overt treasonable act.

Other Wayward Vice Presidents

At least two vice presidents, Daniel D. Tompkins and future president Andrew Johnson, were heavy drinkers who presided over the Senate while drunk.

Both of Grant's vice presidents, Schuyler Colfax and Henry Wilson, were implicated in the Crédit Mobilier scandal related to construction of the Union Pacific Railroad. Wilson, born Jeremiah Jones Colbath, changed his name after reading the biography of an earlier Henry Wilson.

Spiro Agnew's resignation on October 10, 1973, stemmed from a plea bargain with the Justice Department, which prosecuted him for income tax evasion while he was governor of Maryland. He pleaded no contest, agreed to pay $150,000 in back taxes,

and was fined $10,000. Bribery and other charges were dropped.

A Bust in the Wing

Even though he was not the only scandal-tainted vice president, Spiro Agnew was for years the only former vice president not honored with a marble bust in the Senate wing of the Capitol. Congress moved to correct that in March 1993 by approving the sculpting of an Agnew likeness.

Resignations

Agnew was the second vice president to resign. The first, and only other, to resign was John C. Calhoun, Andrew Jackson's first vice president. He quit in 1832 to become a member, from South Carolina, of the Senate he had presided over as vice president. He was the last vice president allowed to appoint Senate committees.

Deaths

George Clinton was the first vice president to die in office, on April 20, 1812. A former governor of New York, Clinton served under both Thomas Jefferson and James Madison—the only president to have two vice presidents die on him. Madison's second vice president, Elbridge Gerry, died November 23, 1814.

Franklin Pierce's vice president, William Rufus de Vane King, served the shortest term as vice president—twenty-five days. By an act of Congress he had been allowed to take the oath of office outside the United States, which no other president or vice president has done. He had gone to Cuba trying in vain to cure his tuberculosis. He returned in time to die on U.S. soil, in Alabama on April 18, 1853.

In all, six vice presidents died in office. The other three were Henry Wilson (who died in 1875 and served under Grant), Thomas A. Hendricks (1885, Cleveland), and Garret A. Hobart (1899, McKinley).

Because of vice presidents' deaths, resignations, or succession to the presidency upon presidents' deaths, the nation was without a vice president for almost thirty-eight years between 1789 and 1993. Fortunately, no president died during those times.

Body Politic or Politic Body? The Congress

UNDER THE Constitution, all legislative power—the power to make laws—is vested in the United States Congress. That body has two chambers: a House of Representatives with 435 members, divided among the states according to population, and a Senate with 100 senators, two for each state. Although the Senate is sometimes called the "upper chamber," the chambers have, in fact, equal status. Representatives understandably resent being called the "lower body."

■ One Person, One Vote
Counting Noses

Every ten years since 1790 a census has been taken of the U.S. population. The process turns up much valuable information about American society, but its main purpose is to determine how many delegates each state will have in the House of Representatives. The size of the house has been fixed at 435 since Arizona and New

Gerrymandering now. The new Twelfth Congressional District of North Carolina snakes 175 miles from Durham to Charlotte along Interstate 85, and at certain points is nothing more than a thin strip along the highway. The district includes nearly every neighborhood with a majority of African-Americans between the two cities to fashion a "majority-minority" district.

New York's Twelfth Congressional District makes its way across Brooklyn, Queens, and Manhattan. By connecting a variety of Latino neighborhoods, the legislature managed to get a district that's 57.2 percent Hispanic.

Mexico joined the Union in 1912 (except for the temporary addition of two seats in 1959 when Alaska and Hawaii became

states), but after each census Congress reapportions that number among the states. (An exception followed the 1920 census, when Congress could not agree on an apportionment plan.) The Constitution guarantees each state at least one representative.

State legislatures then adjust their congressional districts to make each one as nearly equal in population as possible. This equality is required by the Supreme Court's "one person, one vote" decision, handed down in *Gray v. Sanders* (1963). Until then, some rural-dominated legislatures had drawn the lines to make farm districts much smaller than urban dis-

Gerrymandering then

125

tricts, in effect giving the state's city dwellers less representation in Congress.

New computer technology, as well as court decisions requiring equal representation among minority groups, has greatly affected the redistricting process. Some congressional districts are so weirdly contorted that they give new meaning to the term *gerrymandering*—the practice of shaping districts to benefit a particular politician, party, or minority group.

Gerry's Salamander

Before he became vice president under James Madison, Gov. Elbridge Gerry unwittingly added his name to the English language by signing a Massachusetts redistricting law. One of the new districts had an odd shape. Artist Gilbert Stuart added a head, wings, and feet to a map of the district's "dragonlike contour" and exclaimed, "That will do for a salamander!" Editor Benjamin Russell replied, "Better say a Gerrymander!" Gerry hadn't sponsored the bill, but his name evermore has been associated with the drawing of contorted election districts.

The California Powerhouse

In 1993 the state with the most representation was California, with fifty-two districts, an increase of seven since the 1980

census. Next highest was New York, with thirty-one seats. California first surpassed New York as the most populous state in 1970.

The fastest-growing state was Florida, which almost doubled the size of its congressional delegation in thirty years, from twelve seats in 1960 to twenty-three after the 1990 census.

States that gained seats, besides California and Florida, were Arizona, Georgia, North Carolina, Texas, Virginia, and Washington. Losers were Illinois, Iowa, Kansas, Kentucky, Louisiana, Massachusetts, Michigan, Montana, New Jersey, New York, Ohio, Pennsylvania, and West Virginia.

8,500 House Members?

The Constitution originally specified that there would be one representative for every thirty thousand persons, with the House of Representatives to be enlarged as the country grew. If the original ratio were still in force, the House would now have about 8,500 members. But with the 435 limit, each member now represents about 588,000 people.

Each state is guaran-

teed at least one representative under the Constitution, and seven states have the minimum. They include five geographically large states with small populations—Alaska, Montana, North Dakota, South Dakota, and Wyoming—as well as the compact states of Delaware and Vermont.

Besides its 435 voting members, the House has five nonvoting delegates representing the District of Columbia, Puerto Rico, the Virgin Islands, Guam, and American Samoa.

Multimember Districts

Until 1842 several states had districts with more than one member of Congress. As recently as 1838, for example, New York had as many as five multimember districts. Some other states elected their House members at-large, or by a combination of single-member and multimember districts. The multimember system did not affect the number of members each state was entitled to—only how they were elected. In 1842 Congress decided to do away with multimember districts, and it passed a law requiring states to divide themselves into as many districts as the number of representatives to be elected, with one member for each district. Some low-population states have only one House member, who is elected at-large in that state.

■ Measuring Up

It's easy to be a member of Congress—if one can get elected. Members don't have to be smart, educated, or even honest (although they must swear to uphold the laws). The Constitution says in Article I that a senator must be at least thirty years old and have been a citizen at least nine years. A representative must be twenty-five or older and have been a citizen seven years. Members of both chambers must be residents of the state they represent.

These are the only requirements for membership. The Supreme Court ruled in 1969 that it would take a constitutional amendment to add others. In the 1990s that decision posed a potential legal hurdle to proposals being considered in several states to limit the number of terms that members of Congress could serve.

Underage Senators

Republicans Armistead Mason (Virginia) and John H. Eaton (Tennessee)—like the more famous Henry Clay of Kentucky—were below the minimum age of thirty

Profile of the 103d Congress, 1993–1995

	House	Senate
Democrats	257	57
Republicans	176	43
Independent	1	0
Vacancies		
(as of May 8, 1993)	1	0
Average age	51.9	58.2
Men	387	94
Women	47	6
Whites	374	96
African-Americans	38	1
Hispanics	17	0
Asians, Pacific Islanders	5	2
Native Americans	0	1
Religion		
Catholic	118	23
Jewish	32	10
Protestant and others	284	67
Major occupations*		
Law	182	58
Business or banking	130	24
Public service/politics	86	97
Real estate	26	31
Journalism	24	9
Agriculture	19	27

*Totals exceed membership because some members have more than one occupation.

Members of Congress who share legislative interests sometimes form caucuses. The Arts Caucus, Hispanic Caucus, and Children's Caucus are only a few of the caucuses of the 103d Congress. Here, some of the members of the Congressional Black Caucus pose on the steps of the Capitol.

New members of the 103d Congress gather on the steps of the Capitol for the traditional freshman photograph.

when they were sworn in as senators. Mason was twenty-eight years, five months, and eighteen days in 1816, and Eaton was twenty-eight years, four months, and twenty-nine days in 1818, making him the youngest senator in history. Clay was twenty-nine years, eight months when he first entered the Senate in 1806. Since their colleagues did not challenge their qualifi-

cations, all three were sworn in despite the constitutional requirement.

The youngest senator to meet the constitutional age requirement was Virginia Democrat Rush D. Holt, who was twenty-nine when elected in November 1934. He was in no rush, however, to claim his seat—he waited until his thirtieth birthday the following June.

Members in Waiting

Only two senators-elect have been barred from taking their seats because they were not citizens for the mandatory nine years—Albert P. Gallatin of Pennsylvania, a native of Switzerland, in 1793, and Irish-born James Shields of Illinois, in 1849. Gallatin later served in the House and as secretary of the Treasury. Shields became a senator later in 1849 after he won reelection and passed the ninth year of his naturalized citizenship.

No House member has ever been excluded because of the citizenship rule.

■ Terms

House members are elected for two-year terms. Senators are elected for six-year terms, but they are staggered so that only one-third of the hundred members face the voters in election years. To begin the staggering system, the first senators had to draw lots to determine who would serve the shorter two- and four-year terms.

■ Seating Congress

Two Sessions, One Congress

Each two-year Congress is made up of two regular sessions. The first begins at noon on January 3 in odd-numbered years, following the November election of the House of Representatives. Some annual sessions run the whole year, but Congress usually takes a long summer recess in non-election years and goes home in early fall the next year to give members time to campaign.

Some Congresses have had three sessions because the members returned after adjourning one of the annual sessions. After this happened in the Seventy-sixth Congress, the remaining third session, 1940–1941, ran longer than any other in history —366 days.

Sine Die

When Congress completes its two-year session, it adjourns *sine die* (literally, "without a day" set for returning). Since the Watergate emergency of 1973, the language of the sine die resolution has allowed Congress to call itself back into session. But it has not done so since then.

Presidents have the power to call Congress back, but Harry S. Truman was the last to do it, in 1948. It was, however, to little avail. The inaction of the Republican-controlled Congress during the reconvened session incited Truman, a Democrat, to label it the "do-nothing" Eightieth Congress, which may have contributed to his upset win over Thomas E. Dewey that November.

The feisty president's colorful characterization stuck, even though the Eightieth Congress actually produced some landmark legislation, including the Marshall Plan of aid for Europe, the Truman doctrine of aid to Greece and Turkey, and unification of the armed forces under the Defense Department.

■ The Congressional Players: Leading Roles

Mr. Speaker

The Speaker of the House of Representatives holds one of the most powerful positions in the American government. He (all Speakers thus far have been men) wields strong legislative and party leadership powers and, under the Twenty-fifth Amendment to the Constitution, is next to the vice president in the line of succession to the presidency.

There is no constitutional requirement that the Speaker be a member of the House, but no outsider has ever held the job. Members of the majority party members choose the Speaker, subject to confirmation by the whole House. John Bell of Tennessee, a Whig in a House controlled by Democrats, was the sole Speaker (1834–1835) who did not belong to the majority party.

For most Speakers, the position has been the culmination of a long House career rather than a steppingstone to higher office. Only one Speaker, James K. Polk, Democrat from Tennessee, has been elected president, and only two, Republican Schuyler Colfax of Indiana and Democrat John Nance Garner of Texas, have become vice president. The only former Speaker to go on the Supreme Court was Philip P. Barbour of Virginia, appointed in 1830, seven years after his single term as Speaker.

Longevity

Texas Democrat Sam Rayburn served longer than anyone else as House Speaker (eighteen years between 1940 and 1961), but Thomas P. "Tip" O'Neill, Jr., another Democrat but from Massachusetts, had the longest continuous service as Speaker (ten years, 1977–1987).

O'Neill's successor, Jim Wright, also a Democrat from Texas, was the first Speaker to resign in midterm. Facing possible disciplinary action because of his financial affairs, Wright stepped down on June 6, 1989, and left the House June 30.

Bossy Speakers

Two of the most powerful Speakers in history were Republicans Thomas Brackett "Czar" Reed of Maine and Joseph G. "Uncle Joe" Cannon of Illinois. Their iron-

The decline of party discipline has made the job of Speaker much more difficult than it once was. Speaker Thomas P. "Tip" O'Neill's attempts at unity were not as successful as those of legendary Speaker Sam Rayburn, pictured in the painting behind O'Neill.

Thomas Brackett "Czar" Reed. Resented by some for his tremendous power, "Czar" Reed was widely admired for his wit.

fisted control of the House for most of two decades culminated in a 1910 revolt that stripped Cannon of his powers and permanently weakened the Speakership.

Reed, a giant of man who always dressed in black, established rules that gave the majority party virtually absolute control over the legislative process. Can-non did not immediately follow Reed as Speaker but was elected in 1903 when at sixty-seven he was the oldest member of the House. Cannon's use of the Rules Committee to block legislation angered the majority and sparked the revolt that ended his control of the committee. The insurgents stopped short of unseating Cannon, however, and he remained Speaker in title for another year.

Freshman Speakers

No one else has matched Henry Clay's feat of being elected Speaker on his first day in the House in 1811. But Clay, though only thirty-four, was no neophyte. He already had served two brief stints in the Senate—the first one beginning in 1806 when he was technically too young. He had not reached his thirtieth birthday, the constitutional minimum, but no one made an issue of it.

Clay left the House twice but was re-elected Speaker each time he returned. The Kentuckian known as the "Great Compromiser" also served as secretary of state before returning to the Senate, where his death in 1852 closed out one of the most remarkable American public service careers. Congress honored Clay by decreeing that he would be the first person to lie in state in the Rotunda.

One other Speaker, William Pennington, a Whig from New Jersey, was elected in his first term—but for reasons entirely different from those that made Clay so popular.

In the highly charged atmosphere just before the Civil War, the House finally settled on Pennington in 1860 as a bland compromise candidate who presumably could be impartial.

Henry Clay's last great effort to hold the Union together was known as the Compromise of 1850. Visitors packed the galleries during his debate, which marked the last joint appearance in the Senate of Clay, Daniel Webster, and John C. Calhoun.

Rap, Rap

House Speakers go through about a dozen gavels a year—not because they wear out but because some are autographed and given to sponsors of major legislation. The fourteen-inch soft maple gavels are turned out in the Capitol carpentry shop. Even sturdier is the twelve-inch-square iron-wood board the gavels are pounded on. The wood, so heavy it won't float, has not been replaced in at least ten years, according to House gavel maker Bill Beaton.

In the Senate: Vice President as Tie-Breaker

In their role as Senate president, U.S. vice presidents have voted 223 times (as of September 20, 1991) to break ties in that body. When the Senate was smaller, ties were more frequent than they are today. For example, John Adams decided twenty-nine votes and John C. Calhoun, twenty-eight. By contrast, Lyndon B. Johnson and Dan Quayle cast no deciding votes; Spiro T. Agnew, two; Walter F. Mondale, one; and George Bush, eight.

One of Bush's deciding votes came on a tie Senate Republicans forced in 1985 when they wheeled Californian Pete V. Wilson onto the floor in a hospital gurney to vote for a GOP budget plan.

Filling In: The Senate's President Pro Tem

The president pro tempore (usually shortened to pro tem) of the Senate holds a largely ceremonial job. Because the Senate president (the vice president of the United States) usually presides only when a tie vote is expected, the gavel largely rests with the president pro tem or a junior member he or she designates.

Since 1945 the pro tem title has by custom gone to the majority party member with longest service. West Virginian Robert Byrd, the president pro tem since 1989, has presided personally more often than most of his recent predecessors. Whoever holds the office is third in line to succeed the president, after the vice president and Speaker of the House.

Sen. Robert Byrd, left, who served as Senate Democratic leader for a decade, hands the gavel, the symbol of authority, to Sen. George Mitchell after Mitchell's election as majority leader in 1988.

Senate Floor Leaders

In terms of visibility and influence, the majority floor leader comes closest, but in fact the Senate has no post comparable to the House Speaker. The majority leader schedules floor action in consultation with the minority leader.

The Senate's youngest floor leader was Texas Democrat Lyndon Johnson, who was forty-four and still in his first term when he was elected minority leader in 1953. He became majority leader two years later when the Democrats gained control of the Senate.

Democrat Mike Mansfield from Montana served the longest as Senate majority

leader—sixteen years until his retirement in 1977.

Mansfield's successor and fellow Democrat, Robert C. Byrd from West Virginia, was the only senator to serve as minority leader in between stints as majority leader. Byrd was also the first majority leader to resign, stepping down in 1989 to become chairman of the Appropriations Committee. Maine Democrat George Mitchell succeeded Byrd.

Rap, Rap, Rap

The Senate has a cherished symbol—a small silver-capped ivory gavel. Although this gavel was not used after 1954 when it

Vice President John Adams is believed to have used the original ivory gavel in calling the first Senate to order in 1789. His penchant for ceremony earned him the mocking title of "His Rotundity."

began to disintegrate (it has no handle), it is placed on the vice president's desk before the opening of each Senate session. A replica of the old gavel, a gift from the government of India, has been used by the presiding officer of the Senate since 1954.

■ Committees: The Workhorses of Congress

Someone once said that an elephant looks like an animal designed by committee. One could turn that around and say that the congressional committee system resembles an elephant: it is big and powerful but can move quickly when it has to.

In any case, committees are essential to the functioning of Congress. The two chambers simply could not handle the flood of bills that the 535 members introduce each year without splitting them up and parceling them out to committees for initial consideration.

Congress basically has three types of committees: standing, select (special), and joint. Standing, or permanently authorized, committees fall into two types—appropriative or legislative. The Appropriations committees approve spending for programs authorized by the legislative committees, which also deal with general legislation.

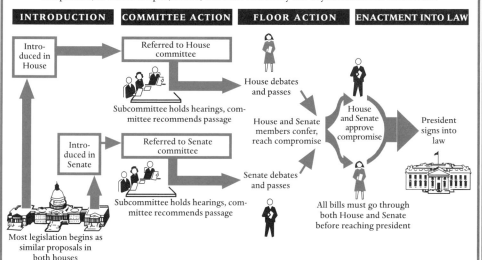

HOW A BILL BECOMES A LAW

This graphic shows the most typical way in which proposed legislation is enacted into law. There are more complicated, as well as simpler, routes, and most bills fall by the wayside and never become law.

INTRODUCTION | **COMMITTEE ACTION** | **FLOOR ACTION** | **ENACTMENT INTO LAW**

Introduced in House

Referred to House committee

Subcommittee holds hearings, committee recommends passage

House debates and passes

Introduced in Senate

Referred to Senate committee

Subcommittee holds hearings, committee recommends passage

Senate debates and passes

House and Senate members confer, reach compromise

House and Senate approve compromise

President signs into law

All bills must go through both House and Senate before reaching president

Most legislation begins as similar proposals in both houses

How a Bill Becomes a Law

Of the thousands of bills introduced in Congress every two-year session, only a handful are enacted into law. The rest are winnowed out through a process that in its simplest form goes like this.

A bill is introduced in the House or Senate (usually in a similar form in both bodies) and referred to the appropriate committee, depending on the subject. The committee passes the proposed legislation on to a subcommittee, which may hold hearings and recommend approval by the full committee. If the committee reports (approves) the bill, it sends it to the full House or Senate with a recommendation for passage. The bill is then debated on the floor and voted on.

Every bill must be passed by the House and Senate in identical form before it goes to the president. If the two approved versions of the bill differ, they are sent to a conference committee of members from both chambers. Any compromise worked out by the conference committe goes back to the House and Senate for final approval.

The bill then becomes law if the president signs it. If the president vetoes the bill, the bill becomes law only if Congress over-rides the veto by a two-thirds majority of each chamber. It also becomes law without a presidential signature if the president takes no action within ten days, excluding Sundays. If the president does not sign the bill and Congress adjourns within the ten-day period, the bill is said to be "pocket-vetoed" and it does not become law.

The Senate Judiciary Committee was thrust into the spotlight when, during Clarence Thomas's nationally televised Supreme Court confirmation hearings, Anita Hill, a former colleague of Thomas's, alleged that he had sexually harassed her.

Select or special committees are supposed to be temporary (although they may be around for years), and their mission usually is to investigate rather than legislate. Joint committees have members from both chambers and usually alternate the chair between the House and Senate.

Below the committee level are subcommittees, which number into the hundreds. In the 103d Congress (1993–1995), there were 290 committees and subcommittees.

To further confuse the picture, there are conference committees, which are created as needed to resolve differences between House and Senate versions of the same bill.

◼ In Congress Assembled . . .

Congress's main job is to pass laws. These can be very simple or they can run to thousands of pages and involve years of work. But from the simplest to the most complex, a federal law must begin with the following words: "Be it enacted by the Senate and House of Representatives of the United States of America in Congress assembled. . . ." Without those words, known as the enacting clause, an act of Congress is just a piece of paper—even though it has been, as required, passed in identical form by both the House and Senate and signed by the president. In the House a quick way to kill a bill is to "omit the enacting clause."

Talkathon

The 100-member Senate, unlike the 435-member House of Representatives, allows virtually unlimited debate on bills. Senators sometimes use this advantage to talk a bill to death. This is known as a filibuster, a delaying tactic to block action on a bill by nonstop speech or procedural delays.

In 1957 South Carolina's Strom Thurmond, a Democrat who later became

---

Say What?

For the most part, Congress uses everyday English as it goes about making laws. But some legislative terms need a little explanation. Here are a few not explained elsewhere in this chapter:

Bill is the legislative form used for most legislation. When passed by both houses in identical form and signed by the president (or repassed by Congress over a presidential veto), bills become laws.

Concurrent resolution is used for a matter affecting the operations of each house, such as fixing the time of adjournment. Such resolutions must be passed in the same form by each chamber but do not require a presidential signature and do not have the force of the law.

Joint resolution is in every respect like a *bill* except that it is generally used when dealing with a single item or issue such as an emergency appropriation bill.

Markup is the painstaking revising of legislation in committee or subcommittee. Members and staff go through the bill line by line, considering each provision to arrive at a version to be sent to the full committee or floor.

Report is a numbered document that a committee or subcommittee issues to explain a bill it has acted on. Sometimes the report also contains statements from those opposing the bill. When a committee *reports* a bill, it usually means it approved it. Sometimes, though, a committee will report a bill unfavorably to bring about floor action on it.

Resolution deals with a matter entirely to do with one house of Congress—such as a rule or procedure—and is not considered by the other house or sent to the president for a signature. (A *joint resolution,* however, requires passage by both houses and the president's signature and carries the force of law.)

Table in effect is the same as *kill.* In the House especially, tabling a bill defeats it. This is not always true in the Senate.

---

a Republican, set the record by speaking twenty-four hours and eighteen minutes against a civil rights bill. But most filibusters are not so dramatic, featuring instead repeated quorum calls or similar tactics.

The Senate now follows a two-track system to prevent a filibuster from bogging everything down. Routine business can proceed while the filibustered bill is being held up.

Sen. Strom Thurmond of South Carolina during his record-setting talkathon in 1957.

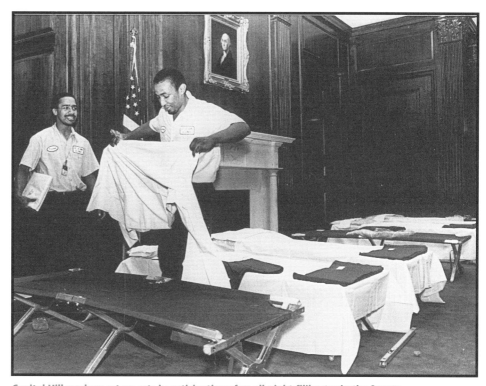

Capitol Hill workers set up cots in anticipation of an all-night filibuster in the Senate.

Senate rules now permit cloture—that is, shutting off a filibuster. If sixty senators vote for cloture, the debate can continue for only thirty more hours. Invoking cloture on changes in Senate rules is more difficult, requiring up to sixty-seven votes (two-thirds of those voting).

In 1993 Senate Republicans used a filibuster to prevent passage of President Bill Clinton's jobs bill package. Although Democrats controlled the Senate, they could not muster the sixty votes needed for cloture. This incident and others like it in the past raised questions about the constitutionality of a rule that permits a minority to thwart the majority will. One drastic proposal: ax the Senate and have a one-house legislature based on population.

Fictional Filibuster

One of the most famous filibusters was not fact but fiction—Jimmy Stewart's in *Mr. Smith Goes to Washington.*

Workload

The Ninetieth Congress (1967–1969) set a record for the number of bills introduced: 26,460. Of these, 1,002 were enacted into

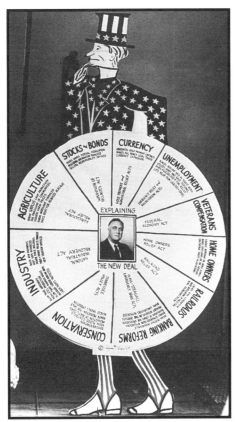

Uncle Sam helps President Roosevelt explain the New Deal.

law, including 362 private bills to help individuals, such as granting an exemption from immigration laws. The Eighty-fourth (1955–1957) enacted the highest number of public laws, 1,028.

Since the 1970s the volume of bills introduced has declined, partly because of changes that have permitted more cosponsors on identical bills. The 100th Congress (1987–1989) had the lowest number of bills introduced in forty years—9,588.

Before World War II, Congress's output was even lower. But in terms of substantial legislation, the first session of the Seventy-third Congress (1933–1935) was perhaps the most productive in history. In one hundred days it passed fifteen major components of Franklin D. Roosevelt's New Deal program.

Committee of the Whole

To help it wade through the huge pile of legislation it must consider each year, the House of Representatives meets as "the Committee of the Whole House on the State of the Union"—known more commonly as the Committee of the Whole. It's the same body as the House, meeting under a different name and under less stringent rules of procedure. It needs only 100 members to make a quorum, versus 218 for the full House, which helps to expedite action.

The committee considers amendments, but it cannot pass a bill. It reports the bill with recommended amendments to the full House for final action. The Speaker does not preside but appoints another member as chairman. The Speaker resumes presiding, however, when the body reconvenes as the House.

Five More Floor Votes

In a historic action, the House changed its rules in January 1993 to permit delegates from the District of Columbia and four territories—American Samoa, Guam, Puerto Rico, and the U.S. Virgin Islands—to vote on the floor in the Committee of the Whole. The action was a victory for D.C. delegate Eleanor Holmes Norton, who argued that they already could vote in legislative committees of the House.

All five delegates were Democrats, and House Republicans unanimously opposed the change as offsetting half of the ten seats they had gained in the 1992 election. To meet their objections, the rule was changed to exclude the delegates from voting the second time around on legislation where their five votes provided the margin of victory in the first vote.

The Mace

In ancient Rome the mace—an ax bound in a bundle of rods—symbolized magisterial power. In the U.S. House, besides standing for power, the mace indicates what kind of session is under way. If the mace is on a tall pedestal beside the Speaker's desk, the session is a regular one.

Here the sergeant at arms bears the mace. On a number of occasions the sergeant at arms has lifted the mace from its pedestal and "presented" it before an unruly member, order is said to have been restored.

Constitution, Jefferson's Manual, and Rules of the House of Representatives. The comparable Senate manual has an even longer full title: *The Senate Manual Containing the Standing Rules, Orders, Laws, and Resolutions Affecting the Business of the United States Senate.*

Time Out of Joint

A *joint session* of Congress is more formal than a *joint meeting*. Only the president addresses a joint session; when other dignitaries are to be heard, each body simply recesses to meet with the other—a joint meeting.

Russian president Boris Yeltsin addresses a joint meeting of Congress in 1992.

If it's on a low pedestal nearby, the House is meeting as the Committee of the Whole.

■ On the Floor: From Rules To Gofers

Jefferson's 'How-to' Book

Thomas Jefferson found little to guide him in 1797–1801 when, as vice president, he was also president of the Senate. So he wrote his own handbook of procedures, now known as *Jefferson's Manual of Parliamentary Practice.* The House of Representatives adopted his manual in part in 1837, and it remains the foundation for many Senate and House practices. The House version states that "the Manual is regarded by English parliamentarians as the best statement of what the law of Parliament was at the time Jefferson wrote it."

For each two-year term of Congress, the House parliamentarian revises the chamber's manual, which bears the formal title

The first foreign dignitary to appear at a joint meeting of Congress was David Kalakaua, king of the Sandwich Islands (now Hawaii), in 1874. Among others so honored have been British prime minister Winston Churchill in 1943, French president Charles de Gaulle in 1960, Polish labor leader Lech Walesa in 1989, Queen Elizabeth of England in 1991, and Russian president Boris Yeltsin in 1992.

In the past Congress usually convened a joint session for presidential inaugurations, but it has not done so since the Johnson-Humphrey inauguration of 1965. It did meet in joint session for Gerald R. Ford's assumption of the presidency on August 12, 1974, following the resignation of Richard Nixon.

Saved by the Bell

Members of Congress can be forgiven if they hear ringing in their ears. An elaborate system of bells, buzzers, and lights tells them what's happening on the floor and summons them to vote. Even the congressional handball court has a buzzer.

The Senate and House use somewhat different codes, up to a maximum of six rings. As befits the larger and more complex body, the House has eleven different combinations of long and short rings. For example, one long ring and three shorts

Since 1973 the House has used an electronic voting system for recorded votes. Members insert plastic cards into voting boxes. Their votes are displayed on a lighted board behind the Speaker's rostrum.

mean a count (known as a quorum call) is being taken to see if enough members (a quorum) are available to conduct business. In both the House and Senate a majority (half plus one) of the members are needed for a quorum. When the House meets as the Committee of the Whole, only 100 of the 435 members make up a quorum.

Five rings tell House members to hurry over to the floor for an electronically recorded vote. In the Senate five rings mean there are five minutes remaining on a yea-or-nay vote. One long ring means the Senate is convening. Six rings signal the end of "morning" (routine) business. In the House, which rarely uses a morning hour, six rings signify recess.

One for the Books

At least one member of Congress could boast of being in the *Guinness Book of World Records*. Rep. William H. Natcher, Democrat from Kentucky, hadn't missed a recorded vote in forty years—and was still going strong in early 1993. As of April 12, 1993, he had voted 17,884 consecutive times, occasionally at considerable personal sacrifice.

The Senate record was held by Wisconsin Democrat William Proxmire, who in 1988 completed the final twenty-two years of his thirty-one year career without missing a roll call.

Most members of Congress have good to excellent attendance records, as measured by their voting participation scores. In 1992 the House had 473 recorded votes, and fourteen members hit every one of them. Eighteen senators scored 100 percent on 270 votes. The average senator voted 95 percent of the time; the average House member, 93 percent. Congress's average reached a low of 79 percent in 1970.

Vice President Thomas Marshall was popular with the pages on the Hill. Here he poses with Senate pages before a holiday party.

Pages

Pages are high school juniors who attend a special school in the morning and run errands for Congress in the afternoon. Nominated by members, they serve for one or two semesters, or during a summer. They report to the House doorkeeper or the Senate sergeant at arms, under whose orders they hand out documents on the House or Senate floor and hurry through the corridors to deliver messages.

The first page was Grafton Hanson, appointed in 1829 by Sen. Daniel Webster of Massachusetts. The second page, appointed by Webster in 1831, was Isaac Bassett, who worked for the Senate the rest of his life, sixty-four years. In 1970 Sen. Jacob Javits of New York appointed the first female page, Paulette Desell.

Former pages who became members of Congress include Senators David Pryor of Arkansas and Christopher Dodd of Connecticut, and Representatives John Dingell of Michigan, Bill Emerson of Missouri, Douglas H. Bosco of California, Paul E. Kanjorski of Pennsylvania, and Jim Kolbe of Arizona.

■ Off the Floor: Oversight and the Home Folks

Besides their committee work on legislation, members of Congress spend many hours in their offices and hearing rooms handling the other activities that go with the job. These include oversight of federal agencies and constituent service.

Looking over Shoulders

Overseeing the work of departmental and independent agencies is one of Congress's most important functions. Even though it's the executive branch's turf, the legislature can safely do this because in almost all cases Congress created the programs and earmarked the money for them.

Congress also exercises oversight through its own agencies, such as the General Accounting Office, and through the budget process.

Shot Down: The Legislative Veto

In 1983 the Supreme Court ruled unconstitutional a device that was becoming increasingly popular as a means of oversight—the so-called legislative veto. This provision, which was inserted into many laws, allowed one or both houses of Congress to overrule actions that the executive branch took to carry out the legislation. In its decision *Immigration and Naturalization Service v. Chadha,* the Court ruled that Congress had overstepped its authority.

Star Makers: Investigations

Congress's broad authority to investigate conditions in society and the Senate's power to confirm presidential appointments have produced dramatic hearings and made celebrities of some participants.

In the 1950s Senators Estes Kefauver and John McClellan became national figures with their televised hearings on crime and labor racketeering. But another Senate chairman of the same era, Joseph R. McCarthy from Wisconsin, drew condemnation from his colleagues for his behavior in probing alleged communism in government. His smear tactics added the term *McCarthyism* to the language.

Sen. Joseph McCarthy

Sen. Sam Ervin, center, and Sen. Howard Baker, left, during the Watergate hearings.

In the 1970s the jowly chairman of the Senate Watergate committee, Democrat Sam Ervin from North Carolina, gained fame and stature from his judicious handling of the investigation that toppled the administration of Richard Nixon.

One congressional investigation that drew great publicity was the 1987 televised grilling of Lt. Col. Oliver L. North and other witnesses in the Iran-contra affair.

In 1991 Anita Hill's allegations of sexual harassment nearly derailed Clarence Thomas's nomination to the Supreme Court. Hill's support from the public

ensured that future witnesses with similar stories would be taken more seriously.

At Your Service . . .

When the Social Security check is late, veterans' hospital care is denied, or the college loan is turned down, the first inclination of many Americans is to call or write their senator or representative. The effort may not get results, but few members of Congress dare ignore these requests from the people they represent. This so-called constituent service is time-consuming for members and their staffs. In fact, the mod-

ern congressional office has been likened to a corporate customer service department.

The steady rise in appeals for help with federal agencies accounts for a large part of the explosion in congressional office staffs, particularly in the state or district offices. In the early 1970s less than 25 percent of congressional staffers worked in home offices. Today 41 percent of representatives' staff work in district offices and 35 percent of senators' staff work in state offices.

Many members offer constituent service with an eye toward reelection. They send newsletters, provide mobile offices, sched-

Whether they are hobnobbing or actually attending to their constituents' requests, members of Congress spend much time at work in their home districts. Here Rep. Mike Synar greets folks back home in Oklahoma.

War Powers

Article I, section 8, of the Constitution gives the Congress the power to declare war, raise and support an army, provide and maintain a navy, and make rules regulating the armed forces. The president, however, is the commander in chief of the military (Article II, section 2). This dual responsibility for the nation's defense has proven over the years to be controversial, and at times downright messy. Since the nation's birth, U.S. armed forces have engaged in many major and minor conflicts overseas, but only on five accasions has Congress formally declared war: the War of 1812 (1812–1814), the Mexican War (1846–1848), the Spanish-American War (1898), World War I (1917–1918), and World War II (1941–1945). Although it was one of the most painful experiences in U.S. history, the war in Vietnam was undeclared.

This famous caricature by David Levine shows Johnson's famous gall bladder scar drawn in the shape of South Vietnam.

ule neighborhood meetings, and appear on radio and TV talk shows—always emphasizing their availability to help.

■ A Favorite Congressional Past-time: Pulling Its Pursestrings

The president and Congress share control of the budget process, which determines how much the government will spend for each fiscal year. (The fiscal year, which begins October 1, is designated by the calendar year in which it ends.) Early in each

calendar year the president sends to Congress a proposed spending plan for the government's fiscal year. Since 1974 Congress has had a mechanism for coming up with its own version of the budget. Months of negotiation then follow in which the two sides try to arrive at a compromise budget before the new fiscal year begins.

The 'D' Words: Deficit and Debt

If the government spends more in a year than it takes in—as it has done almost

every year since the 1960s—it is faced with a *deficit*. Or to put it more simply, the government is "in the red." To make up its shortfall, the government must borrow money. This in turn adds to the *national debt*, the accumulated amount of money the government owes to others. Just paying the interest on the debt costs more than $200 billion a year, making it the third biggest item in the federal budget, exceeded only by defense and Social Security. The entire federal budget for fiscal 1973 was lower than the amount needed for interest on the national debt alone twenty years later.

A River of Red Ink

The last fiscal year the federal budget was balanced was 1969, when it ran a small surplus. That was during the last three months of the Lyndon Johnson administration and the first nine months of the Richard Nixon administration.

For fiscal 1993 President George Bush's budget estimated spending (outlays) at $1.5 trillion and revenues at $1.2 trillion, for a deficit of $319 billion. The actual deficit for fiscal 1992 was lower than expected, $292.4 billion.

In one of his first legislative victories, Bill Clinton won congressional approval of a fiscal 1994 budget that set spending and revenue levels at almost the same level as Bush's for fiscal 1993 but with a lower expected deficit, $247.5 billion.

The last president to pay off the national debt was Andrew Jackson, who served from 1829 to 1837. By the end of the Bush administration, the debt exceeded $4 trillion.

Entitlements

A word often heard in connection with the federal deficit problem is *entitlements*.

President Lyndon Johnson signs legislation in 1965 establishing the Medicare program, as former president Harry Truman, Bess Truman, Hubert Humphrey, and Lady Bird Johnson look on. Entitlement programs such as Medicare make up close to one-half of the federal budget.

An entitlement program is one in which citizens become eligible for benefits simply by reaching a certain age or meeting another requirement. Examples of such programs are Social Security, Medicare, and Medicaid.

Because the government must provide the benefits once eligibility is established, entitlement programs generally are not subject to annual allotments of money (appropriations) from Congress. Thus, they are often described as uncontrollable, making it almost impossible to hold down federal spending.

Social Security, the largest entitlement, was taken "off budget" in 1986, but its spending and revenue figures continued to be counted in deficit calculations. Financed by its own tax, Social Security was running a $52 billion annual surplus in 1992, but budget planners worried that the program could run out of money in the next century as the "baby boomers" of the 1950s reached retirement age.

Gramm-Rudman-Hollings Act

An important piece of legislation in Congress's effort to reduce the federal deficit and sort out the ailing budget process was the Gramm-Rudman-Hollings Act, formally the Balanced Budget and Emergency Deficit Control Act of 1985. The act set a

In 1985 this threesome gave their names to a new antideficit law: from left, Senators Ernest F. Hollings, Phil Gramm, and Warren B. Rudman.

"You know you have my support on pork and beans, but where do you stand on chicken and dumplings?"

timetable for balancing the budget, with automatic spending cuts if necessary. But as the deficit continued to grow, Congress kept pushing back the balanced-budget deadline.

By 1991 the act had been largely replaced by new legislation that allowed the deficit to grow with the economy. President George Bush, who in 1988 had pledged "no new taxes," agreed to the new approach even though it raised some taxes—mostly the "sin" taxes on alcohol and tobacco.

One of the sponsors of the 1985 act,

Republican senator Warren B. Rudman from New Hampshire, gave up his Senate seat in 1993 out of frustration with Congress's inability to control spending, especially for entitlements. The act also was named for Senators Phil Gramm, Republican from Texas, and Ernest F. Hollings, Democrat from South Carolina.

Pork Barrel Politics

George Bush, like many presidents before him, asked for the line-item veto: that is, the power to reject part of an appropriations bill without vetoing the whole bill.

Congress, as it always has, refused. Members prefer the Constitution's existing all-or-nothing system because it protects the "pork barrel" projects for their states or districts. If a pet program is attached to a vital appropriation, such as for defense, the president cannot strike it out without risking loss of the entire bill. A change to "cafeteria" government by item veto would mark a dramatic shift of power to the president.

Many state constitutions require a balanced budget and empower the governor to veto specific spending items. Bush's successor, former Arkansas governor Bill Clinton, said during his presidential campaign that he would seek a constitutional amendment permitting a line-item veto.

Balanced-Budget Amendment

In 1992 Congress rejected proposals for a constitutional amendment requiring the federal budget to be balanced, just as many states require of their budgets. Opponents argued that such an amendment would hamstring the U.S. government in adjusting the budget to economic conditions. Unlike the federal government, they pointed out, states cannot print money and therefore cannot engage in deficit spending for very long. Also, there is nothing to prevent a president from submitting a balanced budget if a way can be found to do so. No recent president has.

Passing Out the $$$$$$

Congress uses a two-step system to approve outlays from the federal Treasury. First, it passes *authorization bills* to approve government programs and set ceilings on expenditures for them. An authorization may last indefinitely.

Second, it passes *appropriations bills,* which tell the various agencies just how much they may spend in that year. As a rule, Congress authorizes more money for a program than it actually appropriates.

By custom, the House votes before the Senate on appropriations bills, which are also called spending bills or money bills. All money bills for raising revenue, as opposed to spending it, must originate in the House under the Constitution.

Budgeting the Bucks

In recent years the congressional budget process has sometimes replaced the traditional appropriations system. Congress created the current budget process in 1974 after President Richard Nixon repeatedly impounded (refused to spend) money appropriated for certain projects and programs. Until then, Congress had merely acted in piecemeal fashion on the president's budget.

The Congressional Budget and Impoundment Control Act of 1974 set up House and Senate Budget committees to consider the budget as a whole. Guided by the committees, Congress was to set spending targets in a budget resolution each year, and the Appropriations committees were supposed to stay within those guidelines.

With the added complications, appropriations bills seldom were passed by October 1, when the new fiscal year began. To keep the government going, Congress relied increasingly on a stopgap device known as a *continuing resolution,* containing

the texts of uncompleted appropriations bills. In the late 1980s all thirteen appropriations bills were folded into one omnibus continuing resolution. In 1988 President Ronald Reagan began his State of the Un-

questration proved inadequate, Congress and President George Bush held a budget summit in 1990 and revised the 1974 act still further. The Budget Enforcement Act capped appropriations in three categories—domestic, defense, and international programs—and made it difficult to shift resources from one category to the other.

Because the 1990 compromise raised some taxes to help reduce the deficit, President Bush in effect reneged on his 1988 campaign pledge in which he said, "Read my lips. No new taxes." Throughout the 1992 presidential campaign, then, Bush had to defend his signing of the bill as something he was forced to do.

ion address by displaying one of the huge bills. He dramatically showed that the process was not working.

'Read My Lips'

The 1985 Balanced Budget and Emergency Deficit Control Act (also known as Gramm-Rudman-Hollings) trundled out a new weapon—sequestration, or across-the-board cuts—into the war on the deficit. If Congress failed to keep spending within limits, sequestration automatically occurred.

But when even the dreaded threat of se-

Budget Timetable

In the nine months leading up to the October 1 start of the federal government's fiscal (financial) year, the president and Congress must meet several deadlines to ensure that the money needed to operate the government will be available when the fiscal year begins.

The first Monday in February, the president submits budget requests. April 15 is the target date for the House and Senate to agree on a budget resolution setting guidelines for spending and taxes. On May 15, House Appropriations committees and

subcommittees begin acting on spending bills. Then during the summer and early fall, House-Senate conferences resolve differences between their versions of the appropriations bills. October 1 is the drop-dead date for the president to sign appropriations bills into law.

If the thirteen regular appropriations bills are not ready, Congress must pass stopgap continuing resolutions or the government must shut down. If any of the bills push government spending over the previously agreed limits and Congress adjourns, the administration after fifteen days must order across-the-board cuts in the overspending category (defense, domestic, or international).

■ A Not-So-Favorite Congressional Pastime: Impeachment

Congress has used sparingly one of its most awesome powers: impeachment. In more than two hundred years, it has actually impeached only sixteen officials (as of mid-1992), and of those only seven—all federal judges—were convicted and removed from office for the constitutional offenses of "Treason, Bribery, or other high Crimes and Misdemeanors." (One of the impeached federal justices, Alcee Hastings, was elected to Congress in 1992 after his conviction was overturned in the courts.)

Impeachment is a two-stage process in which the House of Representatives makes the formal charge, like a grand jury, and the Senate decides the accused's guilt or innocence, much like a regular jury would. Under Article I of the Constitution, the House of Representatives has the sole authority to impeach and the Senate alone tries all impeachments, with a two-thirds majority needed for conviction. If the president is being tried, the chief justice of the United States presides.

Only one president has been impeached and tried, Andrew Johnson in 1868, on charges of violating the Tenure of Office Act by removing Secretary of

War Edwin M. Stanton without Congress's approval. Vehement political tensions after the Civil War were the true basis for the flimsy charges, and the tenure act eventually was declared unconstitutional.

In the Senate trial Johnson escaped conviction by a single vote. His unexpected support from Edmund Gibson Ross, a freshman Republican senator from Kansas, is widely cited as an example of political courage. At the last minute, Ross sided with six other GOP mavericks and the Democrats to make the margin 35–19, one vote shy of the 36 needed to find Johnson guilty.

Except for Johnson, Sen. William Blount (charges dismissed in 1799), and Secretary of War William W. Belknap (acquitted in 1876), all other impeached officials have been members of the judiciary, including Supreme Court jus-

Although President Andrew Johnson did not attend, the two-and-a-half month long Senate trial drew a capacity crowd. Tickets were required for admission.

tice Samuel Chase, acquitted in 1805.

Judges have been targeted for impeachment in greater numbers than any other federal officials because they hold lifetime appointments and cannot be fired. One of those convicted, Harry E. Claiborne of Nevada, was continuing to draw his judge's salary while in prison for tax fraud until he was removed from office.

While few officials have actually been impeached, more than sixty have had impeachment proceedings initiated against them. Some have averted the indignity by leaving office, most notably President Richard Nixon, who resigned facing near-certain impeachment in 1974 for his role in the Watergate burglary coverup.

■ Keeping a Clean House and Senate

Members Only

Congress sometimes tries to bar (exclude) new members whose election is in doubt or who are accused of past misconduct. Only thirteen exclusion efforts have succeeded—three in the Senate and ten in the House.

One of the House's most famous exclusion cases was overturned by the Supreme Court. Flamboyant Harlem Democrat Adam Clayton Powell, Jr., had been a member of the House for more than

Rep. Adam Clayton Powell talks to the press in 1967.

twenty years when that body denied him his seat in 1967. Powell had rubbed many colleagues the wrong way with his absenteeism, disregard for the tax laws, and refusal to cooperate with investigating committees.

The Court ruled in 1969 that the House acted improperly because Powell met the constitutional requirements for membership. But he had already regained his seat through reelection, although he rarely

attended sessions. He lost the seat the following year and died in 1972.

Crime and Punishment

The Constitution allows Congress to write its own rules but also makes it difficult to expel a member for breaking them. A two-thirds majority vote is needed for expulsion.

Only one member, Democrat Michael J. "Ozzie" Myers of Pennsylvania, has been dismissed for corruption. The House ex-

---

Who Said It?

My retainer has not been renewed or refreshed as usual. If it is wished that my relation to the Bank should be continued, it may be well to send me the usual retainers.
—Sen. Daniel Webster, Whig from Massachusetts, to the Bank of the United States, December 21, 1833

On entering the House of Representatives at Washington, one is struck by the vulgar demeanor of that great assembly. Often there is not a distinguished man in the whole number. Its members are almost all obscure individuals. . . . They are mostly village lawyers, men in trade, or even persons belonging to the lower classes of society. . . .

Tocqueville

At few yards' distance is the door of the Senate, which . . . is composed of eloquent advocates, distinguished generals, wise magistrates, and statesmen of note, whose argu-

ments would do honor to the most remarkable parliamentary debates of Europe.
—Alexis de Tocqueville, *Democracy in America,* late 1820s

Congress in session is Congress on public exhibition, whilst Congress in its committee rooms is Congress at work.
—Woodrow Wilson, *Congressional Government,* 1885

It could probably be shown by facts and figures that there is no distinctly native American criminal class except Congress.
—Mark Twain, *Following the Equator,* 1897

But with Congress—every time they make a joke it's a law. And every time they make a law it's a joke.
—Humorist Will Rogers, 1930s

Don't try to go too fast. Learn your job. Don't ever talk until you know what you're talking about. . . . If you want to get along, go along.
—Speaker Sam Rayburn, Democrat from Texas, as quoted by Neil MacNeil in *Forge of Democracy: The House of Representatives,* 1963

Harrison Williams, the only senator caught in the Abscam scandal, resigned to escape expulsion.

Charles H. Keating, Jr., surrounded by press and police, arrives on Capitol Hill to testify before the House Banking Committee.

pelled Myers in October 1980 after he was convicted of bribery in the Abscam (short for Arab scam) scandal of the late 1970s. This FBI sting operation used videotapes to catch members of Congress in the act of accepting bribes from phony Arab sheiks.

Besides Myers, one senator and five other representatives also were convicted in the scandal, and all resigned or were defeated for reelection. The lone senator involved, Democrat Harrison A. Williams, Jr. (New Jersey), was only the fourth senator convicted in office. He resigned to avoid expulsion.

All other expulsions from the House have been for treason or disloyalty, mostly during the Civil War. Only fifteen senators and four representatives have been expelled.

To the Woodshed

Next to exclusion or expulsion, Congress's harshest punishment for errant members is censure or reprimand. The terms mean almost the same thing, but censured House members must stand before their peers and listen to the resolution rebuking them. Reprimanded members are spared this indignity.

No House members have been cen-

sured since 1983, when Democrat Gerry E. Studds of Massachusetts and Republican Daniel B. Crane of Illinois were disciplined for sexual misconduct with young pages—Studds with a male and Crane with a female.

In recent years the Senate has used *condemn, denounce,* or *reprimand* as alternative terms of chastisement. Of the six senators disciplined since 1903, only Thomas J. Dodd, Democrat from Connecticut, has been censured—in 1967 for financial misconduct. The other five cases generally have been regarded as censure by another name.

The Senate's first use of reprimand came in 1991 against Alan Cranston, Democratic member from California, one of the so-called Keating Five senators investigated for accepting help from officers of a failing California savings and loan. It was also the first instance in which the Ethics Committee had acted for the full Senate in rebuking a member.

■ Congressional Scandals

Despite all the jokes to the contrary, most members of Congress are honest, hard-working, decent men and women. But in any large group there are bound to be exceptions, and from time to time some unscrupulous members have brought shame on the national legislature.

Crédit Mobilier

One of the first big scandals arose in the 1870s during the completion of the Union Pacific rail link between the East and West coasts. To undertake the construction, Union Pacific hired a Paris-based company, Crédit Mobilier—a company enriched by lending money backed by mobile property (such as railroad cars) rather than the usual real estate. Crédit Mobilier became a clone of Union Pacific, with the same directors. Several members of Congress, including

ETTA HULME ©1991 FORT WORTH STAR-TELEGRAM NEA

CONGRESS EXEMPTS ITSELF FROM THE LAW OF GRAVITY AND FLOATS AWAY, RESOLVING THE ETHICAL PROBLEM OF CONGRESS EXEMPTING ITSELF FROM LAWS THAT APPLY TO EVERYBODY ELSE.

House Speaker James G. Blaine, a Republican from Maine, were investigated for accepting bribes from the company in the form of money or stock. The scandal also touched executive branch members, including Vice President Schuyler Colfax.

No members of Congress went to jail in the scandal, but it brought about an important Supreme Court decision, *Kilbourn v. Thompson* (1881), that affirmed Congress's constitutional power to punish its own members. Speaker Blaine was cleared, but Vice President Colfax failed to win renomi-

nation and several House and Senate members were disciplined.

'Koreagate'

A more recent major scandal involving a group of lawmakers was dubbed "Koreagate" because it came soon after the Watergate investigation that drove President Richard Nixon from office in 1974. Several House members were disciplined for accepting money and gifts from South Korean businessman Tongsun Park.

Through Park and others, South Korea

PLAYBOY | PENTHOUSE | HUSTLER | CONGRESSIONAL QUARTERLY

© Copley News Service

Sex scandals have hurt or ruined the political careers of several members of Congress. Cavorting with stripper Fanne Foxe cost Wilbur Mills his House Ways and Means chair in 1974. Two years later Wayne Hays lost the House Administration chair for keeping a mistress, Elizabeth Ray, on the payroll despite her lack of clerical or other professional skills. Colleen Gardner charged that she had been kept on the payroll by Rep. John Young of Texas for sex. More recently, beauty queen Tai Collins claimed to have had an affair with Sen. Charles Robb of Virginia.

reportedly dispensed up to $1 million a year in illegal lobbying of Congress. The testimony of Park, who returned after first fleeing the country, helped to convict a former House member who had received $200,000.

The Keating Five

The Senate's most publicized scandal of modern times grew out of the collapse of the savings and loan industry in the late 1980s. The Senate investigated five senators for helping a troubled California S&L headed by Charles H. Keating, Jr., in exchange for campaign funds. Of the so-called Keating Five, only veteran Democrat senator Alan Cranston from California was found to have erred enough to warrant a reprimand. He did not seek reelection the following year, 1992.

'Rubbergate'

Public outrage erupted in September 1991 when Congress's watchdog arm, the General Accounting Office, reported that the House bank had covered thousands of bad checks without penalizing the overdrawn representatives.

Technically, the checks were not "bounced" but floated by the members before their paychecks were deposited. And, strictly speaking, it was not a bank but sort of a "cash club" operated by the sergeant at arms for members' convenience. Whatever the case, the voters were furious that their representatives could freely engage in banking practices that would cost ordinary citizens expensive fees.

Already faced with a strong anti-incumbent mood on the eve of an election year, Speaker Thomas S. Foley, Democrat from Washington, shut down the bank and replaced the sergeant at arms. Within months, the members' worst fears were realized as the voters began picking off the check-kiters. The first to go in a primary defeat was Democrat Charles A. Hayes from Illinois, who had been exposed as floating 716 checks.

In April 1992 the House made public the names of 325 current or former members who had overdrafts between July 1988 and October 1991. The number of overdrafts for individuals ranged from 996 to 1. The overdrafters were members and House leaders from both parties, including Speaker Foley (2 overdrafts) and Minority Whip Newt Gingrich, a Republican from Georgia (22 overdrafts).

House Post Office Scandal

Members of Congress can mail almost anything official without a stamp. All they need is the "frank"—their signature or a facsimile of it on the envelope. Then why were some House members buying thousands of dollars in stamps every year?

That's what federal law enforcers were trying to determine in what began as an investigation of thefts from the House Post Office in 1991. Allegations arose that lax procedures could have allowed vouchers for stamps to be exchanged for cash.

By late 1992 the House postmaster had resigned and several clerks had pleaded guilty to various charges in the case. But a federal grand jury was weighing evidence that higher-ups may have been implicated.

The grand jury subpoenaed the records of three members, including Illinois Democrat Dan Rostenkowski, chairman of the House Ways and Means Committee. A Congressional Quarterly tally showed that Rostenkowski bought $29,672 in stamps from 1986 to 1992.

■ The Supporting Cast on Capitol Hill

Making laws, raising and spending revenues, and representing the interests of 256 million Americans are a complex business. That is why for every one of the 535 members of Congress, there are about 70 congressional employees on Capitol Hill. Some work directly for senators and representatives, but most are on the staffs of the various support units, including House and Senate committees, the Library of Congress, General Accounting Office, Congressional Budget Office, and Capitol police force, among others.

Staffing Up

The explosion of congressional staff began after World War II. For example, from 1930 to 1947 the personal staff of House members increased from 840 to 1,440 and staff of the standing committees from 112 to 193. By 1991 House personal staff had skyrocketed to 7,278 and committee staff to 2,201.

On the Senate side, personal staff grew from 280 in 1930 to 590 in 1947. By 1991, however, they numbered 4,294. Over the 1930–1947 period, standing committee staff increased from 163 to 290, only to balloon to 1,030 by 1991.

Many women have found job opportunities in Washington, D.C., that were not available in their hometowns. These five sisters—all employed as secretaries by five different members of Congress in 1924—posed during their lunch break.

Speaker Thomas Foley's staff, pictured here in 1989, included his wife Heather seated beside him at center right. Under the nepotism rule, she was serving without pay as his chief of staff.

In all, the legislative branch employed about 31,000 persons in 1993.

All Work . . . and Pay, Too

The highest-paid congressional staffers made about $10,000–$20,000 less than their bosses in 1991. The maximum committee staff salary was about $99,200 in the Senate and $115,100 in the House.

For personal staff the maximums were $120,000 in the Senate and $104,000 in the House. By comparison, senators and representatives received $125,000. (The figure increased to $133,600 in 1993.) In the executive branch, the highest senior executive service rate (ES-6) was $115,700. The presi-

dent of the United States received $200,000.

House members were allowed to hire eighteen full-time aides. There was no limit in the Senate.

According to the secretary of the Senate's report, two California members, Democrat Alan Cranston and Republican John Seymour, paid more than $1 million in staff salaries. In the House another Californian, Democrat Henry Waxman, had the highest salary expense, $574,824, according to a newspaper survey.

Interns: 'Camp Congress'

A source of cheap (if not free) labor for Congress is the three thousand to eight

thousand student interns who work on Capitol Hill every summer. The Hill has been dubbed "Camp Congress" for those lucky enough to take part. Sponsoring organizations and congressional offices turn down hundreds of applicants for every one chosen. But for some it pays off. In the 1960s, for example, Bill Clinton, then going to Georgetown University, clerked for the Senate Foreign Relations Committee headed by fellow Arkansan J. William Fulbright.

Library of Congress

From 740 volumes in 1800, the Library of Congress has grown to a collection of more than 100 million books and other holdings. The 100 millionth work was received on April 13, 1993, with new acquisitions still coming in at the rate of ten a minute.

The library has a dual function: providing information for Congress and serving the public as a national library. In its first capacity, the library sends books to the Capitol at the rate of one every ninety seconds, day and night. The library's Congressional Research Service (CRS) handles more than 600,000 congressional inquiries a year.

For scholars and the public, the library provides several reading rooms, exhibits,

Of All the Nerve!

The name should make it clear, but not everyone realizes that the Library of Congress is Congress's library. Take the gentleman who became incensed when told a member was using a book he wanted.

"A congressman!" the man fumed. "Why is a congressman using it? I thought Congress had its own library!"

"You may believe it," the reference librarian replied. "They do. And you're in it."

and access to its computerized listing of books, periodicals, maps, photographs, music, films, and more.

Watching, Counting, Taking Apart

Besides the Library of Congress's Congressional Research Service, three major arms of Congress provide expertise to members and committees: the General Accounting Office, the Congressional Budget Office, and the Office of Technology Assessment.

The General Accounting Office (GAO), oldest of the three groups, is known as

"Congress's watchdog." Established in 1921, the agency has exposed numerous improprieties, such as the House bank scandal and cost overruns on weapons systems. GAO employs five thousand accountants and other investigators, whose boss is the comptroller general of the United States.

The Congressional Budget Office (CBO) was created in 1974 when Congress set up its own system for dealing with the federal budget. CBO presents Congress with options to the president's budget. Its deficit estimates, however, sometimes differ markedly from those of the White House's Office of Management and Budget.

Finding itself having to deal with a more complex world, Congress set up the Office of Technology Assessment in 1972 to help sort through the scientific data involved in such things as nuclear weapons systems and genetic engineering.

◼ Keeping the Home Folks Informed

On the Tube

Based on earlier experimentation with live coverage—ninety days in 1977—the House officially initiated live, gavel-to-gavel television coverage of House floor proceedings on March 19, 1979. The Cable-Satellite Public Affairs Network (C-SPAN)

went on the air two weeks later, on April 3, carrying the broadcasts nationwide.

The Senate began televising its sessions in July 1986, following a test that began June 2, 1986. C-SPAN and the commercial networks broadcast some of the Senate debates.

Q: What Is C-SPAN?

A: C-SPAN is a nonprofit cooperative of the cable TV industry. Its 4,140 affiliated cable systems serve 55 million households. House proceedings account for only 15 percent of programming on C-SPAN 1 and C-SPAN 2. The network also covers speeches, news conferences, and other events related to the federal government and politics.

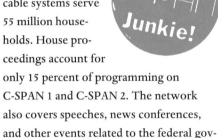

The Official Story

In the early days of Congress, there was no reliable account of House or Senate speeches. Newspapers or shorthand companies reported the debates sporadically. But in 1873 Congress began keeping a verbatim account in the *Congressional Record*, published daily during each session.

Although both chambers now make

available gavel-to-gavel television coverage of floor activity, TV viewers get an entirely different picture than readers of the *Record* where members may insert the texts of remarks or documents not actually read aloud on the floor. Since 1978 inserted remarks have been indicated by a different typeface in the House or black dots in the Senate. Members also may edit their speeches before publication so that an ungrammatical or intemperate remark heard on TV can be cleaned up for publication in the *Record* or deleted entirely.

Although the *Record* has official status as a transcript, the official record of congressional proceedings is each chamber's *Journal,* which does not include debate. The *Congressional Directory,* published at the start of each two-year term, is Congress's official who's who.

■ Congressional Pay and Perks

In 1789 being a member of Congress was a part-time job, and the pay was $6 a day. In 1993 senators and representatives worked year-round, and the pay was $133,600 a year ($366 a day for 365 days).

Until 1991 members supplemented their salaries with fees from speeches and articles (honoraria), but both houses abolished the practice that year in exchange for automatic annual cost-of-living increases. That avoided the public ruckus that arose every time Congress raised its own pay.

The first automatic increase came after the Twenty-seventh Amendment to the Constitution finally kicked in, two cen-

Members of Congress have special parking privileges at busy National Airport in Washington, D.C.

turies after James Madison proposed it. Not until 1992 did a sufficient number of states approve the amendment, which bars midterm congressional pay raises.

Among other perquisites (perks) of being member of Congress are the "franking" privilege, which permits sending official mail with the member's signature in place of a stamp, and allowances for home visits, foreign travel, "clerk-hire" (staff), stationery, offices, telephones, and publications.

Members also have a generous pension plan, life and health insurance, free medical care at work, and a long list of other benefits including free parking, recreation and health facilities, and subsidized stationery stores and restaurants.

The Total Tab

All told, the cost of operating the legislative branch of government came to $2.2 billion in fiscal 1991. House operations amounted to $647.7 million and Senate operations, $437.2 million.

The largest joint operation was the General Accounting Office, $419.1 million.

Vaclav Havel, a Czech playwright who had agitated for human rights under the communist regime, addresses the U.S. Congress on February 21, 1990, after his election as interim president of Czechoslovakia.

The Capitol Hill Crew

Comedians like to joke about Congress, and at times the derision is deserved. But for the most part being a member of Congress is serious business. It is hard work that requires the 535 men and women on Capitol Hill to do a continual balancing act between meeting the demands of lawmaking in Washington and representing the constituents back in the state or district. Since the First Congress in 1789, some eleven thousand individuals have had the privilege of trying to meet that challenge as senators or representatives. They have a lot in common, and that's interesting. But there are also many differences among them, and that's even more interesting.

■ Age and Longevity

Congress is getting older. From 47.0 in 1985, the average member's age climbed to 53.1 by the beginning of the 103d Congress in 1993. The average senator was 58.2 years old; the average House member, 51.9. The oldest person ever to serve in Congress was Democratic senator Theodore Francis Green from Rhode Island, who was ninety-three when he retired in 1961. He lived to ninety-eight.

While he was alive Green was a regular on the Washington social circuit. At his fourth cocktail party one evening he was spotted looking at his schedule and was asked, "Are you trying to find out where you're going next?" "No," he replied. "I'm trying to find out where I am now."

Talk about Seniority

On January 6, 1992, Mississippi Democrat Jamie L. Whitten set a new record for length of House service. At fifty years and two days, he surpassed the previous record held by fellow Democrat and southerner Carl Vinson of Georgia (1914–1965).

Whitten continued to serve, but health problems made it unlikely he would break

Rep. Jamie Whitten and Rep. William Natcher, two senior members of the U.S. Congress.

Carl Hayden's record of almost fifty-seven years' total service in Congress. Hayden, a Democrat from Arizona, served in both houses, from 1912 to 1969. Whitten, born April 18, 1910, was reelected in 1992 but lost the Appropriations chairmanship because of his poor health.

The "new kid" who replaced Whitten as

chairman was actually several months older. He was Kentucky Democrat William Natcher, who was born September 11, 1909.

Dynasties

Some American families might be termed "congressional dynasties" because so many of their members have served in Congress. The Longs, Bakers, and Kennedys are just a few of them.

Longs

Only the Longs of Louisiana can boast of having father, mother, and son senators. When Sen. Huey "the Kingfish" Long was assassinated in 1935, his widow, Rose McConnell Long, succeeded him briefly. Then in 1948 their son, Russell, won election to the seat he held for thirty-eight years until he retired in 1987.

At least seven Long relatives have been in Congress. One of them, Huey, also served as governor of Louisiana, as did his younger brother, Earl. Earl's bizarre relationship with stripper Blaze Starr was chronicled in a movie starring Paul Newman.

Bakers

The Bakers of Tennessee come close to matching the Longs' father-mother-son

Huey "the Kingfish" Long was one of the most flamboyant figures in American politics in the 1920s and 1930s, and one of many Longs to serve in the U.S. Congress.

combination, except that only one served in the Senate. Howard H. Baker, Jr., whose father and stepmother both served in the House, was Senate majority leader when Republicans controlled that body in 1981–1985. His stepmother, Irene Bailey Baker, was elected to serve the remainder of her

deceased husband's term in 1964–1965.

Howard Baker was the son-in-law of former Senate minority leader Everett McKinley Dirksen, Republican from Illinois.

Kennedys

Besides having a record three brothers serve in the Senate, the Kennedy family can claim several House members. John Francis "Honey Fitz" Fitzgerald, the grandfather of senators John F., Edward M., and Robert F. Kennedy, served in the House from 1895 to 1901 and in 1919. And Joseph Patrick Kennedy II, Robert Kennedy's son, was elected to the House in 1986. Both Honey Fitz and Joe Kennedy were Democrats from Massachusetts.

The Family Who Serves Together

Simultaneous Service

Instances of family members serving in Congress at the same time are rare. In the case of the Kennedys, brothers Edward and Robert served simultaneously in the Senate, Edward from Massachusetts and Robert from New York. After Robert Kennedy died, his son Joseph served in the House simultaneously with his uncle, Sen. Edward Kennedy.

Robert Kennedy (below left) was a champion of the poor—both black and white. Here he tours a riot-torn section of Washington, D.C., in 1968 after attending a memorial service for slain civil rights leader Martin Luther King, Jr. Joe Kennedy, shown (above) at a Friends of the Earth rally, followed a family tradition in representing Massachusetts as a House Democrat.

Left to right, Alice Robertson (Oklahoma), Mae E. Nolan (California), and Winnifred M. Huck (Illinois) on the steps of the Capitol in the 1920s.

Philip M. Crane, a House member since 1969, had the company of his younger brother Daniel B. Crane from 1979 to 1985. Both were Illinois Republicans.

Similarly, brothers Phillip and John L. Burton, California Democrats, served together in the House—Phillip from 1964 until his death in April 1983, and John from 1974 to January 1983. Phillip was succeeded for a time by his widow, Sala.

Michigan Democrats Carl M. and Sander M. Levin began overlapping in congressional service in 1983 when Sander entered the House. His brother had been in the Senate since 1979.

Like Father, Like Daughter

The first woman to succeed her father in Congress was Rep. Winnifred Mason Huck, Republican from Illinois. She was elected in 1922 after her father, William E. Mason, died in office. In 1990 Republican Susan Molinari from New York won the House seat vacated when her father, Guy

V. Molinari, resigned to become Staten Island borough president. In 1992 Louise Roybal-Allard was elected to succeed her father, California Democrat Edward Roybal, who was retiring from the House.

A House-Bound Mom

No member of Congress has ever been succeeded by his or her mother. The Boltons of Ohio—Frances and Oliver—came closest. Oliver was in the House, from a different district, during part of the longer time that his mother served (1940–1969).

■ Rhodes to Congress

Several members of Congress shared President Bill Clinton's distinction of having studied at England's Oxford University as a Rhodes scholar. In the 103d Congress all were in the Senate. They were Democrats David Boren of Oklahoma, Bill Bradley of New Jersey, and Paul Sarbanes of Maryland; and Republicans Richard Lugar of Indiana and Larry Pressler of South Dakota. The House's only Rhodes scholar, Tom McMillen, Democrat from Maryland, was defeated for reelection in 1992.

■ Religion on the Hill

Nearly three-fourths of the members of Congress are Protestants, but since 1965 Roman Catholics have outnumbered any

---

Rich as Rockefeller—or Richer

Who are the wealthiest members of Congress? According to a 1992 compilation by the Capitol Hill newspaper *Roll Call*, the following were the top ten:

1. Rep. Amo Houghton *(R-N.Y.)*, $420 million
2. Sen. Herb Kohl *(D-Wisc.)*, $250 million
3. Sen. John D. Rockefeller IV *(D-W.Va.)*, $200 million
4. Sen. Frank R. Lautenberg *(D-N.J.)*, $45 million
5. Sen. Edward M. Kennedy *(D-Mass.)*, $35 million
6. Rep. Norm Sisisky *(D-Va.)*, $30 million
7. Sen. John Danforth *(R-Mo.)*, $30 million
8. Sen. Charles S. Robb *(D-Va.)*, $25 million
9. Sen. Claiborne Pell *(D-R.I)*, $15 million
10. Senators Howard M. Metzenbaum and John Glenn *(both D-Ohio)*, each $13 million.

Houghton disagreed with *Roll Call's* figure, which was based in part on a *Forbes* magazine estimate that he said included Corning Glass stock he controlled for other family members. His Senate financial disclosure form placed his holdings at $7.7 million.

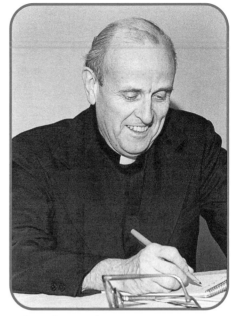

Father Robert F. Drinan

single religious denomination, with Methodists ranking second and Episcopalians and Baptists tied for third.

Charles Carroll of Maryland was the first Catholic in the Senate (1789–1792). He was the brother of John Carroll, the first American Catholic bishop, and a cousin of another Marylander, Daniel Carroll, one of two Catholics who served in the First Congress (1789–1791). The other was Thomas Fitzsimons of Pennsylvania.

The first acknowledged Jew elected to the Senate was Judah P. Benjamin of Louisiana, 1853–1861, a Whig and later a Democrat. In recent times Jews have formed the largest non-Christian group in Congress. In the House the first Jewish member was Israel Jacobs, 1791–1793.

Few clergy members have served in Congress. The first priest in the House, Jesuit Robert F. Drinan, Democrat from Massachusetts, served five terms until Pope John Paul II barred priests from public office in 1980. Another priest, Democrat Robert J. Cornell from Wisconsin, served in the House from 1975 to 1979.

■ Off to War

Despite a clear constitutional ban on dual officeholding by members of Congress (Article I, section 6), many members have fought in American wars without losing their seats. Some of those who left to fight for the South in the Civil War were expelled for disloyalty, but that was a different issue. The Fourteenth Amendment, ratified in 1868, barred reentry to former members who supported the rebellion.

In 1899 the House refused to vacate the seats of four members who had accepted army commissions to fight against Spain. In World War I, House members received their congressional salaries minus any military pay.

In World War II, Texas Democrat Lyn-

don B. Johnson was the first House member to volunteer for the armed forces. He served briefly as a navy officer in the South Pacific before President Franklin Roosevelt called all members back to Congress.

Three years later, in 1944, Henry Cabot Lodge, a Republican from Massachusetts, became the first senator since the Civil War to resign for military service. As an army reservist he had seen action during

Henry Cabot Lodge

recesses, but when forced to choose between the Senate and the army he decided to fight. He was reelected after the war, only to be defeated six years later by another combat veteran, John F. Kennedy.

During the Vietnam War, the Supreme Court declined to revoke the military reserve commissions of 117 House and Senate members.

■ Race and Ethnicity

White Christian males still dominate Congress, but not so exclusively as in the past. At the beginning of the 103d Congress in 1993, thirty-nine members were African-American, seventeen were Hispanic, seven were Asian or Pacific islanders, one was Native American, and fifty-three were women, including several who were also members of racial minorities.

African-Americans in Congress

In all, almost one hundred black Americans have served in Congress since the Reconstruction era after the Civil War. Of these, only three men and one woman have been senators.

Hiram R. Revels, a Republican from Mississippi and a former Union army chaplain, was the Senate's first black member. He served from 1870 to 1871. He was followed in 1875 by another black male from

This Currier & Ives lithograph from 1872 shows Hiram Revels, the first African-American senator (far left), and six representatives serving in the U.S. Congress. Rep. Joseph H. Rainey, the first black representative, is seated second from right.

the same state and party, Blanche K. Bruce, who served six years. It was almost a century later that the Senate gained its third black, Edward W. Brooke, a Republican from Massachusetts, who served from 1967 to 1979. It was only in 1992 that an African-American woman, Democrat Carol Moseley-Braun of Illinois, was elected to the Senate.

South Carolina Republican Joseph H. Rainey, who entered Congress ten months after Revels, was the first black representative. He served until 1879. Another black American, John W. Menard of Louisiana, had won a seat in 1868 but then was excluded because of an election dispute. Exactly one hundred years later, in 1968, the first black woman was elected to the

House—Shirley Chisholm, Democrat from New York.

The first black chairman of a House committee was William L. Dawson, Democrat from Illinois, who headed Government Operations and its predecessor, Expenditures in the Executive Departments, in 1949–1953 and 1955–1971.

Hispanic Members of Congress

As of 1993 thirty Hispanics have been members of Congress, beginning with Rep. Romualdo Pacheco, a Republican from California (1877–1878 and 1879–1889).

Texas Democrat E. "Kika" de la Garza was the first Hispanic to chair a House committee, Agriculture, in 1981. The first Hispanic woman elected to the House was Ileana Ros-Lehtinen, Republican from Florida. She was also the first Cuban-American member of either sex.

Democrat Nydia M. Velázquez from New York, also elected in 1992, was the first Puerto Rican woman in the House.

Two Hispanics, both New Mexico Democrats, have been senators: Dennis Chavez (1935–1962) and Joseph Montoya (1964–1977). Chavez headed the Public Works Committee in 1949–1953 and 1955–1962.

The 103d Congress (1993–1995) had a record number of Hispanics, seventeen, all in the House, not counting two nonvoting delegates, both Hispanic, from Puerto Rico and the Virgin Islands.

Other Minorities

Minorities have more easily gained entry to the House than to the Senate, but the first Chinese-American member of Congress was a senator, Hawaii Republican Hiram L. Fong (1959–1977). The first Asian in

Sen. Hiram L. Fong

Sen. Ben Nighthorse Campbell

Congress was Daliph Singh Saund, a California Democrat of Indian ancestry who served in the House from 1957 to 1963. He was followed in 1959 by the first Japanese-American, Daniel K. Inouye, also from Hawaii but a Democrat, who moved from the House to the Senate in 1963.

The first Korean-American member of Congress was Jay C. Kim, a Republican from California, elected to the House in 1992.

Ben Nighthorse Campbell, a ponytailed Democrat from Colorado, was the second

Native American to serve in the Senate (1993–). The first was Charles Curtis, Republican from Kansas, who served in the House (1893–1907) and the Senate (1907–1913 and 1915–1929) before he became vice president under Herbert Hoover. Curtis was partly Kaw Indian.

Campbell, whose father was Northern Cheyenne, had served earlier in the House, where he received special permission to wear his trademark bolo tie. He was the first part-Indian in the House since Ben Reifel, Republican from South Dakota (1961–1971).

■ Speaking of Women . . .
The Record Holders

By 1993 more than 130 women had served in Congress. Of those, only two had been elected to both chambers: Republican Margaret Chase Smith from Maine and Democrat Barbara A. Mikulski from Maryland. Smith also held records among women senators for length of service (twenty-four years, 1949–1973) and for attendance (2,941 consecutive roll-call votes between 1955 and September 7, 1968, when she missed one because she was hospitalized).

Republican Edith Nourse Rogers from Massachusetts served longer in the House than any other woman (thirty-five years, 1925–1960).

Rebecca Felton in 1922 at the age of eighty-seven at home in Cartersville, Georgia.

Jeannette Rankin as she prepares to leave for the Republican and Democratic conventions in 1932.

First Woman Senator

The first woman senator, Rebecca L. Felton of Georgia, was also the oldest new senator and holds the record for the shortest Senate service. Appointed temporarily to fill a vacancy, she was sworn in November 21, 1922, at the age of eighty-seven. The next day she was replaced by another Democrat, Walter F. George, who had been elected to fill the seat.

Caraway from Faraway Arkansas

Democrat Hattie W. Caraway from Arkansas was the nation's first *elected* senator, in 1931. She was also the first woman to preside over the Senate (1943) and to chair a Senate committee—on Enrolled Bills.

And Rankin Right Up There . . .

The first woman to be elected a representative was Jeannette Rankin, a Republican from Montana, in 1916. Rankin was also the first woman to run for the Senate.

Rankin, who served twice in the House (1917–1919 and 1941–1943), was the only member of Congress to vote against U.S. entry into both World Wars. In 1941 she cast the only vote against declaring war on Japan. In 1968, at the age of eighty-eight, she led a march on Washington to oppose the Vietnam War. She died in 1973.

Nolan in the Chair

The first woman to chair a House committee was Mae Ellen Nolan, Republican from New York, who headed the Committee on Expenditures in the Post Office Department from 1923 to 1925.

Lights, Camera, Vote!

The first movie star elected to Congress was Helen Gahagan Douglas. Voted into the House in 1944, she was defeated in a 1950 bid for the Senate by another California representative, Republican Richard Nixon. Nixon's efforts to link Douglas with communist sympathizers helped to establish his reputation as a ruthless campaigner.

The Other Mrs. Douglas

Another actress, Emily Taft Douglas of Illinois, also was elected to the House in 1944. She served only one term. Both she and Helen Gahagan Douglas had husbands who were well known in their own right. Emily's spouse, economist Paul H. Douglas, was elected to the Senate in 1948 and served eighteen years. Helen's husband was veteran movie actor Melvyn Douglas.

A First for Women Candidates

With two Senate seats to be filled, California elected women to both slots in

No Potty Parity

In her first and only day on the job, the first woman senator, Rebecca Felton, discovered a Senate shortcoming that was not rectified until seventy-one years later—there was no Senate ladies' room. Paul Rhodes of Washington recounted in a December 1992 letter to the *Washington Post* that in 1922 as a fourteen-year-old page he escorted Mrs. Felton to an upstairs "women's retiring room," which no longer exists, so she would not have to use the public restroom. At the time there was a men's room off the Senate floor but no women's room.

The same situation existed until January 1993, when the new Senate women's room opened to accommodate a record-high number of women senators—six, four more than in the previous Congress.

Barbara Boxer and Dianne Feinstein, both of California.

1992—a first for the country. The winners, both Democrats, were former San Francisco mayor Dianne Feinstein and former U.S. representative Barbara Boxer of Marin County. Feinstein defeated the Republican incumbent, John Seymour, for the remaining two years of Pete V. Wilson's term. Wilson, who left the Senate in 1991 to become the state's governor, had appointed Seymour as interim senator.

Boxer defeated TV commentator Bruce Herschensohn, a Republican, for the seat vacated by Democrat Alan Cranston, who had retired after long service in the Senate.

Members of the all-male Senate Judiciary Committee during the Clarence Thomas hearings on his nomination to the Supreme Court.

Record Numbers

Both the House and Senate had record numbers of women members at the opening of the 103d Congress (1993–1995): forty-seven in the House and six in the Senate. Never before had more than two women served in the Senate at the same time.

Besides Boxer and Feinstein, new senators were Carol Moseley-Braun of Illinois and Patty Murray of Washington. They joined incumbents Nancy Landon Kassebaum of Kansas and Barbara Mikulski of Maryland. Kassebaum was the only Republican. Braun was also the first black woman elected to the Senate. The number of women senators rose to seven in June 1993

with the election of Kay Bailey Hutchison, Republican from Texas.

Another Male Bastion Falls

Two of the female freshman senators elected in 1992, Dianne Feinstein and Carol Moseley-Braun, won assignment to the previously all-male Senate Judiciary Committee. In 1991 the committee was widely criticized as sexist in its treatment of Anita Hill, a witness who accused Supreme Court nominee Clarence Thomas of making gross sexual comments when they worked together at federal agencies. The Senate confirmed Thomas's appointment, and he

became the second African-American to serve on the Court.

First Woman to Testify

The first woman to testify before Congress was suffragist Elizabeth Cady Stanton. She appeared before the Senate District of Columbia Committee on January 20, 1869, to speak on behalf of women's right to vote in the District.

The Marrying Kinds

The first marriage between members of Congress took place in 1976 when Rep. Martha Keys, Democrat from Kansas, married fellow Democrat and House member Andrew Jacobs from Indiana. In 1989 Rep. Olympia J. Snowe, Republican from Maine, married a former colleague, John R. McKernan, Jr., then the governor of Maine.

Representative Mom?

The first woman to give birth during her tenure in Congress was Rep. Yvonne Brathwaite Burke, Democrat from California, in November 1973.

■ Personality Contestants

Throughout the history of Congress, certain members have garnered more attention than others by virtue of their personalities or creativity (or lack of either). Some were leaders but others were ordinary members who made headlines by what they did or said.

Davy Crockett, Folk Hero Congressman

David Crockett, Whig from Tennessee, became a hero to millions of youngsters in the 1950s thanks to Walt Disney's TV series "Davy Crockett: King of the Wild Frontier," starring Fess Parker. Although the series touched on Crockett's six years in the House (1827–1831 and 1833–1835), it focused mainly on his legendary (and partly fictional) exploits as a frontiersman and his heroic death at the Alamo. Few of

Davy Crockett

the "baby boomers" who grew up with the series in the 1950s probably even remember the important but less colorful part of Crockett's career—his years in Washington.

He Gave the Dictionary a Bad Name—His

Mc•Car•thy•ism (mə kär'thē iz'm) n. [after J. McCarthy, U.S. senator (1946–57), to whom such practices were attributed] the use of indiscriminate, often unfounded, accusations, sensationalism, inquisitorial investigative methods, etc., as in the suppression of political opponents portrayed as subversive.
—*Webster's New World Dictionary, Third College Edition*

Joseph R. McCarthy, a Republican from Wisconsin, was highly controversial in the 1950s because of his televised Senate hearings on alleged communist infiltration of the State Department, army, and other agencies. He claimed to have lists of known communists who were shaping federal policy, but he produced little or no proof. If colleagues challenged him, he would imply that they were soft on communism. In the fearful atmosphere toward the Soviet Union after World War II, McCarthy's tactics helped to defeat two Democratic senators (Millard Tydings of Mary-

Sen. Joseph McCarthy

land and William Benton of Connecticut) who tried to investigate his charges.

In one of the most dramatic episodes of the 1954 Army-McCarthy hearings, Boston lawyer Joseph N. Welch expressed anguish at McCarthy's attack on a young colleague. "Until this moment, Senator, I think I never really gauged your cruelty or your recklessness. . . . Have you no decency, sir, at long last? Have you left no sense of decency?"

Later that year the Senate officially condemned McCarthy, who quickly faded from the headlines. He died in 1957. Welch died in 1960.

Coiners of Words and Phrases

Sen. Simon Cameron, Republican from Pennsylvania, is remembered for stating in 1860 that "an honest politician is one who, once he is bought, stays bought."

Texas Democrat Maury Maverick made up the word "gobbledygook" while serving in the House, 1935–1939. He used it to describe pompous, wordy, Latin-punctuated language that had the ring of a turkey gobbling.

In her maiden speech to the House in 1943, Clare Booth Luce, Republican from Connecticut, coined the word "globaloney" to describe the world views being pushed by former vice president Henry A. Wallace. A year later Luce, a playwright and wife of publisher Henry Luce, originated the term *G. I. Joe* in a speech to the Republican National Convention.

Split Personalities

Political scientist Richard F. Fenno, Jr., pioneered in the observation that members of Congress have not one personality style but two—a "Hill style" while working on Capitol Hill and a "home style" while back in the state or district with the voters who sent him or her to Washington. The two styles might be completely different. In Washington a congressman, for example, might be urbane, sophisticated, and at ease with scholars and intellectuals. Back home the same legislator might shun big words, wear old clothes, and work at being "just one of the boys." The idea, of course, is to stay close to the voters and get reelected. It usually works.

The so-called Fenno paradox is that most people trust and admire their own senators or representative, while at the same time they distrust Congress as a whole.

Rayburn: Dandy to Dirt Farmer

A prime example of split styles was House Speaker Sam Rayburn, Democrat from Texas, who wore tailored suits, rode in a chauffered limousine, and moved easily in Washington's high society. Back home in Bonham, Rayburn became a plain dirt farmer, wearing old khakis, driving a battered pickup, and spitting from a wad of tobacco that he never seemed to chew in the capital.

LBJ: Rayburn Emulator?

As Senate majority leader before he became vice president and president, Lyndon Johnson emulated his fellow Texan and mentor Sam Rayburn in many ways. He returned often to his ranch on the Pedernales River, spending many hours being just another "good ole boy" with the neighbors.

As Senate majority leader, Lyndon Johnson had an extraordinary ability to persuade in one-on-one encounters, through sheer force of will.

But on the job in Washington LBJ was a tough and intimidating leader, wise in the ways of the Senate. A famous sequence of pictures by *New York Times* photographer George Tames shows Johnson in action, giving his persuasive "Treatment" to Rhode Island senator Theodore Francis Green. By the time he was through, LBJ was almost nose to nose with Green, who was bent backward against a table.

Howard Baker: Republican Folksy Style

Democrats had no monopoly on the folksy, down-home style. When Republicans controlled the Senate in the early 1980s, Majority Leader Howard H. Baker, Jr., could often be found home in Tennessee, chatting on the courthouse steps with some of the locals.

Back home in Tennessee, Sen. Howard H. Baker, Jr., shares a laugh with constituents on the courthouse steps in 1973.

The Greatest Senators

In 1955 a special Senate committee headed by John F. Kennedy chose the five greatest senators of all time after a poll of historians. The committee's job was to select senators to be honored with paintings in the Senate Reception Room. The portraits, shown below, were unveiled in March 1959.

 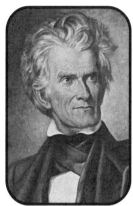   

Henry Clay of Kentucky, known as the "Great Compromiser" for his efforts to heal bitter regional differences over slavery.

Daniel Webster of Massachusetts, an outstanding orator who, like Clay, fought to preserve the Union.

John C. Calhoun of South Carolina, champion of states' rights and gifted spokesman for the South before the Civil War.

Robert M. La Follette, Sr., of Wisconsin, a progressive Republican leader who advocated public ownership of railroads in the early twentieth century.

Robert A. Taft, Sr., of Ohio, known as "Mr. Republican" for his party leadership and conservative politics in the 1940s and early 1950s.

Keep 'em Laughing

One of the quickest wits in Congress belonged to Morris K. "Mo" Udall, Democrat from Arizona, who often turned humor on himself. He liked to tell of the time in 1976 when he walked into a New Hampshire barbershop and said, "Hi, I'm Mo Udall and I'm running for president." "Yeah, we know," the barber replied. "We were laughing about it this morning."

That was Udall's problem. People didn't take him seriously, despite a solid record of thirty years in the House, including fourteen as chairman of the Interior and Insular Affairs Committee. He titled his 1988 memoir *Too Funny To Be President.*

The Lovable Scoundrel

James Michael Curley, better known as the Democratic Boston mayor and Massachusetts governor who was the model for the fictional politician in the book and movie *The Last Hurrah,* served in the House in 1911–1914 and again in 1943–1947, after his service as governor. During his last House term, he went to jail for mail fraud to obtain war contracts. Yet he remained a hero to many for his eloquence, his help for the poor, and his biting wit. Once when he saw John Francis "Honey Fitz" Fitzgerald holding a bookbag for his grandson Teddy (now senator) Kennedy, Curley called out: "Ah, John, I see you still carry your burglar's tools."

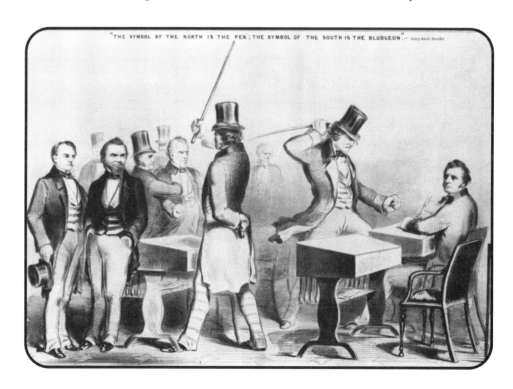

Retirement: 'Here's Your Hat— and Your Moneybags'

Some seventy members of Congress stood to gain $1 million or more each in life-time pension benefits if they chose to retire, said a 1992 survey by the National Taxpayers Union. The estimates were based on the future retirees' length of service, congressional pay, and the expected life span under actuarial tables.

Of the six senators in the $1 million plus pension category, Steve Symms, Republican from Idaho, had the highest potential lifetime benefit. Symms, whose congressional service began in 1973, was listed at $2.7 million. Among the sixty-five House members likely to collect more than $1 million in pensions, Les AuCoin, Democrat from Oregon, topped the list at $2.9 million. AuCoin entered the House in 1975. Eleven other House members were listed in the over $2 million category.

Accidents and Violence

A Spat over a Spitting

In January 1798 Matthew Lyon of Vermont spit tobacco juice in the face of Roger Griswold of Connecticut, who had been taunting Lyon on the House floor for alleged cowardice during the American Revolution. The House's first censure motion, to punish Lyon for a "violent attack and gross indecency," was voted down. A few weeks later Griswold attacked Lyon with a hickory walking stick. The two men fell to the House floor scuffling and had to be pulled apart. Another censure motion—this one against both men—failed, but they pledged not to fight again.

Nonfatal Duel

Congressmen George Washington Campbell of Tennessee and Barent Gardenier of New York fought a duel at Bladensburg, Maryland, in March 1808. Campbell objected to Gardenier's assertions that the House was under French influence. Gardenier was wounded in the duel and left the House in 1811. Campbell went on to become a senator, secretary of the Treasury, and minister to Russia.

Cocked Pistol on the Senate Floor

On April 7, 1850, during one of the furious debates over slavery and the Compromise of 1850, Sen. Thomas Hart Benton of Missouri objected to being called a "calumniator" (slanderer) by Sen. Henry S. Foote of Mississippi. As Benton advanced menacingly toward him, the much smaller Foote drew a pistol, cocked it, and aimed at Benton. Other senators disarmed Foote as Benton roared, "I disdain to carry arms! Stand out of the way and let the assassin fire!" A special committee rebuked both men, but the Senate took no further action.

The Bludgeoning of Sumner

In May 1856 Rep. Preston S. Brooks of South Carolina savagely beat Sen. Charles Sumner of Massachusetts with a cane on the Senate floor. Brooks said he was avenging an attack Sumner had made two days earlier on another South Carolinian, his cousin Rep. Andrew Butler, and other southern supporters of the Kansas-Nebraska Act permitting the two territories to allow slavery.

It was more than three years before Sumner could return to the Senate because of his head injuries. Meanwhile, Brooks resigned his House seat, only to be reelected to fill the vacancy. A vote to expel him had failed along north-south party lines.

Pinned to the Floor

What began as a playful tug ended up as a brawl in 1964 between two sixty-one-year-old senators, Strom Thurmond of South Carolina and Ralph Yarborough of Texas. Yarborough, a liberal Democrat, tried to get Thurmond inside a Capitol meeting room so that enough senators would be present to act on a presidential civil rights nomination. Thurmond, a conservative Democrat who later became a Republican, wanted to block the vote by preventing a quorum. After Yarborough pulled at his sleeve, Thurmond jokingly agreed to go in if the Texan could drag him in. In the brief scuffle that followed, Thurmond pinned his heavier opponent to the corridor floor. Then they both went inside and the nominee was approved with one no vote—Thurmond's.

Incident at Chappaquiddick

Sen. Edward M. Kennedy, Democrat from Massachusetts, was the driver in one of the most publicized auto accidents in congressional history. On July 19, 1969, Kennedy's car plunged off a narrow bridge on Chappaquiddick Island off Martha's Vineyard. Kennedy swam to safety but his companion, Mary Jo Kopechne, drowned. Kennedy pleaded guilty to the charge of leaving the scene of an accident, but he was damaged politically by his failure to report the accident until nine hours later. The incident took him out of contention for the 1972 presidential race.

■ Congressional Deaths

Assassinations

Two senators with national followings died of assassins' bullets:

Huey P. Long, a Democrat from Louisiana, on September 10, 1935, and Robert F. Kennedy, Democrat from New York, on June 6, 1968.

Long died two days after being mortally wounded by Dr. Carl A. Weiss at the Louisiana capitol in Baton Rouge. Long's bodyguards shot and killed Weiss, whose motive was never determined. Former governor Long, then forty-one and a fiery orator, had strong Depression-era appeal with his "share-the-wealth" plan and was preparing to challenge President Franklin Roosevelt for election to the White House when he was gunned down.

Kennedy, too, was running for president when Sirhan B. Sirhan shot him in the head as he was passing through the kitchen of a Los Angeles hotel. The forty-two-year-old senator had just addressed supporters after winning the June 5 California primary and was being led out the back way when Sirhan attacked. Members of Kennedy's entourage subdued Sirhan and took his gun. Kennedy died the next day. Sirhan, a Jordanian said to have been angered by Kennedy's support for Israel, is serving a life term in prison.

Duel on the Pike

One House member killed another in a duel February 24, 1838, on Marlboro Pike, Maryland, outside Washington. The victim, Rep. Jonathan Cilley of Maine, was shot by Rep. William Graves of Kentucky. Cilley had refused to accept a note Graves presented on behalf of a Whig newspaper editor in New York protesting Cilley's criticism of the editor.

A Key Affair

On February 17, 1859, Democratic representative Daniel Sickles from New York shot and killed Philip Barton Key, who had been having an affair with Sickles's wife, Teresa. Sickles, ambitious and busy with legislative work, had tolerated and even encouraged his wife's attendance at social events with Key, a lawyer son of "Star-Spangled Banner" writer Francis Scott Key. But the New York legislator became enraged when he learned the friendship had turned intimate, and, after forcing a written confession from his wife, he shot Key

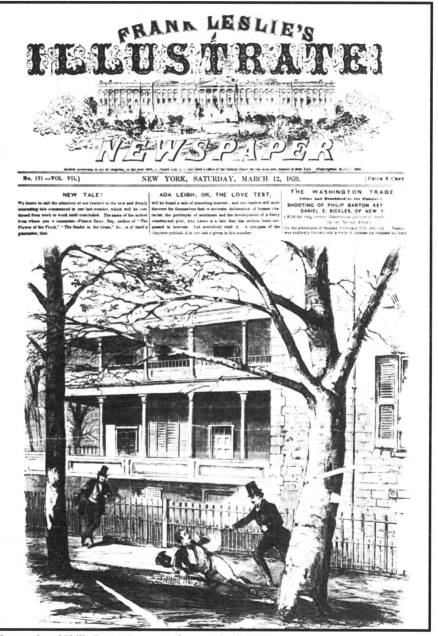

The murder of Philip Barton Key created a sensation in 1859.

outside the National Arts building on La-
fayette Square.

Sickles, who was acquitted as temporarily insane, gained more notoriety as a general in the Battle of Gettysburg, in which
he lost a leg. Sickles and his wife never divorced but neither did they live together
after the affair. He lived to ninety-four; she
died at thirty-one.

Duel in the Sand

On the morning of September 12, 1859,
California senator David Broderick fought
a duel on a Pacific beach with David Terry,
newly resigned as chief justice of the California supreme court. Terry had challenged
Broderick after the antislavery senator
openly accused Terry of corruption.

Broderick fired too quickly and his bullet hit the sand in front of Terry, who then
calmly aimed and gravely wounded Broderick in the chest. After four days of intoler-
able pain, the senator died.

In a classic case of "who lives by the
sword, dies by the sword," Terry himself
was shot and killed nearly thirty years later
when he assaulted a former colleague, Supreme Court justice Stephen J. Field.

Aircraft Fatalities

By unofficial count, eighteen members
of Congress had died in airplane crashes as

Not all foreign trips are the luxurious junkets critics decry. As chairman of the Select Committee on Hunger, Rep. Mickey Leland traveled to parts of the world that were far from glamorous. He was killed in a plane crash in Africa.

of mid-1993. The first senator to be the victim of an air accident was Bronson Cutting,
who was killed May 6, 1935, when his plane
went down near Atlanta, Missouri. Cutting, a Republican from New Mexico, had
been flying back to Washington with records he hoped would prove the legitimacy
of his contested 1934 reelection. His challenger, Dennis Chavez, won appointment
to Cutting's vacant seat and served almost
thirty years as the first Hispanic senator.

House Majority Leader Hale Boggs of
Louisiana and Rep. Nick Begich of Alaska,
both Democrats, disappeared on an airplane flight in Alaska on October 16, 1972,
and were presumed dead.

Killed on the ground as he headed for
his airplane was Rep. Leo J. Ryan, Democrat from California. Ryan had been investigating conditions at Jim Jones's People's
Temple cult in Guyana. Jones loyalists shot
Ryan and several others on November 18,
1978, after which Jones and several hundred followers committed mass suicide.

Another House member, Georgia Democrat Lawrence P. McDonald, was among

the 269 victims of Korean Air Lines flight 007, shot down over Soviet air space on September 1, 1983. On the other side of the globe, Democratic House member George Thomas "Mickey" Leland from Texas died in a plane crash on August 7, 1989, while on a hunger relief mission in Ethiopia.

The most recent victim was Pennsylvania senator John Heinz, who was a passenger in a small plane that crashed April 4, 1991, after colliding with a helicopter. The next day former senator John G. Tower of Texas and his daughter died in another small-plane accident.

Death on the Floor

John Quincy Adams, the only former president elected to the House of Representatives, collapsed February 21, 1848, at his desk in the old House chamber. He was taken to the Speaker's room and died there two days later.

On June 14, 1932, Rep. Edward Eslick, Democrat from Tennessee, dropped dead while speaking on the House floor. His widow, Willa Eslick, who had been listening in the family visitors' gallery, later was elected to complete her husband's term.

Another Tennessean, Sen. Estes Kefauver, suffered a heart attack while making a Senate speech August 8, 1963. Although in obvious pain he managed to finish and then drive to Bethesda Naval Hospital, where he died within two days. Kefauver was the Democratic nominee for vice president in 1956.

Congress's Burying Ground

Of the 60,000 people buried at Congressional Cemetery, fewer than 100 (70 representatives and 19 senators) are members of Congress. Most in fact are children because of the high infant mortality rates of the nineteenth century. The adults interred there also include cabinet members, generals, congressional pages, and people who helped to build the nearby U.S. Capitol.

Although it is private, Congressional bills itself as "the first national cemetery." Unlike the official national cemeteries, however, it is open to nonmilitary men and women.

Located on the Anacostia River south of RFK Stadium at Eighteenth and E Streets SE, the thirty-three-acre facility has been administered since 1976 by the nonprofit Congressional Cemetery Association. The cemetery was established in 1807 with church affiliation but is now nondenominational.

Burial Firsts

The first person buried at Congressional, in 1807, was William Swinton, a Philadelphia stonecutter recruited to work on the Capitol. The first member of Congress interred was Sen. Uriah Tracy of Connecticut.

After the Civil War, most members who died in office were buried in their home states, but Congress continued to erect cenotaphs (empty tombs) at Congressional identical to the tombs of members actually buried there. The practice was halted in 1875 as too expensive, but it was revived in 1972 for two House members lost during an Alaskan plane trip, Hale Boggs of Louisiana and Nick Begich of Alaska.

The first and longest-serving FBI director, J. Edgar Hoover, is buried at Congressional. Nearby is the grave of Leonard Matlovich, known as the "first certifiable gay hero." Matlovich, who died of AIDS in 1988, won the Bronze Star for bravery in the Vietnam War. His headstone reads:

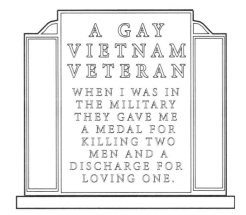

A GAY VIETNAM VETERAN

WHEN I WAS IN THE MILITARY THEY GAVE ME A MEDAL FOR KILLING TWO MEN AND A DISCHARGE FOR LOVING ONE.

'USA Law'
The Supreme Court

William Marbury

Besides being the highest court of appeals, the Supreme Court is the ultimate interpreter of the Constitution. This role gives the Court enormous power because the Framers crafted the charter in broad strokes, leaving most of the details of governing to be worked out by the president and Congress. This is not to say, however, that Congress has too free a hand in its lawmaking "details." The Court made that clear in 1803, when in *Marbury v. Madison* it established its own power to review and declare invalid acts of Congress. *Marbury* was perhaps the single most important decision in the Court's history.

The Court has often overruled the legislative and executive branches on grounds that their actions, or inactions, violated the Constitution. For example, in the early part of this century Congress tried to address the evils of child labor. After the Court struck down a law forbidding the interstate shipment of products made by children, Congress tried again. It imposed a tax on products made by child labor. Again the Court slapped lawmakers down, saying in *Bailey v. Drexel Furniture Co.* (1922) that Congress had overstepped its taxing powers.

In recent years there has been much speculation about the "original intent" of the Founders when they wrote certain provisions of the Constitution, and whether such intent would apply under modern conditions—even if anyone could figure out what the Founders had in mind more than two hundred years ago.

■ Serving on the Court: No Experience Necessary

Article II, section 2, of the Constitution gives the president the power to appoint members of the Supreme Court, subject to their confirmation by two-thirds of the Senate.

Because the Constitution says nothing about qualifications for justices, there is no age requirement or restriction on foreign birth. What's more, a justice doesn't have to have had prior service as a judge—or even a law degree. The Constitution does say, however, that once on the Court, a justice has the job for life with no pay cuts. The one requirement, "good Behaviour," is not defined but generally has been taken to mean not breaking the laws, avoiding scandal, and in general setting a high moral standard.

Foreign-Born Justices

Six justices were in fact born outside the United States: James Wilson, Scotland

Justice Felix Frankfurter and his wife, Marion, at the time of his appointment to the Supreme Court in 1939 to replace Benjamin Cardozo.

(who served on the Court from 1789 to 1798); James Iredell, England (1790–1799); William Paterson, Ireland (1793–1806); David Brewer, Turkey (1889–1910); George Sutherland, England (1922–1938); and Felix Frankfurter, Austria (1939–1962).

All Lawyers but Not Necessarily Benchwarmers

As a practical matter, most justices have been experienced, but some never sat on another bench, including five chief justices: John Marshall, Roger B. Taney, Charles Evans Hughes, Harlan Fiske Stone, and Earl Warren.

All nominees to the Court have been lawyers, but only since the twentieth century have most been law school graduates. In the early days, lawyers studied for the bar in private firms.

First among Equals

Although he has only one of nine votes when it comes to deciding cases, the chief justice is in fact the "first among equals." He (so far there have been no women chief justices) is the administrator of the Court and the traditional head of the American judicial system. As chief justice, he presides at Court sessions, both private and public, and assigns most of the writing of the Court's opinions.

The Constitution mentions the title only once, in Article I, section 3: "When the President of the United States is tried, the Chief Justice shall preside." Most of the chief's duties and influence have evolved over time.

Getting It Right

It is a common mistake to refer to the head of the Court as "chief justice of the Supreme Court." The official title is "chief justice of the United States." Originally, it was simply "chief justice," but Congress added "of the United States" at the urging of Salmon P. Chase, after President Abraham Lincoln named him to that post in

1864. The associate justices (who are "of the Supreme Court") informally call the boss the "chief."

Once the "chief's" coat hook.

■ Taking the Oaths

'Raise your right hand . . .'

Supreme Court justices must take two oaths of office—a "constitutional" oath, which all federal employees take, and a "judicial" oath, required for all federal judges. The judicial oath was included in the Judiciary Act of 1789 and has been changed over the years. In 1993 it read:

I, _____, do solemnly swear (or affirm), that I will administer justice without respect to persons, and do equal right to the poor and to the rich, and that I will faithfully and impartially discharge and perform all the duties incumbent on me as [a justice of the Supreme Court], under the Constitution and laws of the United States. So help me God.

Movable Swearing-ins

Beginning in the early 1970s, the constitutional oath was administered to the new justice in a private ceremony, usually in the justices' robing room. The judicial oath was taken in a special session of the Court before the justice's family and friends. In recent years, however, several justices have taken the constitutional oath in a ceremony at the White House. Justice David H. Souter, for example, took his constitutional oath in the White House East Room. Justice Clarence Thomas took his in a ceremony on the South Lawn. Although the chief justice generally administers the oath of office, in Thomas's case it was administered by Justice Byron R. White; Chief Justice Rehnquist was absent because of the death of his wife.

◼ Sizing Up the Court

Fluctuations

Congress, not the Constitution, determines the size of the Supreme Court. The First Congress set the number of justices at six, but under later statutes the size ranged from five to ten. It has remained at nine for more than one hundred years.

Congress Shrinks the Court

The radical Republican Congress that impeached Andrew Johnson (1865–1869) and almost removed him from office after the Civil War was not about to let him appoint anyone to the Supreme Court be-

THE INGENIOUS QUARTERBACK!

cause of his ongoing political battle with the Congress over Reconstruction. After a justice died in 1865, Congress eliminated the vacancy by reducing the number of seats from ten to seven (actual membership remained at nine). When another justice died in 1867, the membership dropped to eight—still too high for Johnson to make an appointment.

Congress increased the Court to nine seats after the Republicans regained the White House in 1869, allowing President Ulysses S. Grant to make one of the two nominations denied his predecessor. Since

then, the Court size has remained fixed at a chief justice and eight associate justices.

FDR's 'Court-Packing Plan'

During Franklin D. Roosevelt's first term, a closely divided Supreme Court struck down much of his New Deal legislation. After his landslide reelection in 1936, Roosevelt proposed adding one new member to the Court for each one older than seventy. Such a move would have temporarily increased the membership from nine to fifteen and permitted the president to appoint justices favorable to his program.

Harold H. Burton poses with his son, daughter, grandson, and wife shortly after being sworn in as associate justice in 1945.

President Ronald Reagan with Justice Sandra Day O'Connor in 1981.

But the plan was never implemented. While Congress was debating it, some justices softened their opposition, and the president began to get what he wanted without enlarging the Court—prompting the quip "a switch in time saves nine." It was later learned that one justice, Owen Roberts, had changed his mind before FDR announced his plan.

As vacancies occurred, Roosevelt was able to change almost the entire Court. In his four terms he appointed nine justices—second only to Washington's eleven.

◼ Filling Vacancies

The longest the Court has gone without a change of membership has been twelve years, from 1811 when Joseph Story was confirmed to 1823 when Henry Brockholst Livingston died.

Vacancies usually are filled quickly, but it took two years, three months, and twenty-three days to replace Henry Baldwin, who died on April 21, 1844. During that time, the Senate rejected four nominations by presidents John Tyler and James K. Polk, while future president James Buchanan declined the nomination three times. In the end, Pennsylvania judge Robert C. Grier won the nomination and was promptly confirmed.

Harold H. Burton won Senate confirmation as a Supreme Court justice the same day President Harry S. Truman nominated him—September 19, 1945. Burton, a Republican, was a pal from Truman's Senate days.

Opportunities to Appoint

George Washington holds the record for Supreme Court appointments: eleven. He appointed the first six justices and five later to fill vacancies.

Jimmy Carter was the only full-term president who never got a chance to appoint a justice. No one on the Court died or resigned while he was president. His successor, Ronald Reagan, appointed three new members (including the first woman, Sandra Day O'Connor) and elevated William H. Rehnquist to chief justice. Other presidents who made no Supreme Court appointments were William Henry Harrison and Zachary Taylor, who died in office, and Andrew Johnson, who served out all but six weeks of Abraham Lincoln's second term.

Until the Clinton administration, the last justice appointed by a Democratic president was Thurgood Marshall, named by Lyndon B. Johnson in 1967. Marshall, the first black justice, retired in 1991 and died in 1993. The last Democratic appointee still on the Court at the beginning of the Clinton administration was Byron R. White, appointed by John F. Kennedy in 1962. White retired on the last day of the 1992–1993 term, and President Clinton appointed Ruth Bader Ginsburg to his seat.

Cross-Party Nominations

Abraham Lincoln broke precedent in 1863 when he went outside his own Republican party for a Supreme Court candidate. He nominated Democrat Stephen J. Field of California. Since then, a few other presidents, mostly Republicans, have followed suit.

Among them was Republican William Howard Taft, whose six nominations included three Democrats: Horace H. Lurton, 1909; Edward D. White, promoted by Taft to chief justice in 1910; and Joseph R. Lamar, 1910. Other Republicans and the Democrats they appointed were Benjamin Harrison—Howell E. Jackson, 1893; Warren G. Harding—Pierce Butler, 1922; Herbert Hoover—Benjamin Cardozo, 1932; Dwight D. Eisenhower—William J. Brennan, Jr., 1956; and Richard Nixon—Lewis F. Powell, Jr., 1971.

Franklin D. Roosevelt and Harry S. Truman were the only two Democratic presidents to nominate Republicans—Roosevelt in 1941 when he promoted Harlan Fiske Stone to chief justice, and Truman in 1945 when he nominated Harold H. Burton.

Setback for Washington

George Washington is the only president to have a chief justice nominee turned down. In 1795 he nominated former justice John Rutledge to succeed Chief Justice John Jay, who resigned. The Senate rejected Rutledge, partly because he suffered fits of insanity and partly because he openly opposed a treaty that Jay had negotiated with the British to settle financial and maritime matters pending from the revolutionary war. Washington then nominated Oliver Ellsworth, who won easy confirmation after Justice William Cushing declined the promotion.

Rejections

Through mid-1993 twenty-eight nominees had failed to win Senate confirmation to the Supreme Court. Two of those were for the same man, Edward King, nominated twice by President John Tyler, who holds the record for rejected nominations (five). The Senate rejected about a dozen

President Richard Nixon nominated both Lewis F. Powell, Jr. (left), a Democrat, and William H. Rehnquist (right), a Republican, to the Supreme Court on October 21, 1971.

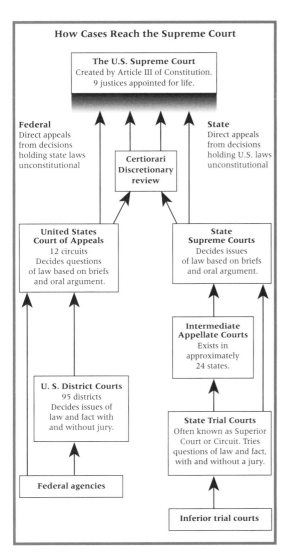

How Cases Reach the Supreme Court

The U.S. Supreme Court
Created by Article III of Constitution.
9 justices appointed for life.

Federal
Direct appeals from decisions holding state laws unconstitutional

State
Direct appeals from decisions holding U.S. laws unconstitutional

Certiorari Discretionary review

United States Court of Appeals
12 circuits
Decides questions of law based on briefs and oral argument.

State Supreme Courts
Decides issues of law based on briefs and oral argument.

Intermediate Appellate Courts
Exists in approximately 24 states.

U. S. District Courts
95 districts
Decides issues of law and fact with and without jury.

State Trial Courts
Often known as Superior Court or Circuit. Tries questions of law and fact, with and without a jury.

Federal agencies

Inferior trial courts

Recent Turndowns

In the twentieth century six nominations failed, beginning with the rejection of Herbert Hoover nominee John J. Parker, a North Carolinian opposed by the National Association for the Advancement of Colored People (NAACP). Parker, a federal judge, went on to write several influential opinions supporting civil rights.

Lyndon Johnson's nomination of Abe Fortas as chief justice was withdrawn in 1968 amid partisan conflict over Fortas's finances and ideology. With Fortas still on the Court, there was no vacancy for his replacement, Homer Thornberry—already nominated by Johnson. Thornberry's nomination, therefore, was not acted on.

After Fortas resigned under fire in 1969, the Senate rejected Richard Nixon's first two nominees to fill the vacancy, Clement F. Haynsworth, Jr., and G. Harrold Carswell, both southern federal judges. Opposition was mostly partisan in both cases, but Carswell's competence and racial tolerance also were questioned.

In 1987 the Senate rejected Ronald Reagan's nomination of federal judge Robert H. Bork, a legal scholar strongly opposed by civil and women's rights groups for his conservative views and refusal to concede a constitutional right to privacy, the keystone of abortion rights.

Reagan's planned nomination of Douglas Ginsburg, also a federal judge, was not submitted after it was disclosed he had used marijuana.

They Died, Declined, or Had Served

Eight men whose appointments were confirmed never sat on the Court. In two cases, the men had been nominated twice. Edwin M. Stanton, Abraham Lincoln's secretary of war, died in 1869 before he could take the seat offered by President Ulysses S. Grant. The other seven declined their appointments: Robert H. Harrison, 1789; William Cushing, 1796; John Jay, 1800; Levi Lincoln, 1811; John Quincy Adams, 1811; William Smith, 1837; and Roscoe Conkling, 1882. Both Jay and Cushing had served on the Court earlier, Jay for six years and Cushing for twenty-one.

■ Types of Cases Taken by the Court

Original Jurisdiction Cases

According to the Constitution, the Court may hear two types of cases without prior review by a lower court: those in which a state is a party and those involving senior foreign diplomats.

Such cases make up a small part of the Court's caseload.

nominees outright. Three were later renominated and confirmed. The others faced near-certain rejection, and their nominations were withdrawn or allowed to lapse.

A Look at Lawyerly Latin

Ex parte "On behalf of." A legal proceeding is said to be ex parte if it occurs at the instigation of one party without notice being given to the opposing party.

Ex post facto "From a thing done afterward." An ex post facto law makes illegal an act that has already taken place or makes the punishment greater than it was at the time of the act. The Constitution prohibits either Congress or the states from passing ex post facto laws.

Habeas corpus "You shall have the body." The writ of habeas corpus is a judicial instrument dating from seventeenth-century England. Used to review the legality of a person's imprisonment by government authority, it is specifically protected by the U.S. Constitution.

Obiter dictum "Said in passing." This is the name given to a statement by a justice expressing an opinion that is included with, but is not essential to, an opinion resolving a case before the Court. Dicta are not construed as precedent and are not binding in future cases.

Per curiam "By the court." A per curiam opinion is an unsigned opinion of the Supreme Court, or an opinion written by the whole Court. Such opinions usually are issued in decisions that apply settled law to the case at hand and are therefore quite short.

Stare decisis "Let the decision stand." This phrase embodies the principle of adherence to settled cases. The Court generally operates under this doctrine, which provides that the principles of law established in earlier judicial decisions should be accepted as authoritative in similar later cases.

Appeals from Lower Federal Courts and State Supreme Courts

Most cases reach the Court on appeals from other courts. A litigant who lost in a lower court may ask the Court for a *writ of certiorari,* setting forth in the petition why he or she thinks the decision should be reviewed. If the Court sees merit, it issues the writ, which orders the lower court to prepare a record of the case and send it up for review. Most Court actions require at least a five-member majority, but four votes are sufficient for a writ of certiorari.

Appeals from state supreme courts usually concern allegations that a person's constitutional right was denied.

Requests for Certification

Though seldom used, certification is a request by a lower court—usually a court of appeals—for a final answer to questions of law in a particular case. After examining the certificate, the Court may order the case argued before it.

Pauper Cases

Most of the cases filed with the Supreme Court come from people who cannot

Clarence Earl Gideon taught himself enough about the law to prepare his own petition to the Supreme Court.

afford the $300 filing fee or the multiple copies required by the Court. These cases from self-described indigents are filed *in forma pauperis* and the costs are waived.

Prisoners seeking to have their convictions overturned account for the biggest share of the so-called pauper's cases and for much of the increase in the Court's caseload in recent years. Criminal defendants who had court-appointed counsel in federal cases automatically are entitled to pauper status. Others must file affidavits to prove their inability to pay.

Since 1984 the Court has been clamping down on use of the pauper filings, issuing blanket denials to large-scale abusers. One criminal defendant had filed seventy-four such appeals. In 1991 the Court began denying pauper status to cases it considers "frivolous or malicious."

Only about 1 percent of the pauper cases are accepted by the Court for review, compared with 6 percent of the paid cases. Paid cases have a better chance of acceptance because they are less likely to be frivolous and almost always are drafted by lawyers.

■ The Court's Caseload

Except for an occasional dip, the Supreme Court's caseload has been climbing steadily, from 4,212 in 1970 to just over

Throughout much of the Court's history the justices have been burdened by a heavy caseload, as depicted in this 1885 *Puck* cartoon.

5,800 in 1991–1992. By comparison, the number of cases on the docket (calendar) was under 2,000 annually until the 1960s.

While the number of cases on the Court's docket continues to go up, the number of cases that the Court schedules for full review has scarcely grown at all. In terms of signed opinions issued, the number has even declined slightly: from 109 in 1970 to 107 in 1992 (down from a peak of 151 in 1982 and 1983). Only a handful (three in 1989) of cases are decided *per curiam* ("by the Court") in brief, unsigned opinions. The vast majority of cases are dismissed, withdrawn, not

acted on, or carried over to the next term.

Since 1789 the Court has declared unconstitutional 126 federal laws and more than 1,200 state and local laws. The decade 1970–1979 saw the highest number of laws overturned: 20 federal and 193 state and local.

Circuit Riding: An Early Hardship

Supreme Court justices have often complained that they have too much work, but things actually used to be worse. The Judiciary Act of 1789 required justices to "ride circuit," which meant that because there was no separate set of judges for the fed-

Rough roads, uncomfortable carriages, and poor accommodations made circuit riding one of the least pleasant parts of a justice's duties.

eral circuit courts, two justices sat with one district court judge at circuit courts in each of three circuits. Thus, in 1792 the six justices were required to attend a total of twenty-seven circuit courts a year and two sessions of the Supreme Court.

As the country expanded westward, circuit riding became even more of a hardship. One justice reported that he had traveled ten thousand miles in 1838. Despite many pleas to Congress over the years to curtail this burdensome activity, it was not until 1891 that Congress passed the Circuit Court of Appeals Act, which created a new level of federal courts—circuit courts of ap-

peals—between the district and circuit courts, on the one hand, and the Supreme Court, on the other. In 1911 Congress finally abolished the old circuit courts.

Law Clerks

Many a famous lawyer, including Chief Justice William H. Rehnquist, has gained valuable experience working as a law clerk to a Supreme Court justice. By the same token, today's overburdened justices could not function without the help of their clerks. By the 1990s there were thirty-three of them, double the number twenty years earlier.

Each clerk is hired for a year by one of the nine justices. Some stay longer. The clerks analyze the thousands of cases handled by the Court, often laying out the options in memorandums to help the justices decide which way to vote. Whether any clerk has ever actually written an opinion is a closely guarded secret.

On the Rehnquist Court, besides the chief justice himself who clerked for Robert H. Jackson in 1952–1953, were two others who had been law clerks: Justice Byron R. White, for Fred M. Vinson, 1946–1947, and Justice John Paul Stevens, for Wiley B. Rutledge in 1947–1948. All three have said that clerks, while helpful, have little influence on the outcome of cases.

How a justice uses a clerk is a personal decision. Justice Louis Brandeis, a stickler for detail, once asked a clerk to check every one of tens of thousands of pages of *United States Reports* for a particular bit of information. In earlier days, when the workload was lighter, some justices wanted their clerks to be tennis partners or walking companions.

Congress first began providing money to hire law clerks in 1886. Four years earlier, Justice Horace Gray had paid $1,600 out of his own pocket to hire the first clerk, a top graduate of Harvard Law School who acted primarily as Gray's barber and servant.

The Court's Schedule

The phrase "first Monday in October," popularized as a play and movie title, makes it easy to remember when the Supreme Court begins its new term. From then until early May, it hears oral arguments two weeks at a time, with two weeks between sessions, tapering off as it begins to announce its decisions. The Court usually recesses in late June, but members continue to work on cases during the vacation months. By recessing, instead of adjourning as it used to do, the Court

avoids the need for special sessions if summer problems arise.

For the Sake of Argument . . .

Getting on the Calendar

Once the Court announces it will hear a case, the clerk of the Court puts the case on the calendar for oral arguments. Cases are argued roughly in the order in which they are granted review, with at least three months between the time the review is granted and the time the argument takes place. Well before the argument, the attorneys in the case provide the justices with briefs and records.

Arguments are heard on Monday, Tuesday, and Wednesday for seven two-week periods beginning the first week of October and ending in late April or early May.

Beating the Clock

Each side has thirty minutes in which to argue its case. At the controls for the warning and stop-speaking lights is the marshal of the court or the marshal's assistant. A white light indicates that only five minutes are left. A red light says that time is up; the attorney may continue talking only to complete a sentence.

An exception to the time limit is sometimes made for an *amicus curiae*—a person who volunteers or is invited to take part in

the case before the Court but who is not a party to it.

No TelePrompTers in Court

Typically only one attorney on a side presents the argument. He or she is strongly advised not to read from a prepared text, but most attorneys do use an outline or notes.

Lawyers begin their presentation by saying, "May it please the Court." The oral arguments are tape recorded and transcripts are available from the National Archives after the term ends.

During oral arguments, the justices are free to wade in with their questions or remarks as often as they wish. Indeed, questions take up about ten minutes of the allotted half-hour.

How often questions are asked and the manner in which they are asked depend on the style of a justice and his or her interest in a case. Chief Justice Warren E. Burger asked very few questions, but Justice Antonin Scalia has from his first day on the Court peppered attorneys with questions. Justice Sandra Day O'Connor is also known for asking many questions from the bench.

The Court's Many Friends

Individuals or groups interested in the outcome of a case often file briefs as an *amicus curiae,* friend of the court, even though they are not directly involved in the litigation. For example, the 1954 school desegregation case, *Brown v. Board of Education of Topeka,* drew fifty-one amicus briefs, a record at that time.

More recently, cases that could overturn *Roe v. Wade,* the 1973 case legalizing abortion, were apt to generate even more arguments. The 1989 case of *Webster v. Reproductive Health Services* brought a new record of eighty outside briefs to the Court, many of them joint submissions from dozens of interest groups on both sides of the abortion issue.

■ Arriving at a Decision

Conferences

Once the oral arguments are over, the case is considered in closed conference. The four cases argued on Monday are discussed and decided at a Wednesday afternoon conference. The cases argued on Tuesday and Wednesday are discussed and decided at Friday conferences that last all day. At these conferences justices also consider new motions, appeals, and petitions.

The chief justice is the first to indicate his view of the case and how he plans to vote; the other justices follow in order of seniority. Although the justices can speak as long as they wish, in the interests of effi-

ciency long speeches are discouraged. Justices are not supposed to interrupt one another.

Other than these procedural arrangements, little is known about what actually goes on in these secret conferences.

Next Step: Writing Opinions

An opinion is a reasoned argument explaining the legal issues in the case and the precedents (earlier decisions, for example) on which the opinion is based.

Soon after the case is decided in conference, one justice is assigned the task of

writing the majority opinion. The chief justice makes the assignment when he has voted with the majority. If he is in the minority, the justice in the majority with the most seniority assigns the job.

Opinion-writing can be long and tedious. Draft copies are circulated secretly among the justices, and new drafts are then written and rewritten to accommodate their comments.

Occasionally justices who voted with the majority in conference change their votes because they find the majority opinion unpersuasive or a dissenting opinion particularly convincing.

One such change of mind came to light in May 1993 when the Library of Congress made public thousands of pages of files it had received from Justice Thurgood Marshall, who had died earlier that year. The Marshall papers revealed much about the Court's decision processes, including a disclosure that in 1989 the Court came close to overturning *Roe v. Wade,* the 1973 decision legalizing abortion.

According to the papers, an eleventh-hour shift by Justice Sandra Day O'Connor, an abortion opponent, weakened the antiabortion side in *Webster v. Reproductive Health Services.* Although the final decision upheld Missouri's restrictions on abortion, it stopped short of sweeping away *Roe,* as had appeared nearly certain in the Court's secret deliberations.

Thumbs Up, Thumbs Down Opinions

Any justice can write a separate opinion. Justices who agree with the Court's ruling but disagree with some of the reasoning in the majority opinion may write concurring opinions. Those who disagree with the decision are free to write dissenting opinions or go on record as dissenters without an opinion. More than one justice can sign a concurring or dissenting opinion. Justices may concur with or dissent

from only a portion of the majority opinion.

Justice-friendly Software

Draft opinions used to be printed in a print shop in the basement of the Supreme Court Building. Strict security precautions were taken, and each copy was numbered to prevent extra copies from being removed from the building. In 1980 the Court began to use word processors to prepare draft opinions—some justices even using them themselves.

The Big Day: Announcing Opinions

The amount of time that passes between the vote on a case and the announcement of the decision varies from case to case. In simple cases where few points of law are at issue, the opinion can sometimes be written and cleared by the other justices in a week or less. In more complex cases, especially those with several dissenting or concurring opinions, it can take six months or more. Some cases may have to be reargued or the initial decision reversed after the drafts of the opinions have been circulated.

When an opinion has been finalized, it is printed—but only after the reporter of decisions has added a "headnote," or syllabus, summarizing the decision and a "lineup" at the end showing how each justice voted.

Opinions are released only on Tuesdays and Wednesdays during the week the Court is hearing oral arguments. In other weeks, opinions are released on Mondays.

The public announcement of opinions in Court is probably the Court's most dramatic moment. Justices do not elaborate on their written opinions because the Court has long held that its opinions must speak for themselves.

■ Major Decisions
Judicial Review

The Court staked out its power to review and declare invalid acts of Congress in

Marbury v. Madison (1803). Without its precedent, many of the other historic decisions may never have been handed down.

The first law struck down as unconstitutional was a relatively minor part of the Judiciary Act of 1789, in which Congress authorized the Supreme Court to order federal officials to undertake particular tasks. Citing that act, William Marbury sued to force the new Jefferson administration to honor his appointment to a government job by the previous administration of John Adams, even though the commission, albeit signed and sealed, had not been delivered.

According to Chief Justice John Marshall, in empowering the Court to issue such orders, Congress illegally expanded on the powers given by the Constitution. More-over, he declared, "It is, emphatically, the province and duty of the judicial department to say what the law is."

States' Rights

It wasn't long after *Marbury* that the Court extended its power of judicial review to include state and local laws. The issue came up in the celebrated case of *McCulloch v. Maryland* (1819).

James McCulloch headed the Baltimore branch of a congressionally chartered national bank, which Maryland tried to tax.

Civil Rights and Civil Liberties—So What's the Difference?

Many people think *civil rights* and *civil liberties* mean about the same thing. Wrong—their meanings are distinctly different.

On December 1, 1955, Rosa Parks refused to relinquish her seat to a white person and move to the back of a Montgomery, Alabama, bus. Her arrest and trial sparked a bus boy-cott, one of the first organized civil rights protests in the South.

A "bugged" telephone. Court opinions evolved on whether eavesdropping constituted an unreasonable search as such devices became more sophisticated.

Civil rights refers to the concept of being free from discrimination when engaging in public activities, such as voting, or participating in other aspects of civic life; using public transportation or other public accommodations; buying or renting a home; or looking for or working in a job. In the United States since the end of the Civil War, the term *civil rights* has referred in particular to the effort to eliminate racial discrimination against African-Americans.

Civil liberties have been defined as claims of right that a citizen can assert against the government. Most of the civil liberties Americans enjoy today are embodied in the Bill of Rights. These include the freedoms of expression guaranteed by the First Amendment; the Fourth Amendment protection against unreasonable searches and seizures; and the rights in criminal and civil trials set out in the Fifth, Sixth, Seventh, and Eighth amendments.

HISTORIC MILESTONES IN COURT RULINGS

1803

Marbury v. Madison—establishes the Court's power to declare an act of Congress unconstitutional.

1819

McCulloch v. Maryland—upholds the establishment of a national bank and supports a broad construction of Congress's power under the "necessary and proper" clause of the Constitution.

1824

Gibbons v. Ogden—strikes down a New York steamboat monopoly law, saying it conflicts with Congress's power to regulate interstate commerce. The decision establishes the federal commerce power as superior to that of the states but allows states to regulate commerce within their borders if Congress has not acted.

1852

Cooley v. Board of Wardens of Port of Philadelphia—settles on a doctrine of "dual federalism," giving the states greater power to regulate commerce where local interests outweigh national interests.

1857

Scott v. Sandford—provides that Congress cannot bar slavery from the territories and that slaves are not citizens of the United States. The decision hastens the onset of the Civil War.

1865–1870

The three Civil War amendments abolish slavery, limit state action restricting individual rights, and guarantee voting rights for blacks. Subse-

quent Court rulings make the amendments virtually useless in protecting the rights of blacks.

1873

Slaughterhouse Cases—limit the scope of the Fourteenth Amendment by narrowly defining the "privileges and immunities" of U.S. citizenship.

1883

Civil Rights Cases—strike down the Civil Rights Act of 1875, which prohibited racial discrimination in public accommodations, as lying beyond Congress's power under the Thirteenth or Fourteenth Amendment.

1895

Pollack v. Farmers' Loan and Trust Co.—finds the federal income tax unconstitutional. The decision, which feeds charges that the Court favors business and propertied interests, is later reversed by the Sixteenth Amendment (1913).

1896

Plessy v. Ferguson—upholds legally mandated racial segregation in public

transportation. The "separate but equal" doctrine provides a legal basis for segregation in the South and elsewhere to continue for the next sixty years.

1905

Lochner v. New York—adopts a broad "freedom of contract" theory to strike down a state law regulating working hours for bakers. The doctrine is used over the next three decades to strike down several other state and federal laws regulating economic activity.

1918

Hammer v. Dagenhart—strikes down a federal law designed to outlaw child

labor on the grounds that it lies beyond Congress's commerce power. Four years later the Court invalidates a second law imposing a prohibitive tax on goods manufactured with child labor.

1935–1936

The Court strikes down key parts of Franklin D. Roosevelt's New Deal program. Roosevelt strongly criticizes the justices and privately considers way to circumvent the Court.

1943–1944

The Court unanimously approves a wartime curfew placed on Japanese-Americans (*Hirabayashi v. United States*). By a 6–3 vote, the Court also upholds relocation of Japanese-Americans from the West Coast to inland internment camps (*Korematsu v. United States*).

1952

Youngstown Sheet and Tube Co. v. Sawyer—nullifies Harry S. Truman's seizure of steel mills to avert a wartime shutdown due to a strike. The decision rejects the theory that the president has inherent power to act in an emergency without authority from Congress.

Linda Carol Brown in 1952 at age nine. Her father's suit against the Topeka, Kansas, board of education led to the 1954 decision that integrated the nation's schools.

1954

Brown v. Board of Education of Topeka—unanimously declares racial segregation in public elementary and secondary schools unconstitutional because it violates the equal protection clause of the Fourteenth Amendment. One year later the Court says school desegregation must be carried out "with all deliberate speed."

1960

Elkins v. United States—requires states to enforce the exclusionary rule, barring use of illegally seized evidence in criminal trials. Over the next eight years the Court issues a series of decisions requiring states to give criminal defendants other safeguards set out in the Bill of Rights.

1962

Baker v. Carr—permits federal court suits to require reapportionment and redistricting by state legislatures. Later rulings establishing the principle of "one person, one vote" force reapportionment in every state but one during the 1960s.

1962–1963

In two cases the Court bars official prayer or Bible reading in public elementary and secondary schools.

1963

Gideon v. Wainwright—holds that states must provide lawyers for indigent criminal defendants in felony cases. The Court extends the decision in 1972 to any case in which a jail sentence is imposed.

1964

Congress passes the Civil Rights Act of 1964, prohibiting racial and other forms of discrimination in employment, public accommodations, and federally funded programs. This is followed by the Voting Rights Act of 1965, which establishes strong safeguards for blacks wanting to vote, and by the Fair Housing Act of 1968, which bars discrimination in the sale or rental of housing. The Supreme Court upholds these laws and interprets them broadly.

1971

Swann v. Charlotte-Mecklenburg County Board of Education—upholds use of court-ordered busing to achieve school desegregation. In later rulings the Court limits the power of lower courts to order busing between cities and suburbs.

1972

Furman v. Georgia, Jackson v. Georgia, Branch v. Texas—rules, 5–4, that capital punishment as then administered amounts to unconstitutional cruel and unusual punishment. The Burger Court decision—with the five justices in the majority holdovers from the Warren Court—invalidates all existing death sentences and touches off strong debate. The states begin to re-enact death penalty laws.

Norma McCorvey, surrounded by reporters in 1989, was the real "Jane Roe" of *Roe v. Wade*.

1973

Roe v. Wade—guarantees a woman's right to an abortion during most of her pregnancy.

1974

United States v. Nixon—upholds the special prosecutor's subpoena to President Nixon for tapes of his conversations relating to the Watergate break-in and coverup. Nixon, facing impeachment, releases the tapes, which show that he approved "hush money" to silence the burglars. He resigns

1976

By a 7–2 vote (*Gregg. v. Georgia, Proffitt v. Florida, Jurek v. Texas*), the Court upholds new state death penalty laws that allow juries to impose the death sentence under court guidelines. The Court, however, votes 5–4 (*Woodson v. North Carolina, Roberts v. Louisiana*) to

overturn mandatory death penalty statutes.

Allan Bakke in 1982

1978

University of California Regents v. Bakke—says colleges and universities can consider an applicant's race as one factor in the admissions process but cannot set rigid quotas for minority students.

1983

Immigration and Naturalization Service v. Chadha—provides that Congress's use of the legislative veto to override executive branch decisions without action by both chambers violates the principle of separation of powers.

Despite the Supreme Court's decision in *McCulloch v. Maryland*, the bank of the United States remained under attack. This cartoon depicts President Andrew Jackson attacking the bank with his veto stick. Vice President Martin Van Buren, center, helps kill the monster.

the Tenth Amendment, which reserves to the states all powers the Constitution does not give to the federal government, as "but a truism that all is retained which has not been surrendered."

The Worst Decision: Dred Scott?

Dred Scott was a Missouri slave whose effort to win his freedom led to a Supreme Court decision, *Scott v. Sandford* (1857), which denied Congress the power to ban slavery in the territories and barred slaves from citizenship.

The decision for the 7–2 Court majority was written by Chief Justice Roger B. Taney (pronounced tawny), a Marylander who had freed his own slaves thirty years earlier. Taney and his brother-in-law, Francis Scott Key, actively worked for the welfare of freed slaves.

McCulloch refused to pay, contending that the tax on a federal entity violated the Constitution. Daniel Webster defended the bank's constitutionality against Maryland's claim that Congress overstepped its bounds. Chief Justice John Marshall's opinion for the Court upheld Congress's creation of the bank and struck down Maryland's law imposing the tax. The ruling strengthened the "implied powers"

doctrine that Congress was not limited to the powers spelled out in the Constitution.

More than a century later, in 1941, the Court further diminished states' rights in areas such as child labor and minimum wages and hours. In *United States v. Darby Lumber Co.* the Court unanimously upheld the Fair Labor Standards Act of 1938 as being within Congress's power to regulate interstate commerce. The opinion viewed

Dred Scott

WORDS THAT LIVE

Many Supreme Court decisions are historic because of what they did. A few contain lines that are remembered more than the decision itself. Some examples:

The power to tax involves the power to destroy.
—Chief Justice John Marshall in *McCulloch v. Maryland*, 1819

The most stringent protection of free speech would not protect a man in falsely shouting fire in a theatre and causing a panic. . . . The question in every case is whether the words used are used in such circumstances and are of such a nature as to create a clear and present danger that they will bring about the substantive evils that Congress has a right to prevent. It is a question of proximity and degree.
—Justice Oliver Wendell Holmes in *Schenck v. United States, Baer v. United States,* 1919

The power to tax is not the power to destroy while this Court sits.
—Justice Oliver Wendell Holmes dissenting, in *Panhandle Oil Co. v. Mississippi,* 1928

One who belongs to the most vilified and persecuted minority in history is not likely to be insensible to the freedoms guaranteed by our Constitution. . . . But as judges we are neither Jew nor Gentile, neither Catholic nor agnostic. . . .
—Justice Felix Frankfurter in a rare reference to his Jewish heri-

Justice Oliver Wendell Holmes

tage, dissenting from the Court's ban on mandatory flag salutes, in *West Virginia State Board of Education v. Barnette,* 1943

[The states should proceed on school desegregation] with all deliberate speed.
—Chief Justice Earl Warren in *Brown v. Board of Education of Topeka,* 1955

But implicit in the history of the First Amendment is the rejection of obscenity as utterly without redeeming social importance.
—Justice William J. Brennan, Jr., in *Roth v. United States,* 1957

The conception of political equality from the Declaration of Independence, to Lincoln's Gettysburg Address, to the Fifteenth, Seventeenth, and Nineteenth Amendments can mean only one thing—one person, one vote.
—Justice William O. Douglas in *Gray v. Sanders,* 1963

[Before a suspect is questioned] the person must be warned that he has a right to remain silent, that any statement he does make may be used against him, and that he has the right to the presence of an attorney, either retained or appointed.
—Chief Justice Earl Warren in *Miranda v. Arizona,* 1966

Taney's decision, which was strongly criticized in the North on legal and political grounds, hastened the onset of the Civil War by fueling sectional animosity, widening the split between northern and southern Democrats, and contributing to the election of Republican Abraham Lincoln as president in 1860. It was overturned by the Fourteenth Amendment after the war ended.

One Person, One Vote

According to Chief Justice Earl Warren, who spoke for the Court in the momentous 1954–1955 cases ending school segregation (*Brown v. Board of Education of Topeka,* 1954 and 1955, and *Bolling v. Sharpe,* 1954), even more important than the desegregation cases was the 1962 case that led to the Court's insistence on "one person, one vote."

Until then, increasing urbanization had led to gross imbalances between city and rural districts. Every state had some districts for the state legislature that had at least twice as many people as the smallest district. And rural-dominated legislatures refused to redraw the districts to give urban areas more representation.

The situation was almost as bad in congressional districts, which the state legislators also designed. One urban Texas

district had four times more people than a rural district, yet each had one representative in Congress.

In the 1962 decision cited by Warren, the Tennessee case of *Baker v. Carr,* the Court for the first time rejected the notion that apportionment disputes are "political questions" outside the reach of federal courts. Chief Justice Warren voted with the 6–2 majority.

One year later Justice William O. Douglas set out the Court's "one person, one vote" belief in *Gray v. Sanders,* a Georgia elections case. "The conception of political equality from the Declaration of Independence to Lincoln's Gettysburg Address, to the Fifteenth, Seventeenth, and Nineteenth

Amendments can mean only one thing—one person, one vote," Douglas wrote.

In 1964 the Court extended the doctrine to congressional districts and both houses of state legislatures.

Although the ruling is widely referred to as "one man, one vote," Douglas actually used the nonsexist *person* and not *man.*

'Read 'em their rights....'

In 1963 Ernesto Miranda abducted a teenage girl from a Phoenix movie theater and later raped her in the nearby desert. When his criminal record landed him in a police lineup, he was identified by the victim. Although Miranda stated in a written confession that he had been advised of his rights by police, his court-appointed attorney argued that his client had not been told of his right to legal counsel. But that did not prevent Miranda's conviction and forty- to forty-five-year prison sentence.

The American Civil Liberties Union carried the case all the way to the Supreme Court, where in 1966 the Warren Court made perhaps its most controversial decision. The 5–4 ruling extended constitutional protections to criminal defendants and suspects. Arresting police officers must tell suspects that they have the right to remain silent, the right to consult with a lawyer, and the right to have a lawyer appointed for them if they cannot afford one. They are also warned that the government can use any statement they do make against them at trial.

The five-justice majority in the *Miranda v. Arizona* decision, lead by Chief Justice Earl Warren, stated that such warnings were needed to offset the coercive nature of police interrogations. The dissenting justices faulted the ruling on constitutional and practical grounds.

As for Miranda, he was convicted again on the same charges of kidnapping and rape, but he did not stay in prison long. After being paroled, he died of a knife wound received in a barroom brawl—just ten years after he and the Warren Court made legal history.

■ Beneath the Bench

Reporter of Decisions

Besides the case name, each Supreme Court decision carries a citation, such as 462 U.S. 919, that pinpoints its location in the law books. The codification is consistent and, once learned, easy to remember. But this isn't so with the cases from the Court's formative years. Then the cases carried the name of the official Court reporter—resulting in a curious system of abbreviations and numbers.

Since 1790 there have been fifteen re-porters of decisions, beginning with Alexander J. Dallas and ending with Frank D. Wagner, the reporter since 1987. The first four volumes of Court decisions were titled Dal. 1–4, for Dallas. His successors until 1874 were William Cranch (Cr. or Cranch), Henry Wheaton (Wheat.), Richard Peters, Jr. (Pet.), Benjamin C. Howard (How.), Jeremiah S. Black (Black), and John W. Wallace (Wall.). Wallace in 1874 was the last to have his name on the reports' cover.

The first reporters held other jobs and sold their reports in lieu of pay. Dallas was Treasury secretary and Cranch a federal judge. Wheaton, the first formally appoint-ed reporter, sometimes argued the cases he reported for the Court.

Clerk of the Court

The clerk keeps the Court's judicial house in order by administering the Court's dockets and argument calendars; receiving and recording all motions, peti-tions, jurisdictional statements, briefs, and other documents filed on the various dock-ets; distributing these papers to the jus-tices; and collecting the filing fees and assessing other court costs.

The clerk also prepares and maintains the Court's order list and journal, which contains all the Court's formal judgments and mandates. In these and other duties,

the clerk is assisted by a twenty-five-person staff and a computerized information sys-tem installed in 1976.

By mid-1992 there had been only nine-teen clerks of the Court, all men.

Oyez, Oyez, Oyez

With those words (an Old French word meaning "hear ye"), the marshal of the Court calls the Supreme Court to order. The marshal wears many hats—general manager, paymaster, and chief security officer. Sporting the traditional cutaway suit (like the clerk), the marshal attends all the Court's sessions (or is represented by an assistant), manages approximately 200 employees, supervises the Supreme Court building and grounds, and pays the person-nel and the bills. As for security, the marsh-al oversees the Supreme Court Police Force, composed of a chief of police and seventy-five officers.

For the Government . . .

The solicitor general represents the U.S. government before the Supreme Court. The solicitor general's office, which is part of the Justice Department, decides which cases the government should ask the Court to review and determines the govern-ment's legal position on any case in which it is involved (which amounts to about

Justice Hugo Black (right) swears in the new solicitor general of the United States, Thurgood Marshall, August 24, 1965, as President Lyndon B. Johnson, Marshall's wife, Cecilia, and their two sons look on. Two years later, Johnson appointed Marshall to the Supreme Court.

two-thirds of the cases heard during the term). The solicitor general's staff of about two dozen attorneys petition for hearings, prepare the government's briefs and supporting facts, and argue the government's case. For the latter, the solicitor general is often represented by one of the staff lawyers. If a case of special importance is before the Court, the attorney general of the United States, the solicitor general's superior, presents the argument.

Solicitors general have, for the most part, been pretty anonymous figures. But several—William Howard Taft, Charles Evans Hughes, Stanley Reed, Robert H. Jackson, and Thurgood Marshall—later became justices of the Supreme Court. Robert H. Bork, who held the post from 1973 to 1977, actually gained notoriety because of his role in the infamous "Saturday night

massacre" following President Richard Nixon's decision on October 12, 1973, to fire the special prosecutor in the Watergate affair, Archibald Cox, who was himself a former solicitor general. Attorney General Elliot Richardson and Deputy Attorney General William Ruckelshaus resigned rather than obey Nixon's order to fire Cox. As the next highest ranking official left in the Justice Department, Bork then took command and fired Cox.

The current solicitor general, Drew S. Days, is the second African-American to hold the post. The first was Thurgood Marshall, from 1965 to 1967.

Bar of the Supreme Court

The U.S. solicitor general also serves as head of the Bar of the Supreme Court. When the Supreme Court initially con-

vened in February 1790, one of its first actions was to establish qualifications for lawyers who wished to practice before it. Those requirements—acceptable personal and pro-fessional character and qualification to practice before a state's or territory's highest court—have remained the same since 1790. In all, some 180,000 attorneys have been admitted to the bar. About 5,000 are admitted each year.

Although some lawyers seek admission to the bar merely for personal prestige, membership does have a real function. Attorneys cannot process any case to completion by themselves unless they are members of the Supreme Court bar. A nonmember may work on a case, but at least one member of the Court bar must sponsor any case filed with the Court.

Traditions of the Court

The Supreme Court is steeped in tradition. Its insistence on the historic continuity of its procedures and its strict adherence to secrecy and formal decorum have yielded little to the changing world outside its chambers.

This fondness for traditions gives the Court an aura of substance, dignity, and caution that befits the nation's highest institution of law. It also encourages public

Occasionally a Supreme Court justice will step out into the Washington social circle. At the Washington Press Club's Salute to Congress dinner in 1985, Justice Sandra Day O'Connor took it in stride when her tablemate, John Riggins, suggested, "Come on Sandy baby, loosen up. You're too tight." After dinner the flamboyant Washington Redskins fullback dropped to the floor and fell asleep. He was later helped out of the hotel by his hosts from *People* magazine.

confidence in the integrity of the justices, the seriousness with which they undertake their jobs, and their independence from outside pressures.

Traditions affect justices' behavior outside the Court as well as on the bench. For example, justices seldom participate in Washington's cocktail party circuit, unlike members of Congress, diplomats, and administration officials.

Some traditions of the Court are rather quaint, such as the white quill pens still placed at every chair at the attorneys' tables in the courtroom on argument days. In this era of ballpoints and felt-tips, however, quills have fallen from favor; they serve instead as mementos of an appearance before the high court.

Seniority

The seniority system affects many Court procedures such as conference discussions and voting, announcement of opinions, and seating in the conference room and courtroom. During the Court's conferences, discussions of cases begin with the chief justice and proceed by seniority to the junior member. At the same time, justices typically indicate their position on the case. Reverse seniority is followed when opinions are announced in the courtroom.

Office assignments, seating on the bench—even the justices' placement in official photographs—are all determined by seniority. For example, in the courtroom the chief justice is seated in the center behind the winged mahogany table. The senior associate justice is seated at the immediate right and the second senior associate justice at the immediate left. The other justices take their places in alternating order of seniority, with the newest associate justice at the far left.

'I won't tell if you won't . . .'

Secrecy applies not only to formal deliberations but also to disclosure of personal disagreements and animosities among the justices. The unwritten code of secrecy has made the Court the most leakproof of government institutions.

The practice of allowing no one but justices into the conference room began years ago when it was thought—mistakenly—that pages had leaked a decision. Later leaks, including several in the 1970s, prompted the justices to take measures to prevent further premature disclosures or gossip.

Courtesy

Before they enter the courtroom and at the beginning of every private conference, the justices shake hands with one another. This practice began in the late nineteenth century when Chief Justice Melville W. Fuller decided it was a good idea to remind the justices that while they may have had differences of opinion, they did have to get along with one another.

■ Pay and Perks

Sages and Wages

In 1993 the chief justice earned $171,500 a year and the associate justices, $164,100.

The Court depends on Congress to adjust its salaries, and, like most working folk, the justices have not always been happy with their pay. In 1816, for example, Justice Joseph Story complained the cost of living had doubled and the expenses of the justices had quadrupled since their pay had

Chief Justice Melville W. Fuller photographed in his Supreme Court chambers.

been set in 1789. Congress ignored him.

At least one justice has resigned from the Court because of the low pay—Benjamin R. Curtis, who at the time (1857) was making $4,500 a year. He said he couldn't maintain his family in the style he wished on his Court salary.

Chief Justice William H. Rehnquist

broke precedent in 1989 by lobbying for pay raises for lower court federal judges. He was the first sitting chief justice to testify before a committee of Congress, the House Post Office and Civil Service Committee.

Perks

Besides their prestigious jobs, justices have several perquisites, including the help of up to four law clerks, two secretaries (the chief justice has three), and a messenger. Justices also have access to the Court dining room, exercise room, and library, as well as the services of the Court barber (for which they pay). The government provides the chief justice with a car, and the Court maintains a small fleet of cars for the official use of the other justices. But most justices drive themselves back and forth to work.

Retirement Goodies

For its first eighty years the Court had no retirement plan. Until 1869 justiceswho were unable to carry out their duties because of age or disability often hesitated to submit their resignations, knowing they would receive no retirement benefits. Because justices are appointed for life, they cannot be forcibly retired when they reach a certain age.

Justices' Salaries

Years	Chief justice	Associate justices
1789–1819	$4,000	$3,500
1819–1855	5,000	4,500
1855–1871	6,500	6,000
1871–1873	8,500	8,000
1873–1903	10,500	10,000
1903–1911	13,000	12,500
1911–1926	15,000	14,500
1926–1946	20,500	20,000
1946–1955	25,500	25,000
1955–1964	35,500	35,000
1964–1969	40,000	39,500
1969–1975	62,500	60,000
1975	65,625	63,000
1976[a]	68,800	66,000
1977	75,000	72,000
1978[a]	79,100	76,000
1979[a]	84,700	81,300
1980[a]	92,400	88,700
1981[a]	96,800	93,000
1982–1983	100,700	96,700
1984	104,700	100,600
1985–1986	108,400	104,100
1987–1989	115,000	110,000
1990	124,000	118,600
1991	155,000	148,300
1992	166,200	159,000
1993	171,600	164,100

[a] Cost-of-living adjustment.

Justice Stephen J. Field in his library on his eightieth birthday in 1896. Field managed to avoid the issue of his retirement when his fellow justice, John Marshall Harlan, attempted to raise the subject. Field finally retired in 1897 after thirty-four years of service on the Court.

It was largely the incapacity of Justices Samuel Nelson (1845–1872) and Robert C. Grier (1846–1870) that prompted Congress to set up a retirement system for the Court. The new system, enacted in 1869, stipulated that any justice who reached age seventy and had served on the Court for ten years could resign and continue to receive full salary. Congress has since modified that law to ensure that justices who retire at age seventy with at least ten years of service or at age sixty-five with at least fifteen years of service will receive their full salary. Justices with fewer than ten years of service who retire because of disability may receive one-half of their annual salary.

■ Justice on a 'Shoestring'

When compared to the president and the Congress, the Supreme Court seems to operate on a shoestring. In fiscal 1992, for example, Congress appropriated $24.6 million for the Court to pay the salaries of the nine justices and Court employees and to cover operating costs, including care of the Supreme Court building and grounds. For the same fiscal year, the Executive Office of the President had a budget of $298 million and Congress, $1.6 billion.

Composite picture of Supreme Court justices around 1926. From left, Louis D. Brandeis, Edward T. Sanford, James C. McReynolds, Harlan Fiske Stone, Chief Justice William Howard Taft, Oliver Wendell Holmes, Pierce Butler, Willis Van Devanter, and George Sutherland.

William H. Rehnquist   **Harry A. Blackmun**   **John Paul Stevens**   **Sandra Day O'Connor**   **Antonin Scalia**

The members of the Supreme Court in 1993 arranged in order of their seniority. The chief justice of the United States is at the far left.

JUSTICES *for All*

No job in the United States government, perhaps even the presidency, receives more scrutiny than that of Supreme Court justice. Presidents have at most eight years to leave their marks on history. But justices, like diamonds, are forever; they may remain on the bench for decades, making decisions that affect everyone's lives.

Is it any wonder, then, that the Senate Judiciary Committee digs so thoroughly into the background of every nominee for the Court? It pores over everything he or she has written, searching for clues as to how the nominee might vote on a controversial issue such as abortion. The news media also probe candidates' backgrounds. Reporters even have been known to check their video stores to see what kinds of movies they rent.

In 1991 it was neither the committee nor the press that initiated the most personal probe yet of a nominee to the Supreme Court. It was a former colleague, Anita F. Hill, who stepped forth and accused Clarence Thomas of inappropriate sexual speech. Thomas nevertheless was confirmed by the Senate, closing out one of the most unusual episodes in the selection of "justices for all."

Anthony M. Kennedy

David H. Souter

Clarence Thomas

Ruth Bader Ginsburg

The Court Today

Over the Supreme Court's first two centuries (through August 1993), only 107 persons have served as justices. Of these, two were women (Sandra Day O'Connor and Ruth Bader Ginsburg) and two were African-American (Thurgood Marshall and Clarence Thomas). All except fourteen were Protestants.

In 1993 the Court looked like this: Chief Justice William H. Rehnquist (initially confirmed 1971, promoted 1986), Byron R. White (1962; retired June 28), Harry Blackmun (1970), John Paul Stevens (1975), Sandra Day O'Connor (1981), Antonin Scalia (1986), Anthony Kennedy (1988), David Souter (1990), Clarence Thomas (1991), and Ruth Bader Ginsburg (sworn in August 10 to replace Byron White).

All in the Family

Several Supreme Court justices have been related. Among them are two with the same name: John Marshall Harlan, who were grandfather (served 1877–1911) and grandson (1954–1971). Stephen J. Field (1863–1897) and a nephew, David J. Brewer (1890–1910), served together for seven years. The two Lamars—Lucius Quintus Cincinnatus Lamar (1888–1893) and Joseph Rucker Lamar (1910–1916)—were cousins.

Characterizing Justices

Age and Longevity

The youngest justice ever appointed was Joseph Story (1804). He was a month younger than William Johnson (1811), who was also thirty-two.

The oldest appointee was Horace H. Lurton (1910), sixty-five; the oldest justice, Oliver Wendell Holmes, was ninety when he retired in 1932.

William O. Douglas, who at forty was the youngest justice appointed in the twentieth century, served longer than any member—thirty-six years and seven months, from April 1939 until he resigned in November 1975.

James F. Byrnes served the shortest time, from July 8, 1941, to October 3, 1942, when he resigned to become director of the World War II Office of Economic Stabilization. He later became secretary of state in the Truman administration.

Degreed or Not Degreed?

Of the sixty justices who attended law school, the largest number (fifteen) went to Harvard. Yale taught nine and Columbia, six. Two of the early justices, John Rutledge and John Blair, studied at the Inns of Court, England, as did Francis W. Murphy, who served in the 1940s.

Tapping Reeve's law lectures in the late eighteenth century were in such great demand he built a one-room schoolhouse next to his house in Litchfield, Connecticut.

Stanley F. Reed (1938–1957), the last justice without a law degree, attended two law schools (University of Virginia and Columbia) but received a degree from neither.

Not until 1957 was the Court for the first time entirely composed of law school graduates. The last justice who never atten-

The justices that make up the members of today's Supreme Court are all law school graduates. The Stanford Law class of 1952 boasted two future Supreme Court justices: William H. Rehnquist (back row, far left) and Sandra Day, who became Sandra Day O'Connor (first row, second from left).

ded law school—nor graduated from high school—was James Byrnes, who was mostly self-taught and passed the bar when he was twenty-four.

Religion Courtside

The first non-Protestant on the Court was Chief Justice Roger B. Taney, a Roman Catholic nominated by Andrew Jackson in 1835. Other Catholic members have been Edward D. White, Joseph Mc-Kenna, Pierce Butler, Frank Murphy, William J. Brennan, Jr., and two current justices, Antonin Scalia and Anthony Kennedy. Clarence Thomas was raised a Catholic but became an Episcopalian.

Woodrow Wilson's nomination of Louis D. Brandeis as the first Jewish justice was controversial more because of Brandeis's liberal views than his religion. He was confirmed 47–22 in 1916. Other Jewish justices were Benjamin Cardozo, Felix Frankfurter, Arthur J.

The nomination of Louis D. Brandeis to the Supreme Court in January 1916 set off a four-month confirmation battle, in which conservative forces in industry and finance vigorously fought to keep Brandeis, a Jew, off the bench. President Woodrow Wilson and a host of progressive reform groups prevailed, and the Senate confirmed him by a wide margin.

Goldberg, and Abe Fortas. Ruth Bader Ginsburg, also Jewish, is also only the second woman appointed to the Court. A justice's religion rarely if ever influences him or her in deciding cases. Brennan, for example, supported women's abortion rights despite his church's strong antiabortion stance.

Speaking Geographically . . .

Justices have come from thirty-one of the fifty states, and states have not been represented in any particular appointment pattern. New York has been the home of sixteen justices, Pennsylvania of eleven. Ten justices have come from Massachusetts, nine from Ohio, and six each from Virginia and Kentucky. No other states have been so frequently represented on the Court.

Early in the Court's history, geographic balance was a major consideration in selecting nominees. Because the justices also served as circuit judges, it was popularly assumed that each region should have a spokesperson on the Court. Until the Civil War this custom resulted in a "New England seat," a "Virginia seat," a "New York seat," and a "Pennsylvania seat." With the nation's post–Civil War expansion and the end of the justices' circuit-riding duties, this tradition faded.

Marshall and Thomas

President Lyndon B. Johnson nominated the first black Supreme Court justice, Thurgood Marshall, on June 13, 1967. Marshall, a noted civil rights lawyer, was quickly confirmed by the Senate, 69–11. But it was a different story in 1991 when Marshall retired and George Bush named a conserv-

ative black, Clarence Thomas, to replace him. The subsequent confirmation hearings were the strangest in U.S. history. Millions of television viewers around the world watched as the senators and witnesses discussed genitalia and other delicate matters after a former colleague, Anita Hill, accused Thomas of sexual harassment. The Senate ultimately confirmed Thomas by a narrow margin, 52–48.

Women of the Court

President Ronald Reagan nominated the first female justice, Sandra Day O'Connor, on August 19, 1981. O'Connor, an Arizona judge, won unanimous Senate approval for the high court.

Ironically, although she was one of the outstanding students in her law school class, O'Connor had trouble landing a job in 1952 because women had made no inroads into the legal profession. When she applied to one law firm to work as an attorney, she was offered the position of legal secretary instead.

In 1993 President Bill Clinton nominated Ruth Bader Ginsburg to the Court to replace the retiring Byron White. Ginsburg, a judge on the U.S. Court of Appeals, is the first Democratic appointee to the Court in twenty-six years. She was confirmed 96–3 by the Senate on August 3.

■ Chief Justices

Up the Ladder

Only four sitting or former justices have become chief justices. Edward D. White, appointed by President William Howard Taft in 1910, was the first. White had been on the Court since 1894, a nominee of Grover Cleveland. Next was Charles Evans Hughes, who left the Court to run for president in 1916 and was brought back as chief justice by Herbert

Hoover in 1930. Third was Harlan F. Stone, a 1925 Calvin Coolidge appointee promoted by Franklin D. Roosevelt in 1941. And fourth was conservative William H. Rehnquist, a 1971 Richard Nixon appointee moved up by Ronald Reagan in 1986.

Chief Justices of the United States

Name	Years served	Appointed by	Home state
John Jay	1789–1795	Washington	New York
John Rutledge	1795*	Washington	South Carolina
Oliver Ellsworth	1796–1800	Washington	Connecticut
John Marshall	1801–1835	Adams	Virginia
Roger B. Taney	1836–1864	Jackson	Maryland
Salmon P. Chase	1864–1873	Lincoln	Ohio
Morrison R. Waite	1874–1888	Grant	Ohio
Melville W. Fuller	1888–1910	Cleveland	Illinois
Edward D. White	1910–1921	Taft	Louisiana
William Howard Taft	1921–1930	Harding	Ohio
Charles Evans Hughes	1930–1941	Hoover	New York
Harlan Fiske Stone	1941–1946	Roosevelt	New York
Fred M. Vinson	1946–1953	Truman	Kentucky
Earl Warren	1953–1969**	Eisenhower	California
Warren E. Burger	1969–1986	Nixon	Minnesota
William H. Rehnquist	1986–	Reagan	Arizona

*Rutledge accepted a recess appointment and presided over the Court at its August 1795 term, at which two cases were decided. In December 1795, however, the Senate refused, 10–14, to confirm him.

**Warren accepted a recess appointment as chief justice in September 1953 and was confirmed by the Senate in March 1954.

Former U.S. president William Howard Taft signing the oath of office as the tenth chief justice of the United States, July 11, 1921.

Chief Justices and Politics

Charles Evans Hughes resigned from the Court in 1916 to run for president against Democrat Woodrow Wilson. He returned in 1930, appointed by Herbert Hoover as chief justice to replace William Howard Taft. Hughes retired in 1941.

Earl Warren, then governor of California, was Thomas E. Dewey's running mate in his ill-fated 1948 race against Harry S. Truman. After President Dwight D. Eisenhower suffered a heart attack, Warren was widely considered a possible Republican

Earl Warren's handsome family was not only a great asset in his political campaigns but also the foundation for his sense of values. This photograph, taken when Warren was attorney general of California, was used in his successful 1942 gubernatorial campaign.

JIM CROW LAW.

UPHELD BY THE UNITED STATES SUPREME COURT.

Statute Within the Competency of the Louisiana Legislature and Railroads—Must Furnish Separate Cars for Whites and Blacks.

Washington, May 18.—The Supreme Court today in an opinion read by Justice Brown, sustained the constitutionality of the law in Louisiana requiring the railroads of that State to provide separate cars for white and colored passengers. There was no interstate, commerce feature in the case for the railroad upon which the incident occurred giving rise to case—Plessey vs. Ferguson—East Louisiana railroad, was and is operated wholly within the State, to the laws of Congress of many of the States. The opinion states that by the analogy of the laws of Congress, and of many of states requiring establishment of separate schools for children of two races and other similar laws, the statute in question was within competency of Louisiana Legislature, exercising the police power of the State. The judgment of the Supreme Court of State upholding law was therefore upheld.

Mr. Justice Harlan announced a very vigorous dissent saying that he saw nothing but mischief in all such laws. In his view of the case, no power in the land had right to regulate the enjoyment of civil rights upon the basis of race. It would be just as reasonable and proper, he said, for states to pass laws requiring separate cars to be furnished for Catholic and Protestants, or for descendants of those of Teutonic race and those of Latin race.

nominee in 1956. But Eisenhower, recovered, ran again, and won. As chief justice, Warren headed the commission that investigated the assassination of President John F. Kennedy.

Most chief justices were politically active before reaching the high court. Taft was president; Edward D. White, a senator; Warren, a governor; and several, cabinet members.

■ Associate Justices
The Great Dissenter

The first justice John Marshall Harlan (there were two) is known as the Supreme Court's "great dissenter." In his thirty-four years on the Court (1877–1911), Harlan dissented from the majority 380 times. He is best remembered for his lone dissent in *Plessy v. Ferguson* (1896), in which the Court sanctioned "separate but equal" public facilities for blacks and whites.

Harlan, a former slaveholder, wrote that "in view of the Constitution, in the eye of the law, there is in this country no superior, dominant ruling class of citizens. There is no caste here. Our Constitution is colorblind, and neither knows nor tolerates classes among citizens."

Fifty-eight years later in *Brown v. Board of Education of Topeka,* the Court vindicated Harlan's viewpoint by overturning *Plessy* as a defense for segregated schools.

"We conclude that in the field of public education the doctrine of 'separate but equal' has no place," wrote Chief Justice Earl Warren.

The Erratic, . . .

In August 1795 President George Washington appointed former justice John Rutledge (1790–1791) to succeed John Jay as chief justice. Although Rutledge presided unofficially during the Court's August term, the Senate rejected his nomination by a 10–14 vote the following December. When he heard what had happened, Rutledge tried to drown himself. He suffered from periodic bouts of insanity until his death in 1800.

Justice Henry Baldwin was one of the most erratic justices to ever serve on the Supreme Court. During his fourteen years there (1830–1844), he suffered from periods of mental illness, had screaming arguments with his colleagues, and was said to be occasionally violent.

Indeed, he missed a whole term of the Court after a mental breakdown in the winter of 1832–1833. After he died, his friends were forced to take up a collection to pay for his funeral because he was heavily in debt.

John Rutledge

Henry Baldwin

the Violent, . . .

Eight years before Thomas Jefferson appointed him to the Court, Henry Brockholst Livingston (who served from 1807 to 1823) killed a man in a duel. Apparently he fought several other duels as well. Livingston was known as a genial man who also had a violent streak.

. . . and the Just Plain Nasty

James Clark McReynolds may be the nastiest person to ever serve on the Court (1914–1941). He also turned out to be one of the most conservative justices to serve during the twentieth century, much to the surprise of President Woodrow Wilson, who appointed him.

Antisemitic, McReynolds openly shunned the Court's two Jewish justices, Louis Brandeis and Benjamin Cardozo. He even refused to speak to Brandeis during the first three years of Brandeis's tenure—and to sit next to Brandeis for a group photograph. McReynolds also wouldn't speak to Justice John H. Clarke. He considered Clarke dimwitted.

Justice Congeniality

As chief justice (1930–1941), Charles Evans Hughes was known for the conciseness and clarity with which he was able to summarize the essential points of a case—

Henry Brockholst Livingston

James C. McReynolds

Charles Evans Hughes, Jr., (left) was serving as solicitor general in 1930 when President Herbert Hoover appointed his father to be chief justice of the United States. Because the solicitor general argues cases for the government before the Supreme Court, the younger Hughes resigned his position to avoid any appearance of conflict of interest. A third generation of Hughes men is represented here by Stuart Hughes, born in 1916.

and for his consideration toward others. For example, during oral arguments attorneys who were nervous or long-winded were often saved by a simple question from Hughes that sought to clarify or rephrase arguments they had presented poorly.

He was also extremely considerate of the other justices. At that time the Court held Saturday conferences, and Hughes ordinarily had the opinion-writing assignment delivered to the appropriate justice later that day. Knowing that Justice Benjamin N. Cardozo, who had had a heart attack before coming to the Court in 1932, would begin working on an assignment as soon as he received it, Hughes had Cardozo's assignments delivered on Sunday. And so that Cardozo would not be aware of this special treatment, Hughes also delayed delivering assignments to Justice Willis Van Devanter, who lived in the same apartment house as Cardozo.

Hughes is the only justice to have served two separate terms on the Court. President William Howard Taft named him associate justice in 1910, but he resigned in 1916 to run for president against Democrat Woodrow Wilson (Hughes lost the election by only twenty-three electoral votes). Hughes rejoined the Court in 1930 when President Herbert Hoover appointed him chief justice. He served until his retirement in 1941.

John McLean

Justice McLean: A Four-Time Loser

In 1829 President Andrew Jackson made a bargain with the politically ambitious John McLean. Jackson promised to appoint McLean to the Supreme Court if McLean would give up his yearning to be president. Jackson was true to his word, but McLean went back on his. During the thirty-two years (1829–1861) he was on Court, McLean ran for president four times, changing political parties with each race. He lost all four times.

Cramming for the Court

When Joseph McKenna was nominated to the Court in 1897, he decided he needed to brush up on his law before stepping up

Joseph McKenna

Edward T. Sanford

happened to be on the same day, March 8, 1930.

The Justice Who Wanted to Be a Soldier

Francis "Frank" William Murphy was nominated to the Supreme Court in 1940 by President Franklin Roosevelt. But Murphy was disappointed; he really wanted to be secretary of war. Indeed, Murphy was so eager to become involved in World War II that he spent Court recesses serving as an infantry officer at Fort Benning, Georgia.

to the high court. So, like many people these days, he went back to school. Despite studying for a few months at Columbia University Law School, his poor education and writing ability severely handicapped him during the early years of his twenty-six-year stay on the bench.

Friends to the End

Chief Justice William Howard Taft must have been delighted in 1923 when his close friend Edward Terry Sanford was named to the Court. Indeed, Court-watchers observed that they appeared to be such good friends that Taft in effect had two votes at the Court. They remained close friends until they died—which

Frank Murphy reviews the local constabulary in the Philippines during his stint there as governor-general in the mid-1930s. Later, after his appointment to the Court and during World War II, he would beg President Roosevelt for an assignment back in the islands. But it was not to be. He became high commissioner of the islands when they attained commonwealth status in 1935.

How the Supremes Are Rated

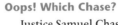

In 1970 sixty-five law school deans and other judicial experts evaluated the Court's first one hundred justices. Based on their ratings, the "greats" were Chief Justice John Marshall, Joseph Story, Chief Justice Roger B. Taney, the first John Marshall Harlan, Oliver Wendell Holmes, Chief Justice Charles Evans Hughes, Louis D. Brandeis, Harlan F. Stone, Benjamin Cardozo, Hugo L. Black, Felix Frankfurter, and Chief Justice Earl Warren.

Rated as "failures" were Willis Van Devanter, James C. McReynolds, Pierce Butler, James F. Byrnes, Harold H. Burton, Chief Justice Frederick M. Vinson, Sherman Minton, and Charles E. Whittaker.

■ Impeached!

Justice Chase

The only justice ever impeached, Samuel Chase, was charged with harsh and partisan conduct on the bench. Chase, a Federalist, was himself the target of Jeffersonian Democrats who viewed the Court as the last bastion of Federalist influence. Chase's support of the Alien and Sedition acts and his death sentence for the farmer who led Pennsylvania's largely nonviolent Whiskey Rebellion gave his political enemies ammunition for removing him. The House impeached Chase in January 1804, but the Senate acquitted him in 1805. Chase remained on the Court until his death in 1811.

Oops! Which Chase?

Justice Samuel Chase should not be confused with Chief Justice Salmon P. Chase, who served on the Court from 1864 until his death in 1873. Chief Justice Chase is one of only two justices whose face has appeared on U.S. currency—the $10,000 bill, which is no longer printed. The other justice is John Marshall who appeared on the $500 bill.

Federal Judges Impeached

The Senate has convicted only seven officials on impeachment

charges, and all were federal judges. Five other judges were tried but acquitted, maing the judiciary the largest single category of persons formally accused under Congress's constitutional impeachment power.

In all, sixteen officials had been impeached by the House through mid-1993, including Supreme Court Justice Samuel Chase in 1804–1805 and President Andrew Johnson in 1868. Of the fifteen tried by the Senate, eight were acquitted. (There was no Senate action on one of the sixteen impeached officials, federal judge Mark H. Delahay, who resigned before the House charged him in 1873.)

Charges against those found guilty included misconduct, treason, tax fraud, perjury, and bribery. The seven judges removed from office on one or another of these charges were John Pickering, 1803–1804; West H. Humphreys, 1862; Robert W. Archbald, 1912–1913; Halsted L. Ritter, 1936; Harry E. Claiborne, 1986; Alcee L. Hastings, 1988–1989; and Walter L. Nixon, Jr., 1989. (Hastings's conviction was overturned, and he ran for and won a House seat from Florida in 1992.)

Claiborne, of Nevada, was the first sitting federal judge ever to be jailed. He was in prison on criminal tax fraud charges when the House impeached him. Hastings, of Florida, was the first federal official impeached after being acquitted by a jury. Suspicions that he lied to the jury were a factor in his being tried on impeachment charges.

The judges acquitted, besides Justice Chase, were James H. Peck, 1830–1831; Charles Swayne, 1904–1905; George W. English, 1926 (charges dismissed); and Harold Louderback, 1933.

Hastings's Comeback

Former federal judge Alcee L. Hastings made history in 1993 by returning to the chamber of Congress that impeached him five years earlier. In 1992 he was elected as a Democratic member of the House of Representatives from Florida, making him one of the first two blacks from the state since 1873.

In September 1992 a federal court overturned Hastings's conviction for perjury and corruption on grounds that the full Senate had not tried him. He had been tried by a special twelve-member committee as part of the Senate's effort to streamline the handling of impeachment cases. The full Senate had, however, found Hastings guilty. The Supreme Court later upheld the Senate procedure.

Alcee Hastings

Fortas: Impeachment Threatened

Eight months after he was nominated for chief justice in 1968, Abe Fortas became the first person to resign from the Supreme Court under threat of impeachment. Fortas resigned May 14, 1969, ten days after *Life* magazine disclosed that Fortas had accepted $20,000 in 1966 from Lewis Wolfson, an industrialist later convicted of illegal securities sales. Fortas denied any wrongdoing and said he had returned the money after Wolfson was indicted. Questions over Fortas's other financial dealings

Abe Fortas's close friendship with Lyndon B. Johnson began when Fortas was a Washington attorney and Johnson a little-known representative from Texas. The advisory relationship continued throughout Fortas's tenure on the Supreme Court.

had sidetracked his nomination by President Lyndon Johnson to succeed Chief Justice Earl Warren. The delay enabled the new Republican president, Richard Nixon, to make the nomination, and Warren Earl Burger became chief justice.

Douglas: Stood His Ground

Another justice faced with impeachment, William O. Douglas, withstood criticism from future president Gerald R. Ford and remained on the Court five more years. Ford, then House minority leader, accused Douglas of showing "gross impropriety" by not disqualifying himself from obscenity cases involving a publisher Douglas had written for, and of illegally practicing law through a foundation. A House subcommittee investigated and cleared Douglas in 1970.

Douglas, an outspoken liberal and environmentalist, had been briefly threatened with impeachment in 1953 after he temporarily delayed the executions of convicted spies Julius and Ethel Rosenberg.

Douglas was also controversial because of his four marriages, the last two to very young women. His first marriage ended in divorce after thirty years. His second, to a Washington socialite, lasted nine years. Then he married a twenty-four-year-old student, but she didn't like life in Washing-

An ardent outdoorsman and conservationist, William O. Douglas spent most of his leisure time hiking in wilderness areas all over the world. He published several books on nature preservation and on his travels.

ton and divorced him after only three years. At age sixty-eight he married Cathleen Ann Heffernan, a twenty-three-year-old college student who became a lawyer and, eventually, his widow. Fortunately for Douglas, serial marriage is not an impeachable offense.

Murder, She Almost Wrote

Until 1891 Supreme Court justices were required to ride circuit, hearing appeals in various parts of the country. On one such trip to California in 1888, Stephen J. Field angered Sarah Althea Hill by invalidating her marriage to a wealthy mine owner who had since died. Hill meanwhile had married David Terry, a former colleague of Field's. She threatened to kill Field for denying them the estate.

For protection Field traveled with federal marshal David Neagle on his return to California in 1889. At one train stop the Terrys spotted Field, and David Terry struck him. Neagle pulled his gun and killed Terry when it appeared he was going for a weapon. California officials tried to charge Neagle with murder, but the Supreme Court ruled in 1890 that he had acted under federal authority, even though there was no specific law authorizing him to protect Field.

Sarah Althea Hill

American Political Parties since 1789

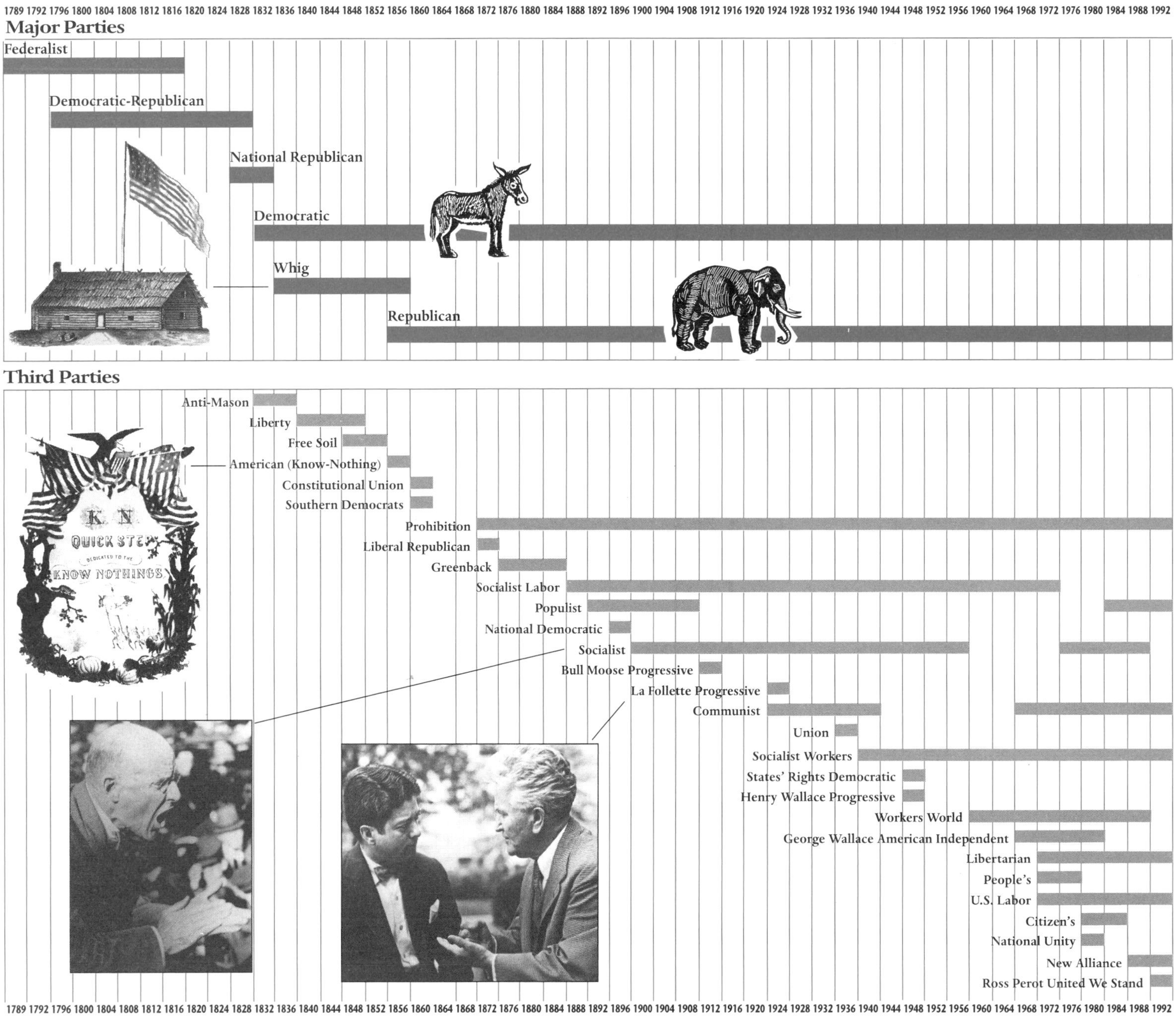
1789 1792 1796 1800 1804 1808 1812 1816 1820 1824 1828 1832 1836 1840 1844 1848 1852 1856 1860 1864 1868 1872 1876 1880 1884 1888 1892 1896 1900 1904 1908 1912 1916 1920 1924 1928 1932 1936 1940 1944 1948 1952 1956 1960 1964 1968 1972 1976 1980 1984 1988 1992
Major Parties
Federalist
Democratic-Republican
National Republican
Democratic
Whig
Republican
Third Parties
Anti-Mason
Liberty
Free Soil
American (Know-Nothing)
Constitutional Union
Southern Democrats
Prohibition
Liberal Republican
Greenback
Socialist Labor
Populist
National Democratic
Socialist
Bull Moose Progressive
La Follette Progressive
Communist
Union
Socialist Workers
States' Rights Democratic
Henry Wallace Progressive
Workers World
George Wallace American Independent
Libertarian
People's
U.S. Labor
Citizen's
National Unity
New Alliance
Ross Perot United We Stand
K N
QUICK STEP
DEDICATED TO THE
KNOW NOTHINGS
1789 1792 1796 1800 1804 1808 1812 1816 1820 1824 1828 1832 1836 1840 1844 1848 1852 1856 1860 1864 1868 1872 1876 1880 1884 1888 1892 1896 1900 1904 1908 1912 1916 1920 1924 1928 1932 1936 1940 1944 1948 1952 1956 1960 1964 1968 1972 1976 1980 1984 1988 1992

The Political Party Scene

The he American political party system was not created, it evolved. In fact, the Constitution doesn't even mention parties, and what little the Founders thought about them was probably negative. One example: "If I could go to heaven but with a party, I would not go there at all," declared Thomas Jefferson in 1789.

Yet Jefferson and James Madison came to be identified with a party that opposed strong central government—known as the Jeffersonian or Democratic-Republican party. In the opposite camp were the Federalists led by Alexander Hamilton and John Adams.

From 1801, when Jefferson replaced Adams as president, the Democratic Republican party gradually became dominant. It controlled both the White House and Congress for three decades and for a time after 1816, when the Federalists faded away, it was essentially the only party. In the 1820s the country began to settle into

the two-party system still dominant today—first with the Democrats, the party of Jefferson and Andrew Jackson, and later with the Republicans, the party of Abraham Lincoln.

In the meantime, various third parties came and went to promote this or that cause. The oldest of these still in existence is the Prohibitionist party, which seeks to prohibit the sale of alcoholic beverages.

Whigs

In the mid-1820s the National Republicans emerged as a challenger to the Democrats, as the Democratic-Republicans began to be known. In 1834 the National Republicans led by Henry Clay and Daniel Webster changed their name to Whigs to signify their opposition to what in their view was populism under Andrew Jackson. (The term Whig was taken from English politics, where the Whigs opposed strong central authority, and from Colonial

The Whigs were able to win the White House twice by nominating the famous Indian fighter William Henry Harrison in 1840 and the Mexican-American War hero Zachary Taylor in 1848.

America, where the Whigs opposed the Tories loyal to the British Crown.) The Clay-Webster Whigs captured the White House twice—in 1840 (William Henry Harrison) and 1848 (Zachary Taylor)—but then dwindled away.

■ Democrats and Republicans

The Democrats, strongest in the agricultural South and West, gained control of Congress in 1826 and the presidency in 1828 with the election of Andrew Jackson.

The Republicans, at first an antislavery third party, gradually replaced the Whigs as the Democrats' chief rival. They elected their first president, Abraham Lincoln, in 1860.

Nicknamed the "Grand Old Party" (GOP), the Republicans controlled Congress and the presidency for most of the next seventy years, until Democrat Franklin D. Roosevelt's landslide victory in the Great Depression year of 1932. Since World War II, the United States has generally experienced "divided government," with the presidency in Republican hands most of the time and Congress, especially the House, almost always under Democratic control. The Republicans have not had a majority in the House since the 83d Congress (1953–1955).

Party Organization

Cowboy humorist Will Rogers used to say, "I am not a member of any organized party—I am a Democrat." It's a funny line but in truth it could apply to the Republicans as well. Political parties in the United States are very loosely organized. Anybody can join. In fact, anyone can be a Democrat or Republican simply by saying so. Of course, both parties welcome those who want to join formally and pay dues, but it's not required. Most states require voters wishing to participate in a state's primaries or caucuses to register as a Democrat or Republican, but some states have primaries open to voters of either party or, in some cases, to independents as well as party members.

> "I don't belong to any organized political party, I'm a Democrat."
> Will Rogers

Parties purposely keep their rolls open to all comers (the more votes the better), but their main objective is to win elections and to do that they need an organizational structure, which both parties have. It is a loose federation, however, reflecting the fragmented character of American politics. Every four years the party organization comes together to try to elect a president,

but in the meantime the organization is basically a series of progressively larger units, beginning at the neighborhood or precinct level and rising through committees at the county, legislative and congressional district, and state levels to the national committee.

There is no "chain of command." Each unit is more or less independent. The national chair exerts influence mainly through leadership and force of personality, rather than through any specified powers. The chair is elected by the national committee, but for the party holding the White House the president actually designates the chairperson.

The Democratic National Committee, with about 400 members, is more than twice the size of the 162-member Republican National Committee. But the commit-

tees seldom meet; the day-to-day work is done by the chair and the headquarters staff.

Party Identification

Although more Americans call themselves Democrats than anything else, they usually vote Republican in presidential elections. In the forty-eight years from 1945 to 1993, Republicans held the White House twenty-eight years to the Democrats' twenty years.

Polls consistently show that most voters identify themselves as Democrats. In a 1990 Gallup poll, for example, 39 percent said they were Democrats; 31 percent, Republicans; and 30 percent, independents.

Where Did That Donkey and Elephant Come From?

How did the donkey and elephant become symbols of the Democratic and Re- publican parties? Political cartoonist Thomas Nast popularized them in his drawings for *Harper's Weekly* in the late 1880s. The Democratic donkey appeared first, in 1870, followed by the GOP's elephant four years later. Nast, a Republican, also made the tiger a symbol of Tammany Hall, the Democratic machine that dominated New York politics for years under William Marcy Tweed. In fact, Nast regularly assailed the Tweed Ring in his cartoons.

In this self-portrait for *Harper's Weekly* in 1875, Thomas Nast sketches himself sketching what would become the symbol of the Democratic party for more than a century.

The Mugwumps

A *mugwump,* in the definition of Princeton president Harold Willis Dodds, "is a fellow with his mug on one side of the fence and his wump on the other." But in the 1884 presidential election the Mugwumps were righteous Republicans who bolted from the party rather than support James G. Blaine, whose ethics were in question. The term comes from *mugwomp,* the Algonquin word for chief.

Blaine also was hurt by his failure to disavow a supporter's effort to label the Democrats as the party of "rum, Romanism, and rebellion." Grover Cleveland won, despite his admission that he was supporting an illegitimate son.

■ Third Parties and Independents

Two parties, not always the same ones, have dominated American politics almost from the beginning. Yet few presidential elections have passed without participation by a third party. Some have championed good ideas that the major parties adopted later on.

Beginning with the Anti-Masons' William Wirt, who won almost 8 percent of the vote in 1832, third-party or independent candidates have achieved 6 percent or more of the vote in twelve elections. The most

Some of the More Mentionable Third Parties

Free Soil—1848, Martin Van Buren, 10.1 percent. Former president Van Buren bore the standard for the Free Soilers, who wanted to keep slavery out of the new Southwest territories. In the 1850s, no longer a separate party, the Free Soilers strengthened the antislavery Republican party.

Know-Nothing—1856, Millard Fillmore, 21.5 percent. The American "Know Nothing" party nominated former president Fillmore, who had moved up to the presidency when the second and last Whig president, Zachary Taylor, died. Hostile to Catholic immigrants and pledged to support only native Protestant Americans for office, the Know Nothings were named for their practice of responding "I know nothing" to questions about their rituals. By 1860 most northern Know Nothings had joined the Republican party. The remainder joined the short-lived Constitutional Union party, which backed antiwar candidate John Bell and thus helped elect Abraham Lincoln by splintering the vote.

Southern Democratic—1860, John C. Breckinridge, 12.6 percent. Rebuffed in their efforts to have the party platform protect slavery in the territories, southerners bolted the Democratic convention that nominated Stephen A. Douglas. They nominated their own presidential candidate, Vice President Breckinridge. After the Civil War the Southern Democrats rejoined the national party.

Populist—1892, James B. Weaver, 8.5 percent. Economic hardship persisted in the South and Midwest long after the Civil War. Blaming their plight on high railroad rates and the tight money supply, farmers organized first the Greenback Labor and then the People's or Populist party. Besides government takeover of the railroads, the Populists advocated an income tax, direct election of senators, and free coinage of silver. They ran Weaver, a former Greenback candidate, in 1892 but backed Democrat William Jennings Bryan in 1896.

Progressive—1912, Theodore Roosevelt, 27.4 percent. Former president Roosevelt broke with his handpicked successor, William Howard Taft, and organized his Progressive "Bull Moose" party to oppose the GOP candidate. Roosevelt succeeded in outpolling Taft, but the split benefited the winner, Democrat Woodrow Wilson. Theodore Roosevelt took six states with eighty-eight electoral votes.

Socialist Labor—1912, Eugene V. Debs, 6.0 percent. Socialist Debs, making his fourth try for the presidency, also did well in 1912, although it's doubtful he took many votes away from Taft.

Progressive—1924, Robert M. La Follette, 16.6 percent. Wisconsin Republican senator La Follette sought reforms popular in the farm belt, such as nationalization of the railroads. He appealed more to farmers and workers than to the middle-class former Bull Moosers. He won his own state's thirteen electoral votes.

American Independent—1968, George C. Wallace, 13.5 percent. Wallace, famous as the Democratic Alabama governor who turned black students away from the state university in 1963, rode the "white backlash" against civil rights activism to his surprisingly strong showing. He won five southern states with forty-six electoral votes. Wallace tried to run again in 1972, this time as a Democrat, but he dropped out after being wounded in an assassination attempt at an outdoor rally in Maryland.

National Unity—1980, John B. Anderson, 6.0 percent. Anderson ran after failing to get the GOP nomination.

recent to do so was Texas billionaire Ross Perot, who won 18.9 percent of the popular vote in 1992. Perot's 19.7 million vote total was the third highest in history for an independent. Perot's percentage was also the highest for a candidate who was not a former president. The only third-party candidates who did better were ex-presidents Millard Fillmore in 1856 (21.5 percent) and Theodore Roosevelt in 1912 (27.4 percent).

Here Today, Gone Tomorrow

Most third parties are one-election wonders. They generally disappear or join forces the next time around. In 1836 the Anti-Masons went with the Whigs; in 1984 independent John B. Anderson, who took 6 percent of the vote four years earlier, endorsed Democrat Walter F. Mondale.

He Kept Going and Going

As the Energizer bunny of presidential politics, Harold E. Stassen is likely to be remembered longer than the inexhaustible battery-powered toy in the TV commercials. The former "boy wonder" of Minnesota, who was elected governor when he was thirty-one, ran for president in almost every election from 1948 through 1992 (he sat out 1956 and 1972 when Republican presidents Eisenhower and

---

Independent Candidacies: An Impossible Dream?

The independent candidacy of Texas tycoon Ross Perot in 1992 ended as implausibly as it began. It started with a seemingly impromptu remark on the Larry King talk show, when Perot said he would run if enough volunteers backed him. And it ended with Perot amassing the third largest vote for an independent in history—18.9 percent.

Such a result seemed impossible—even nutty, as Perot acknowledged on election eve as he danced with his wife to his theme song, Patsy Cline's "Crazy." It was an impressive vote, and it set up Perot for his new role as Clinton administration gadfly at the head of a new political organization, United We Stand America.

Yet Perot failed as every other independent candidate has failed in recent history. He, like John B. Anderson in 1980, did not carry any states or win any electoral votes (270 are needed to win). Anderson, then a Republican congress-

man from Illinois, ran as an independent after losing his party's nomination to Ronald Reagan. Anderson won 6 percent of the vote—next to Perot's the best showing for an independent or a third-party candidate since former Alabama governor George C. Wallace took 13.5 percent in 1968.

Anderson was the first independent to be helped financially by the public funding of presidential campaigns, which began in 1976. His campaign cost $15 million. Perot, the first billionaire candidate, turned down the federal grants and therefore did not have to limit his spending or disclose the amount.

Perennial presidential candidate Harold Stassen was also governor of Minnesota (1939–1943) and president of the University of Pennsylvania (1948–1953).

Socialist leader Eugene Debs was convicted for inciting insubordination, disloyalty, and mutiny in the armed forces, and for obstructing military recruitment, when he told his listeners, "You need to know that you are fit for something better than slavery and cannon fodder."

Nixon were up for reelection). At age eighty-four, still active in his Philadelphia law practice, he paid $1,000 to register in the 1992 New Hampshire primary, listing his residence as Sunfish Lake, Minnesota.

They Did, Too

Two perennial candidates, Eugene V. Debs and Norman M. Thomas, often bore the Socialist banner in one of the longest third-party campaigns for the presidency.

Railway union leader Debs ran in 1900 as the candidate of the Social Democratic party, which merged the following year with a Socialist Labor faction to form the Socialist party. Debs was then the Socialist nominee for president four times, beginning in 1904. Imprisoned in 1918 for his criticism of World War I, Debs nevertheless received almost a million votes in his last election, 1920. President Warren G. Harding freed him from prison in 1921.

Thomas, a writer-editor and former Presbyterian minister, was the Socialist nominee in six elections from 1928 to 1948. After a two-decade hiatus, the party resumed running presidential candidates in 1976.

They WON'T Drink to That

Prohibitionists have been the most persistent third party, with candidates in every election since 1872. Their long ef-

forts to curtail alcohol consumption finally paid off in 1919 with ratification of the Eighteenth Amendment, which barred the manufacture, sale, or transportation of intoxicating beverages in the United States. The victory was short-lived, however, and after fourteen years of massive disobedience to Prohibition it was repealed by the Twenty-first Amendment.

The party had its best showing in 1892 when its nominee, John Bidwell, received 2.2 percent of the popular vote. In 1992 it received less than .1 percent of the total vote.

■ The Old Way of Nominating Candidates: Caucuses

Before there were political party conventions there were caucuses—informal party groupings in Congress that picked the nominees for president. Then after the popular vote in the general election, the members of the electoral college from each state formally elected the president from among the nominees.

What the Framers Had in Mind

But even caucuses were a change from what the Framers of the Constitution envi-

sioned when they called for selection of the president by the electoral college rather than by direct vote of the people. They had hoped that "factions" or parties would play no part and that the state electors would both nominate and elect the president. But the parties' congressional caucus system quickly developed, taking the presidential nomination—but not the election itself— away from the state electors.

From 1789 to 1804

In the first election, 1789, there were no formal nominations and George Washington received all sixty-nine electoral votes. The Democratic-Republican and Federalist parties began to emerge in the second election, 1792, but it was not until 1800 that both parties used the congressional caucus to choose their nominees.

That election was the first that failed to produce a majority of electoral votes for any candidate, throwing the election into the House of Representatives. Under the Constitution as then written, each elector cast two ballots and the person receiving the greatest number of votes and a majority became the president. The runner-up became vice president. But the Democratic-Republican electors, intending Thomas Jefferson to be president and Aaron Burr to be vice president, unintentionally created a tie between them. In the House, thirty-six ballots were taken before the deadlock was settled in Jefferson's favor, making Burr the vice president.

After that, the system was changed by the Twelfth Amendment, and since 1804 electors have voted separately for president and vice president.

Another Tossup: The 1824 Election

Between 1800 and the 1830s, when conventions replaced congressional caucuses as the nominating body, one other election failed to produce a majority candidate, and it, too, was thrown into the House. The 1824 election caused particularly great turmoil. Of several Democratic-Republicans nominated, John Quincy Adams won the House vote even though Andrew Jackson had led in both the electoral vote (but with less than a majority) and popular vote. Although Adams won on the first ballot in the House, his election was clouded by allegations that he had made a deal with another contender, Henry Clay, whom Adams later appointed as secretary of state. After that the caucus system was dead, even though the convention system was not yet born. As a step in that direction, however, in 1828 the Tennessee legislature nominated Jackson, and he won the presidency.

Andrew Jackson en route to Washington, D.C., for his presidential inauguration in 1829.

◼ The New, 'Conventional' Way

The first national political convention was held in Baltimore in 1831 by what was a third party even then—the Anti-Masons. They nominated for president a former Mason, William Wirt, who received only 7.8 percent of the 1832 vote in a three-way contest won by incumbent Democrat Andrew Jackson. The runner-up was the National Republican candidate, Henry Clay. The Democrats had nominated Jackson earlier in 1832 at their first convention, also held in Baltimore.

The Republicans, who later replaced the National Republicans and Whigs as the second major party, held their first convention in Philadelphia in 1856. In 1860 in Chicago, they named their first winning ticket—Abraham Lincoln and Hannibal Hamlin. Since then there have been eighteen GOP presidents and eight Democratic presidents.

Convention Firsts

Here are a few firsts of the many in the history of national political conventions:

★ Republican nominated with 100 percent of the vote on the first ballot: Ulysses S. Grant in 1868.

★ Woman nominated for president: Victoria Claflin Woodhull, on the Equal Rights party ticket in 1872. Black leader Frederick Douglass was her running mate.

★ Incumbent governors nominated for president: Republican Rutherford B. Hayes of Ohio and Democrat Samuel J. Tilden of New York in 1876.

★ Conventions to have women delegates: 1900, when each party had one. Substantial numbers of women were delegates for the first time in 1920. Beginning in 1980, the Democratic party required its national nominating conventions to be equally divided among men and women delegates.

★ Vice president nominated in his own right after succeeding the dead president: Theodore Roosevelt at the 1904 GOP convention.

★ Entire tickets renominated: Republicans William Howard Taft and James S. Sherman in 1912 and Democrats Woodrow Wilson and Thomas R. Marshall in 1916.

★ Nominees to accept the nomination in person: Democrat Franklin Roosevelt at Chicago in 1932 and Republican Thomas E. Dewey at Chicago in 1944.

★ Televised convention: 1940 Republican, live from Philadelphia.

★ Woman placed in presidential nomination by a major party: Sen. Margaret Chase Smith of Maine, Republican, in 1964. She received twenty-seven votes, but the nomination of Sen. Barry Goldwater of Arizona was made unanimous.

★ Woman nominated for vice president: Rep. Geraldine Ferraro of New York, Democrat, in 1984.

Delegates and Primaries

The scholarly president, Woodrow Wilson, wished never to put another candidate through the agony he endured in 1912, when he won the Democratic nomination on the forty-sixth ballot. Although his idea of a direct national primary never caught on, most states today select their national convention delegates in presidential primaries rather than in state party caucuses

"There ought never to be another Presidential nominating convention," wrote Woodrow Wilson after his election experience in 1912. "The nominations should be made directly by the people at the polls."

or conventions. In 1992 each party held forty primaries, including those in the District of Columbia and Puerto Rico. The Democrats selected 66.9 percent of their convention delegates in primaries and the Republicans, 83.9 percent. State caucuses elected 15.1 percent of the Democratic delegates and 16.1 percent of the Republicans. The remaining 18.0 percent of Democrats went to the convention as "superdelegates," party and elected officials with reserved slots. The Republicans had no superdelegates.

Primaries Wax and Wane . . .

The use of primary elections to choose convention delegates arose around the turn of the century as an alternative to the "smoke-filled rooms" where party bosses and business bigwigs chose the nominees and cronies followed their bidding on the convention floor.

Originally aimed at state and local political corruption, the primary idea soon spread to presidential elections. Florida enacted the first presidential primary law in 1901. It allowed party leaders to select convention delegates in primary elections, but like other early primary laws, the Florida system did not permit delegate candidates to have their presidential candidate preference shown on the ballot.

Robert La Follette

Progressive leader Robert M. La Follette gained a delegate-selection primary in Wisconsin in 1904, and his supporters pushed the concept in other states. In 1910 in Oregon they succeeded in enacting the first primary in which voters could indicate their presidential preference in choosing delegates. By 1916 presidential primaries in twenty-six states permitted direct election of delegates, a preferential vote for president, or both.

But enthusiasm for the primary system

waned as election after election produced candidates who did well in the primaries but failed to win the convention nomination. By 1935 eight states had repealed their primary laws.

. . . and Wax Again

The primary movement regained strength after World War II as reform zeal spread and old-style political bosses began to lose influence. In 1960 John F. Kennedy popularized the primary route to the presidency with his successful uphill campaign for the Democratic nomination.

Combined with other reforms, particularly in the Democratic party, that called for more delegate representation among women and minorities, the primary system helped to produce nominees who were unlikely to have been the choice of the traditional political machines. Among them were Democrats George McGovern in 1972, Jimmy Carter in 1976, and Bill Clinton in 1992.

The number of presidential primaries dipped slightly after hitting a high of thirty-seven in 1980, but it rose to set a new record with the forty held in 1992.

The Scramble to Be First

New Hampshire traditionally has the first primary of the presidential election

Known for his charm and charisma, John Kennedy campaigns for the presidency in West Virginia in 1960.

Among nonprimary states, Iowa usually is the first to hold its delegate-selection caucus, beating the New Hampshire primary by a week in 1992. With its own senator Tom Harkin an easy winner, the Iowa caucus did not have the impact it had twenty years earlier when George McGovern's suprisingly good showing propelled him toward the Democratic nomination.

Super Tuesday

A southern strategy to counter the Yankee head start was devised in the 1980s as "Super Tuesday" (it falls about three weeks after the New Hampshire primary), when many states in the South and elsewhere hold their presidential primaries. In 1988 twenty states participated, making it the closest ever to a national primary. In 1992 Super Tuesday shrank to about half its original size as several states opted to vote later than March 10.

Rules, Rules, Rules

From the outset, Democrats have had more stringent convention and delegate-selection rules than the Republicans. One

year, and officials there keep making it earlier and earlier (February 18 in 1992) to prevent any other state from gaining the lead-off spot.

With only a handful of convention delegates at stake (twenty-four Democratic and twenty-three Republican), the New Hampshire primary is more a media event and test of popularity than a major election. But its proven ability to thin out the pack makes it a must for anyone intent on

becoming president. In forty years only one person—Bill Clinton in 1992—managed to win the presidency without winning the New Hampshire primary. (He placed second to former senator Paul Tsongas of neighboring Massachusetts.)

Another loser in New Hampshire, Sen. Eugene McCarthy in 1968, did so well as an anti-Vietnam War candidate that incumbent president Lyndon B. Johnson decided to drop out of the race.

of the toughest, adopted in 1832 at the Democrats' first convention, required a two-thirds majority vote to capture the party's nomination. Until it was dropped in 1936, the two-thirds rule cost two candidates the nomination. Martin Van Buren lost it to James K. Polk in 1844 after winning majorities in the early votes, and Champ Clark lost it to Woodrow Wilson in 1912 after similarly being ahead in early votes.

For most of its history, until 1968, the Democratic party also had a unit rule that enabled a split delegation—if authorized by the state party—to give all votes for the candidate favored by the delegation majority.

More recently the Democrats have overhauled their rules several times to permit broader representation and openness. By contrast, the Republican rules have gone largely unreformed.

The GOP, for example, allows winner-take-all primaries, which the Democrats banned in favor of proportional representation. In other words, each delegation goes to the Democratic convention divided in proportion to the candidates' share of the vote in the state's primary or caucus.

The 1924 Yawner

The longest national party convention was held by the Democrats at New York in 1924. It lasted seventeen days and required a record 103 roll-call votes to nominate John W. Davis for president over another New Yorker, Gov. Alfred E. Smith. In the fall election, Republican Calvin Coolidge defeated Davis and Progressive Robert M. La Follette.

Four years later, Smith won the Democratic nomination, the first Roman Catholic nominated for president by a major party. He lost to Republican Herbert Hoover.

Planked Words

Crafting a platform—what the party stands for—has touched off some of the ugliest fights at political conventions. But once the planks are all nailed into place, they are seldom mentioned again.

The first platform, under 1,000 words long, was adopted by the Democrats in 1840. By contrast, the 1984 Democratic platform—the longest ever—ran more than 45,000 words.

Chairwomen

The first woman to chair a national party committee (the Democratic National Committee) was Jean Westwood of Utah in 1972. She was chosen by presidential nominee George McGovern.

At the bidding of President Gerald R. Ford, Mary Louise Smith of Iowa was the first woman to serve as chair of the Republican National Committee, from 1974 to 1976. Both Westwood and Smith had been state organizational leaders.

Ron Brown

The Democratic National Committee made history in February 1989 by electing Ronald H. Brown as the first African-American chairman of a major political party. Brown, then forty-seven, was a Washington, D.C., lawyer who had held several lesser jobs in the party leadership. As chairman, Brown masterminded the 1992 New York City convention that nominated Bill Clinton of Arkansas for president and Al Gore of Tennessee for vice president. After the election, Clinton chose Brown as his secretary of commerce.

■ Conventional Oratory

G.I. Joe's Mother

Playwright Clare Booth Luce, then a member of Congress from Connecticut, coined the term *G.I. Joe* in a speech to the 1944 Republican convention. The G.I. stood for government issue.

'I Give You a Man Who . . .'

Arkansas governor Bill Clinton gave one of the longest nominating speeches on record—thirty-five minutes—for presidential nominee Michael Dukakis at the 1988 Democratic convention. The crowd cheered when Clinton finally said, "And in closing. . . ."

In July 1992, when he accepted his own

Barbara Jordan at the 1976 Democratic convention.

nomination to the presidency, Clinton joked, "I wanted to come back to this convention and finish that speech I started four years ago." Then he went on to outdo himself: he spoke for fifty-four minutes.

Barbara Jordan

The first and second black women to keynote a major party national convention were the same person: Barbara C. Jordan of Texas. In her second term as a member of Congress, Jordan delivered the keynote address at the Democratic nominating convention in 1976. Her dramatic speech so impressed the delegates that she received twenty-four and a half votes for the vice-presidential nomination, which was won by Walter F. Mondale.

Sixteen years later, Jordan was one of three keynoters at the 1992 convention that nominated Bill Clinton for president. By then Jordan had left the House, in 1979,

Keynotes and Sour Notes

Most of the oratory that delegates hear—or ignore—at national party conventions is routine and forgettable. But some convention appearances live on in memory.

★ William Jennings Bryan electrified the 1896 Democratic convention with his "Cross of Gold" speech condemning opposition from the GOP and the so-called Gold Democrats to ex-

pansion of the money supply by the free coinage of silver. "You shall not press down upon the brow of labor this crown of thorns," he roared, "you shall not crucify mankind upon a cross of gold." The gold plank was defeated and Bryan won the nomination on the fifth ballot.

★ In 1932 Franklin Roosevelt broke with tradition and flew to Chicago to accept the Democratic nomination in person. There he pledged "a new deal for the American people."

★ The man Roosevelt replaced in the White House, Herbert Hoover, spoke to every Republican convention from 1936 through 1952.

★ In 1948 Hubert H. Humphrey, then mayor of Minneapolis and running for the Senate, delivered to the Democrats what might have been the most persuasive convention speech since Bryan's "Cross of Gold." The convention adopted a liberal civil rights plank after hearing Humphrey say, "There will be no hedging . . . no watering down, if you please, of the instruments and the principles of the civil rights program."

★ Reluctant nominee Adlai E. Stevenson, dubbed an "egghead" because of his intellectual speeches, quoted Jesus in accepting the 1952 Democratic nod. "I have asked the Merciful Father—the Father of us all—to let this cup pass from me," he said. "But from such dread responsibility one does not shrink in fear, in self-interest, or in false humility. So, 'If this cup may not pass from me, except I drink it, Thy will be done.'"

★ Many have tried, but candidates can't seem to match the catchiness of FDR's "New Deal" slogan. John F. Kennedy came close in 1960 when he told the Democratic convention, "We stand today on the edge of a new frontier . . . a frontier of unknown opportunities and perils—a frontier of unfulfilled hopes and threats." By contrast, Bill Clinton's "New Covenant" was never heard from after the 1992 Democratic convention.

✷ Defending his strong conservatism, Sen. Barry Goldwater of Arizona accepted the GOP nomination in 1964 by saying: "I would remind you that extremism in the defense of liberty is no vice. And let me remind you also that moderation in the pursuit of liberty is no virtue."

✷ In 1968, six years after he briefly retired from politics by saying "you won't have Nixon to kick around anymore," Richard Nixon capped a remarkable comeback with an eloquent speech accepting the GOP presidential nomination. Recounting his own achievement of the American dream, he asked his listeners "to help make that dream come true for millions to whom it's an impossible dream today."

✷ New York governor Mario Cuomo vaulted to national prominence with his keynote speech to the 1984 Democratic convention. Citing President Ronald Reagan's description of America as "a shining city on a hill," Cuomo said, "the hard truth is that not everyone is sharing in this city's splendor and glory. . . . There is despair, Mr. President, in the faces that you don't see, in the places that you don't visit in your shining city."

✷ Democratic nominee Walter Mondale learned the hard way in 1984 that frankness is not always good politics. In his acceptance speech he said, "Let's tell the truth. It must be done. It must be done. Mr. Reagan will raise taxes, and so will I. He won't tell you. I just did."

✷ Jesse Jackson, the first African-American seriously in contention for the presidency, addressed the 1988 Democratic convention after losing the nomination to Michael Dukakis. "We must never surrender," he concluded. "America will get better and better. Keep hope alive. Keep hope alive. Keep hope alive. On tomorrow night and beyond, keep hope alive."

✷ In 1988 the Democratic keynoter, Texas treasurer Ann Richards, skewered GOP nominee George Bush as having been "born with a silver foot in his mouth." In 1990 Richards was elected governor of Texas.

✷ The most famous line of George Bush's 1988 acceptance speech—"Read my lips. No new taxes."—came back to haunt him four years later when he signed a deficit-reduction bill that contained new taxes.

and was teaching at the University of Texas, where she held the Lyndon B. Johnson Chair in National Policy.

◼ Going on Location

In the early 1900s Chicago edged out Baltimore as the most popular convention site. Chicago has been home to twenty-four major party conventions—fourteen Republican and ten Democratic, including the riotous 1968 Democratic gathering marked by Vietnam War protests. Neither party

has returned to Chicago since.

Until its last one in 1912, Baltimore had hosted ten conventions, nine Democratic and one Republican.

Five national conventions, all Democratic, have been held in New York City, most recently in 1992. That year the Republicans met in Houston, George Bush's home city. It was Houston's second convention and the first since the Democrats gathered there in 1928.

Party Time, Party Time

When the political parties throw a party, it's a lulu. In 1992, for example, the major parties each spent some $40 million to throw their convention bashes in New York (Democrats) and Houston (Republicans).

About $11 million of each tab was picked up by the federal government through the $1 tax return checkoff that subsidizes presidential campaigns. Corporate sponsors such as AT&T, American Express, and

Coca-Cola also put up some $6.5 million for each convention.

Just to rent Madison Square Garden cost the Democrats $4 million, plus $175,000 for parking. Other major expenses included the massive podium, a 400-piece band, 1,843 folding chairs, and 60,000 balloons. Figuratively speaking, estimates of the GOP's expenses for its grand old party were in the same ballpark. In fact, the party itself was held in a real ballpark—Houston's Astrodome.

■ The Nominees

Dark Horse

The first "dark horse" or compromise candidate for president was James K. Polk, nominated by the Democrats in 1844 on the ninth ballot. Former president Martin Van Buren, the front-runner, lost his lead after opposing the annexation of Texas, and a deadlock loomed. Polk went on to win the election, the only former House Speaker to become president.

Thrown Riders

In 1856 Democrat Franklin Pierce became the only elected president denied renomination by his own party. A New Hampshire Yankee, he enraged fellow northerners by signing the Kansas-Missouri Act, which repealed part of the Missouri Compromise outlawing slavery north of 36° 30'. The act turned the Kansas territory into a bloody battleground for opposing forces on the slavery issue. Pierce lost the nomination to James Buchanan, who had been kept away from the slavery furor as ambassador to Britain.

The only other sitting president denied renomination was Chester A. Arthur, who had not been elected to that position. As vice president, he had succeeded the assassinated James A. Garfield in 1881. Arthur lost the 1884 Republican nomination to James G. Blaine.

The Nominee's Choice

In 1940 Franklin Roosevelt wanted to dump his two-term vice president, John Nance Garner, in favor of the more liberal Henry A. Wallace. But party leaders protested; always before, they had chosen the vice-presidential candidate. Roosevelt got his way, however, by threatening to refuse renomination, and presidential nominees ever since have picked their own running

mates. An exception was 1956, when Democrat Adlai E. Stevenson left the choice to the convention, which nominated Estes Kefauver.

Texans All

Only three men, all Texans, have tried to win the presidential nomination, accepted the second spot after failing, and then been elected vice president later that year. They were Democrats John Nance Garner in 1932 and Lyndon Johnson in 1960, and Republican George Bush in 1980.

Out-of-the-Running Mates

Vice President James S. Sherman died after he was renominated at the 1912 Republican convention. Because he had been in poor health, the delegates empowered the GOP national committee to fill the vacancy if it occurred. The committee chose Nicholas Murray Butler, president of Columbia University, who substituted as William Howard Taft's running mate on the losing ticket.

Sen. Thomas F. Eagleton of Missouri withdrew as the Democratic vice-presidential nominee in 1972 after it was disclosed that he had received electroshock therapy for depression several years earlier. George

★ Campaign Slogans

Keep cool with COOLIDGE in WISCONSIN this Summer

It's Always Wonderful in Wisconsin

The slogans of political campaigns sometimes are remembered longer than the candidates themselves. Here are some and the candidates associated with them:

★ "Tippecanoe and Tyler, Too" *(William Henry Harrison, 1840)*

★ "Back to Normalcy" *(Warren Harding, 1920)* (He meant to say "normality.")

★ "Keep Cool with Coolidge" *(Calvin Coolidge, 1924)*

★ "A Chicken in Every Pot, a Car in Every Garage" *(Herbert Hoover, 1932)*

★ "Don't Be a Third Termite" *(Wendell Willkie, 1940)*

★ "Let's Get the Country Moving Again" *(John F. Kennedy, 1960)*

★ "Let Us Continue" *(Lyndon Johnson, 1964)*

★ "Four More Years" *(Richard Nixon, 1972)*

★ "Come Home, America" *(George McGovern, 1972)*

★ "It's the Economy, Stupid" *(Bill Clinton, 1992)*

McGovern, who had chosen Eagleton as his running mate, said he was "1,000 percent for Tom Eagleton and I have no intention of dropping him from the ticket." But as the controversy mounted, Eagleton resigned and was replaced by former Peace Corps director R. Sargent Shriver.

■ African-Americans in Presidential Politics

Frederick Douglass

The first black to receive a vote for the presidential nomination was Frederick Douglass, at the 1888 GOP convention.

Jesse Jackson

Jesse Jackson, a clergyman and civil rights activist, was the first black man to make a serious bid for the presidential nomination of a major party. Jackson unsuccessfully sought the Democratic nomination in 1984 and 1988, but while losing he enhanced his reputation as a political leader and a spokesman for the black community.

He drew 3,282,431 votes or 18.2 percent of the total vote in the 1984 Democratic primaries, placing him third behind Walter Mondale, the eventual nominee, and Colorado senator Gary Hart. In 1988 Jackson did even better, running second to the eventual nominee, Michael Dukakis, with 6,685,699 primary votes or 29.1 percent of the total.

Jackson's strong pleas for unity at the 1984 and 1988 Democratic conventions provided some of the most memorable political oratory of modern times. In 1992 Jackson sat out the presidential race as the District of Columbia's "shadow" senator, but he again gave a rousing speech at the party's national convention.

The Postconvention 'Bounce'

The Democratic or Republican candidate who is ahead in the polls before the parties' conventions usually bounds even higher afterward and goes on to win the election. In ten of the twelve presidential elections since World War II, including 1992, the preconvention Gallup poll leader won the White House. The exceptions were in 1948 when Thomas E. Dewey, the Gallup leader both before and after the GOP convention, lost to President Harry S. Truman, and in 1988 when Michael Dukakis bounced to a seventeen-point lead over GOP nominee George Bush, only to drop rapidly and lose the election.

Shirley Chisholm

Democratic representative Shirley Chisholm of New York was the first black woman to contend seriously for a presidential nomination, in 1972. She received 430,703 votes or 2.7 percent of the total vote in the party's primaries. The nomination went to George McGovern.

OUR TIME HAS COME

Electoral Engineering

Every four years the world witnesses an American phenomenon—a presidential election. From every hamlet across the country, citizens trek to the polls to cast their votes in privacy. When it is over—without a shot being fired or any violent show of force—the nation may have a new leader. Or the current president may have gained a vote of confidence and a second term in office.

Nearly 200 million Americans are eligible to vote in presidential elections, but barely half that number take advantage of the privilege. About 104 million voters—55 percent of the 189 million registered—voted to elect Bill Clinton president in 1992. It was the first presidential election to top 100 million votes, and the turnout was a bit better than four years earlier. The upturn, 5 percentage points over 1988, marked the first increase in almost three decades. Until then, the turnout had been dropping steadily since the post-Depression high of 62.8 percent reached in the Kennedy-Nixon contest of 1960.

No less remarkable are the elections held every two years to elect a new House of Representatives and one-third of the Senate. They, along with the many elections for state and local officials, play an extremely important role in the United States's unique system of democratic government—a system still alive and healthy after more than two hundred years of oftentimes stressful operation.

■ Extending the Franchise

Today nearly every man and woman over age eighteen has the right to vote in the United States, but it wasn't always so. The original thirteen states limited the voting privilege to adult male property owners, excluding women, slaves, indentured servants, and certain religious minorities. In other words, of the total adult popu-

Susan B. Anthony fought for equal rights for women for more than fifty years. In addition to her crusade for a woman's right to vote, she championed a woman's right to own property and to custody of children in the case of divorce.

lation, only one person in four could vote.

As the country grew westward, barriers to voting gradually fell, but some lingered on. Some states dropped property ownership as a qualification but still required taxpayer status. Religious restrictions faded, but Rhode Island, home of the first American synagogue, barred Jews from voting until 1842.

After the Civil War the Fourteenth and Fifteenth amendments to the Constitution technically opened the electorate to black men, although state poll taxes and other restrictions denied them the vote in practice. The Twenty-fourth Amendment abolishing the poll tax in 1964 and the Voting Rights Act of 1965 removed most of the major voting barriers related to race.

Women gained the right to vote in 1920 with the Nineteenth Amendment, and District of Columbia residents were enfranchised in 1961 by the Twenty-third Amendment. The last major group excluded from the polls—eighteen- to twenty-year-olds—won the right to vote in 1971 with ratification of the Twenty-sixth Amendment.

Lowering of the barriers to women and African-Americans led to a steady upsurge of both groups in electoral politics, with record numbers reaching Congress in 1993. Women governors are no longer a rarity, but so far Virginia's Douglas Wilder is the only African-American governor.

Federal-State Division of Labor

Holding elections, even for national officials, is a responsibility divided between the federal and state governments. Under the Constitution, states set the time, place, and manner of presidential and congressional elections, subject to regulation by Congress. Congress has done that a few times—notably setting the November election date and lowering the voting age to eighteen—but registration requirements, the makeup of the ballot, the use of primaries or caucuses, and other election rules are mostly left to the states.

Getting Out the Vote

The differences among states in their election rules help to account for the wide differences in how many of their people participate in voting. Some states such as Maine and Minnesota consistently turn out 60 percent or more of their voters in presidential elections—better than the national average of about 50 percent and well above the 30–40 percent range of some Deep South states.

One reason for the higher turnouts is

Voter turnout increased significantly in 1992. Attributed to several factors including an energized electorate, a lingering recession, and the independent candidacy of Ross Perot, the increase may have been the beginning of a trend or an isolated phenomenon.

that some states make it easy to get on the election rolls. Before President Clinton signed legislation May 20, 1993, only a few states had "motor voter" registrations tied in with auto license renewals. Now a voter can even register at a welfare office. Maine, Minnesota, and Wisconsin permit registration at the voting place on election day. North Dakota has no voter registration at all.

Education levels, economic status, race, and age are other factors that influence turnout rates. Educated working people tend to vote more than the unemployed and less schooled. Whites vote more than blacks, and blacks more than Hispanics. Older people have a much higher voter participation rate than people just entering voting age. And people of all ages and backgrounds generally turn out in greater numbers for presidential races than for elections at the local level.

The First Election: Unanimous

In the first election, the American people had no problem selecting a president. George Washington was the unanimous choice, winning sixty-nine electoral votes —the maximum number possible in 1789. No other president has matched that feat, although Franklin D. Roosevelt came close

Just before fleeing the White House as British troops invaded Washington in August 1814, Dolley Madison demanded that this portrait of George Washington by Gilbert Stuart be cut out of its frame so she could take it with her. Today the portrait hangs in the East Room of the White House.

in 1936 with 98.5 percent of the electoral vote. Most other presidential elections have been more competitive, sometimes causing difficulties the Founders did not foresee.

Electoral College System

Americans do not vote directly for their president; they vote instead for the 538 electors who make up the electoral college. After each election, the members of the electoral college from each state—whose number equals the state's total number of senators and representatives—meet in their respective states and vote for a president and vice president. Usually, but not always, their votes go to the two candidates who won the popular vote in their state.

Factions at the 1787 Constitutional Convention settled on the electoral college as a compromise. It reduced the big-state advantage. No matter how small its population, a state started out with three votes (based on two senators and at least one representative). From there on, larger states would gain more electors, based on the size of their delegations in the House. And electors, the Founders felt, would be guided more by reason and less by emotion than would the mass of voters.

In the first presidential election, held in 1789, only four states chose electors by direct popular vote. State legislatures, or some combination of direct and indirect voting, elected the others. Since the Civil War (South Carolina was the last holdout), all states have picked electors by popular vote.

Slicing Up the Pie

The number of presidential electors, based on the size of the Senate (100 members) and the House of Representatives (435 members), has remained at 538 since 1961, when the Twenty-third Amendment gave the District of Columbia three electors, the number it would have if it were a state (two senators and one representative).

A state's share of the 435 electors corresponding to the representatives, however, can change after each ten-year census, if the state gains or loses population. Big gainers for the 1992 election included California (seven more electors), Florida (four), and Texas and Utah (three each). Among the losers were New York (down three) and Illinois, Michigan, Ohio, and Pennsylvania (each losing two). Several states gained or lost one elector, with most of the additions going to Sun Belt states at the expense of those in the older industrial Midwest and Northeast.

Minority Presidents

Controversial from its birth, the electoral college has withstood numerous attempts to abolish it—most recently in 1977 by President Jimmy Carter. The system has permitted fifteen presidents to be elected without a majority of the popular

'Minority' Presidents

Under the U.S. electoral system, fifteen presidents have been elected, either by the electoral college itself or by the House of Representatives, who did not receive a majority of the popular votes cast in the election. Three of them—John Quincy Adams, Rutherford B. Hayes, and Benjamin Harrison—actually trailed their opponents in the popular vote.

The following table shows the percentage of the popular vote received by candidates in the fifteen elections in which a "minority" president (designated by red boldface type) was elected:

Year				
1824	Jackson	Adams	Clay	Crawford
	41.34	30.92	12.99	11.17
1844	Polk	Clay	Birney	
	49.54	48.08	2.30	
1848	Taylor	Cass	Van Buren	
	47.28	42.49	10.12	
1856	Buchanan	Fremont	Fillmore	
	45.28	33.11	21.53	
1860	Lincoln	Douglas	Breckinridge	Bell
	39.82	29.46	18.09	12.61
1876	Tilden	Hayes	Cooper	
	50.97	47.95	0.97	
1880	Garfield	Hancock	Weaver	Others
	48.27	48.25	3.32	0.15
1884	Cleveland	Blaine	Butler	St. John
	48.50	48.25	1.74	1.47
1888	Cleveland	Harrison	Fisk	Streeter
	48.62	47.82	2.19	1.29
1892	Cleveland	Harrison	Weaver	Others
	46.05	42.96	8.50	2.25
1912	Wilson	T. Roosevelt	Taft	Debs
	41.84	27.39	23.18	5.99
1916	Wilson	Hughes	Benson	Others
	49.24	46.11	3.18	1.46
1948	Truman	Dewey	Thurmond	Wallace
	49.52	45.12	2.40	2.38
1960	Kennedy	Nixon	Others	
	49.72	49.55	0.72	
1968	Nixon	Humphrey	Wallace	Others
	43.42	42.72	13.53	0.33

The first tie in a presidential election was between Thomas Jefferson (left) and Aaron Burr. The tie was settled by the House of Representatives.

vote, and in three cases the winner actually came in second.

Under the Twelfth Amendment, the presidential election is thrown into the House of Representatives if no candidate gets a majority (half the total number plus one) of the electoral votes. The House then elects a president from among the top three contenders, with each state having one vote. This has happened only twice in U.S. history: in the 1800 election that brought about the Twelfth Amendment (the one change made in the electoral college system) and in the 1824 election,

when the House chose John Quincy Adams over popular vote winner Andrew Jackson.

Election by the House: 1800

As originally written, the Constitution called for the electoral college to vote for two persons for president. The top vote-getter would be president and the runner-up, vice president. And it worked that way in the first three elections. But in 1800, Thomas Jefferson and Aaron Burr received the same number of votes, throwing the election into the House of Representatives. The House chose Jefferson,

and Burr automatically became vice president.

As this situation clearly demonstrated, the system was flawed. But by 1804 it had been corrected by the Twelfth Amendment. Electors have voted separately ever since for president and vice president.

Election by the House: 1824

The only other election to be settled by the House was the one of 1824, when none of the four major candidates received an electoral vote majority. Under the Twelfth Amendment, the House had to choose from among the three highest vote-getters. It selected John Quincy Adams, who had run second to Andrew Jackson in both the popular and electoral votes. The third contender was Secretary of the Treasury William H. Crawford, who was paralyzed from a recent stroke. Henry Clay, who had run fourth in the electoral vote, helped swing the House vote to Adams.

Hayes-Tilden Contest: 1876

The 1876 electoral battle between Republican Rutherford B. Hayes and Democrat Samuel J. Tilden was so close and so bitterly partisan that it threatened to touch off another civil war. More voters turned out than for any other presidential election: 82.6 percent. Tilden won the popular vote,

Counting electoral votes in Congress is not always just a formality. In 1876 three electoral votes were disputed, and a special commission awarded the disputed votes to Rutherford Hayes.

The 1992 Scare

The likelihood of a third presidential election being thrown into the House loomed for a time in 1992. Polls at midyear showed none of the three major candidates—Republican incumbent George Bush, Democrat Bill Clinton, or independent Ross Perot—headed for a majority in the electoral college.

Had the election turned out that way, chaos might have resulted. In an election in the House, each state has only one vote, raising the prospect of a furious political battle to gain the needed majority.

Although Perot did well, garnering 18.9 percent of the popular vote, he failed to win a single state. With 43.0 percent, Clinton was able to swing an overwhelming electoral vote victory, 370 to Bush's 168.

Senate Election of Vice President

Only once has the Senate had to elect a vice president—in 1837 after Martin Van Buren won the presidency. His running mate, Richard M. Johnson, fell one vote short of an electoral vote majority because Virginia's electors gave their votes to another candidate. They objected to Johnson's reputed fondness for slave mistresses. Required by the Twelfth Amendment to choose between the two top contenders, the Senate voted along party lines for Dem-

but the electoral vote outcome hung on a single vote, with the votes of three southern states in dispute.

A special fifteen-member commission awarded the vote to Hayes, 185–184, after his forces reached an agreement with conservative southern Democrats. The compromise, under which Hayes removed federal troops from the South, ended Reconstruction. Southern whites gained domination of Congress, and Republican industrial interests solidified a hold on presidential politics that lasted until Franklin Roosevelt was elected in 1932.

HE'S BOUND TO MAKE A MISTAKE SOMETIME, AND WHEN HE DOES... WE'LL.... WE'LL.. UM... WE'LL WAIT TO SEE IF HE GOES AWAY...

ROSS

ocrat Johnson over Whig Francis Granger, 33–16.

'Faithless Electors'

The electoral college system, for all its controversy, usually works out the same as if Americans were allowed to vote directly for the president and vice president. The electors almost always vote as expected, so that the nominee of the party that carried the popular vote wins all of the state's electoral votes (the winner-take-all system).

Exceptions are rare, with only nine so-called faithless electors among the more

than seventeen thousand electors chosen since 1789. Most recently, in 1988, Democratic nominee Michael Dukakis was denied one of his 112 electoral votes when a West Virginia elector cast her ballot for the Duke's running mate, Lloyd Bentsen. She gave her vice-presidential vote to Dukakis.

Two states, Maine and Nebraska, use a district system instead of winner-take-all.

Two electoral votes go to the winner of the state's popular vote, but the rest are allocated according to who won the popular vote in each congressional district.

■ Financing the Run for the Presidency: Big Bucks

Each presidential election costs more than the one before it. Adjusted for inflation, using 1960 as the base year, the 1988 election cost four times the $30 million actually spent in 1960. Unadjusted campaign spending in 1988 amounted to $500 million; adjusted it was $126.5 million. The 1992 figures would be still higher.

Private Campaign Financing Nixon Style

The last presidential election wholly funded with private money was the Watergate election of 1972, by far the most expensive one up to that time. The two campaigns together spent $138 million, compared with $100 million four years earlier.

In their corner, the Republicans heavily outspent the Democrats, raising $63 million to help reelect Richard

Nixon over George McGovern. Huge individual and corporate donations accounted for much of the GOP's massive fund, and its misuse was at the core of the scandal that drove Nixon from office.

Post-Nixon Public Financing

Public outrage over testimony that tied Nixon campaign money to the Watergate break-in at Democratic headquarters, and to the subsequent cover-up efforts, led to a sweeping reform of the American campaign system in 1974. The act set up the Federal Election Commission, limited individuals to contributions of $1,000 to one candidate and $25,000 to all candidates in a single year, and provided funds for presidential campaigns.

The law also specified how much candidates could personally spend on their campaigns, but the Supreme Court struck down these limits in *Buckley v. Valeo*, in 1976. The Court did, however, uphold other parts of the law, including spending limits on presidential candidates who accepted federal matching grants.

A $1 checkoff on income tax forms, passed in 1971, fueled the presidential campaign fund. Beginning in 1976, both major party nominees received $22 million. By 1992 the amount had swelled to $55 million because of inflation.

Self-Financed Texans

To be free of spending limits attached to public funding, former Texas governor John B. Connally, Jr., spurned federal matching grants in his 1980 campaign for the Republican presidential nomination. He raised and spent $12 million but gained only one convention delegate.

The second candidate to turn down the money since public financing began in 1976 was another Texan, Ross Perot, in 1992. Running as an independent, Perot took almost 19 percent of the popular vote. But he won no states or electoral votes.

The Thoreau-Perot Connection

Besides having similar names that rhyme, Henry David Thoreau and Henry Ross Perot share an approach to life. Thoreau gained fame by living alone by a pond and writing about it in *Walden*. Perot, inspired by Thoreau's observation that "the mass of men live lives of quiet desperation," quit IBM and founded the computer company that made him rich. In 1992 the Texas billionaire mounted history's strongest individual campaign for the presidency.

The PAC Impact

The use of tax money to finance presidential campaigns has leveled the playing

'Your honor, my client believes that campaign spending limitations are a curb on free speech because everybody knows money talks!'

field and diminished the role of "fat cat" donors. Likewise, contribution limits and disclosure of gifts have opened the process and eliminated many past abuses in federal elections. But by no means have any of the 1970s reforms driven private special-interest money out of the picture. Rather, they have channeled more private money into independent efforts in behalf of this or that candidate or this or that cause, largely through political action committees (PACs). Barred by law from contributing directly to campaigns, businesses and unions can set up PACs for contributions from their executives or members. Professional and trade groups also can support campaigns through PACs.

The number of PACs has mushroomed from 608 in 1974 to 4,677 in 1990, with corporate PACs outnumbering labor PACs about five to one. Originally, unions had twice as many committees as businesses. In 1984 PACs spent $7.2 million to help re-elect Ronald Reagan, compared with only $657,000 spent by committees for Walter F. Mondale.

By law, individuals can contribute more to a PAC ($5,000) than to a presidential candidate ($1,000), which has spurred the explosive growth of PACs. This in turn has made PACs highly controversial, particularly in congressional campaigns.

'Soft Money' Talks Loudly

There is more than one way for parties to skin a fat cat. One way is to hit him up for some "soft money," which can be poured through a giant loophole in federal campaign spending rules. So-called soft money is earmarked for parties' administrative and party-building activities. Unlike other donations to federal candidates, it is unrestricted. While individuals can give no more than $1,000 to a presidential campaign or $20,000 to a party for candidate support, they can give as much as they wish to the soft money account. Gifts over

Home of Bess and Harry Truman in Independence, Missouri

$100,000 have become common. This indirectly helps candidates by freeing up other party funds.

Corporations and labor unions, which are barred from making political contributions, are allowed to donate soft money. Companies and chief executives have been the leading donors of GOP soft money; unions lead for the Democrats.

■ Presidential Campaigns

It's a Long, Long Road

Presidential campaigns are getting longer. Until the 1980s, most would-be presidents formally announced their candidacies early in the election year or late the year before. Since then, most announcements have come more than a year before the

election. By the time Bill Clinton threw his hat in the ring on October 31, 1991, four other Democratic hats were there. Incumbents generally declare later, as Bush did on February 2, 1992. By then his main challenger, Pat Buchanan, had been campaign-ing for several months.

Labor of Love

The first Monday in September, Labor Day, traditionally has been the kickoff date for presidential campaigns. For years Democratic nominees seeking the union vote made blue-collar Detroit their first stop, with a pitch to the auto workers. More recently, Democratic candidates have paid homage to party heroes Franklin Roosevelt and Harry Truman by making Labor Day visits to Warm Springs, Georgia, where FDR died, and Independence, Missouri, Truman's hometown.

Still more recently, the nominees have hit the road even before Labor Day. In 1992 Bill Clinton and running mate Al Gore took off right after the July Democratic convention on a bus trip through the northeastern states representing a large number of electoral votes. After the GOP convention in August, President George Bush headed for Florida—a state reeling from the devastation of Hurricane Andrew but also representing a cache of twenty-five electoral votes.

Mining the Mother Lode

When asked why he robbed banks, Willie Sutton had a ready answer: "That's where the money is." For presidential candidates a similar reply explains why they campaign so heavily in big states: that's where the electoral votes are. The pursuit of electoral votes drives campaign strategy.

In 1992 the big prizes, reflecting reallocation of House seats after the 1990 census, included California, 54 electoral votes; New York, 33; Texas, 32; Florida, 25; Pennsylva-nia, 23; and Illinois, 22.

Clinton captured thirty-two states—including most of the big ones—for a total of 370 votes, even though he took only 43.0 percent of the popular vote.

Ah, Those Numbers Crunchers

Once upon a time public opinion pollsters were pulse-takers. Now they are regarded almost as white-coated scientists who, as one of them put it, can suddenly look "like witch doctors." Modern campaign strategists scrutinize the polls and try to learn what the numbers mean for their clients. Most major campaigns go even further. They have their own pollsters, and they rely on them for advice as well as information.

Chairman Pollster, . . .

Late in his unsuccessful 1992 reelection campaign, George Bush railed at "those crazy pollsters" and accused them of trying to persuade the American people that he was going to lose. Yet the same George Bush months before had shown unusually strong faith in his own pollster, Robert M. Teeter. He made Teeter the first of his craft to chair a president's reelection campaign.

In the final weeks, James A. Baker III took over Bush's campaign, but Teeter could draw some comfort from the credibility his profession gained by predicting the outcome accurately. In the end, all the major polls came close to the actual popular vote.

Nothing Can Go Wrong . . . Go Wrong . . . Go Wrong

Although public opinion polling has a high degree of accuracy, it can yield widely divergent results. In late August 1992, for example, polls by ten leading organizations showed Bill Clinton's lead in the presidential race ranging from a high of 19 percentage points (ABC/Washington Post) to a low of 5 points (Lou Harris). The polls had margins of error of 3 to 5 points for each candidate.

Debates

The famed debates between Abraham Lincoln and Stephen Douglas took place in 1858 when they were Senate candidates. Up to then, Lincoln had been a heckler, shouting questions at Senator Douglas from the audience. Once Douglas agreed to

Stephen Douglas

Abraham Lincoln

meet him on stage, Lincoln stopped stalking the senator.

The first presidential candidates to debate were Richard Nixon and John Kennedy, who dueled four times in 1960. Most television viewers thought Kennedy won the crucial first debate with Nixon, who looked ashen, five-o'clock shadowish, and nervous. Many who heard it on radio and were not influenced by appearances thought Nixon scored more points. (The pair actually had debated at least once before, in 1947, when they were House freshmen. The place was McKeesport, Pennsylvania, and their topic was the Taft-Hartley labor bill.)

Sixteen years elapsed before the next presidential debate, between Gerald Ford and Jimmy Carter in 1976. Four years later, Ronald Reagan debated independent John B. Anderson alone when Carter, then president, refused to participate. One Carter-Reagan debate was held before the election.

The first three-way presidential and vice-presidential debates were held in 1992. President George Bush debated Democrat Bill Clinton and independent Ross Perot three times in varying formats. Vice President Dan Quayle, Democrat Al Gore, and Perot's running mate, James Stockdale, debated once.

Oddities and Novelties

Campaign buttons first appeared in the 1896 William McKinley-William Jennings Bryan race for president. Bryan also began the tradition of back-breaking campaign travel and speeches from the rear platform of a train. Although he stayed home in Canton, Ohio, talking to visitors on his front porch, McKinley won. His campaign promised "a full dinner pail" for all Americans.

The first campaign buttons were made of celluloid, a tough plastic invented in 1870 and better known for its use in early movie films. Later buttons were made of stamped, enameled metal. Buttons of both types remain collectors' items. One button featuring the 1920 Democratic ticket of James Cox and Franklin Roosevelt reportedly was worth $36,000 in 1991.

A car bumper sticker that appeared in 1964 said simply: "Au-H$_2$O '64." Anyone who knew their chemistry and politics recognized that as a combination of two elements—gold (Au) and water (H$_2$O)—and as a sign of support for the Republican presidential nominee, Barry Goldwater.

■ On Election Day

Picking the Date

Why do Americans vote when they do? In January 1845 Congress settled on a November date after taking into account several factors. For example, November was thought to be the best for turnout because there are fewer problems with agricultural work then. But what week and what day? It couldn't be Sunday because of religious complications. Or Monday because it's the beginning of the week. Or Thursday because the British vote then. Or Friday because it's the end of the week. Or Saturday because that's the day to shop. That left Tuesday or Wednesday, and who knows why they chose Tuesday. But which Tuesday? If Tuesday fell on November 1, that wouldn't do because it would mess up accountants trying to close out the books for October. That, then, is why Americans go to the polls the first Tuesday AFTER the first Monday in November in even-numbered years.

Exit Polls

A controversial technique employed by the news media is the exit poll, in which people who just voted are asked who they voted for. With enough answers, the television networks are able to project winners long before the votes are counted. In 1980 President Jimmy Carter conceded defeat to Ronald Reagan while the polls were still open in California. Many voters waiting in line there went home, angering Demo-

"What factors influenced your decision to use this particular exit?"

President Lyndon Johnson's landslide victory in 1964 had long coattails, dramatically increasing his party's margin in Congress. Johnson's reward was the Great Society legislation of 1965 and 1966.

cratic candidates who might have gotten their votes. Since then, the TV networks have refrained from "declaring" a winner until after the polls have closed.

Landslides

Measured by popular votes, incumbent Democrat Lyndon B. Johnson scored the biggest landslide in presidential history in 1964. He took 61.1 percent of the vote to Republican Barry Goldwater's 38.5 percent. Johnson's margin surpassed the previous record set in 1936 when Democrat Franklin Roosevelt defeated Republican challenger Alfred M. Landon 60.8 percent to 36.5 percent.

FDR's 523 electoral votes in 1936 (98.5 percent of the 531 total; then there were

only forty-eight states), remain the largest electoral college percentage after George Washington's 100 percent in 1789. Republican Ronald Reagan won 525 electoral votes in his 1984 defeat of Democrat Walter F. Mondale, but Reagan's 97.6 percent of the 538 total still ranked behind Roosevelt's 98.5 percent.

Mondale won only his own state of Minnesota and the District of Columbia for a total of 13 electoral votes (2.4 percent). Reagan was the first presidential candidate to receive more than 50 million votes.

Clinton's Firsts

Bill Clinton was the first Democrat to win the presidency without carrying Texas, which joined the Union in 1845. Clinton lost the state to George Bush, one of two Texans in the three-way race. The other was Ross Perot.

Clinton was first in two other ways as well. He was the first candidate of either party since 1952 to be elected without having won the New Hampshire primary. And he was the first candidate in 164 years to head a successful all-southern ticket. Clinton, of Arkansas, and running mate Al Gore, of Tennessee, matched the 1828

In 1944 Harry Truman had the last laugh on the press and his opponent, Thomas Dewey.

Cheap, It Ain't

Wanna buy a Senate seat? Be prepared to spend from $800,000 to $11.3 million to win one, based on the actual costs of the 1992 campaigns. The biggest spender that year was an incumbent, Alphonse M. D'Amato, Republican of New York, who won reelection. Another Republican, freshman Judd Gregg of New Hampshire, spent the least.

On a per-vote basis, it cost Democrat Thomas A. Daschle $17.72 for each vote to

Sen. Alphonse D'Amato of New York—money talks.

victory of Tennessean Andrew Jackson and South Carolinian John C. Calhoun.

Premature Presidents

A valuable item of political memorabilia is the famously wrong issue of the *Chicago Daily Tribune* that carried the front-page headline "Dewey Defeats Truman." In an equally famous photograph, it was held aloft by a smiling President Harry S. Truman after he fooled the pollsters and defeated Thomas E. Dewey in 1944. The faulty polls also burned *Life* magazine, which captioned a picture of Dewey "the

next president of the United States."

An even more embarrassing prediction was made in 1936 by the now-defunct *Literary Digest,* which forecast a landslide for Kansas governor Alfred M. Landon over incumbent Franklin Roosevelt. FDR won by what was then the biggest popular vote margin in history, taking all but two states (Maine and Vermont) and 60.8 percent of the vote. The election also shattered Maine's reputation as an indicator of how the rest of the nation will vote. "As Maine goes, so goes Vermont," quipped Democratic chairman James A. Farley.

Sen. Judd Gregg of New Hampshire—money isn't everything.

keep his South Dakota seat. Newcomer Patty Murray, Democrat from Washington, spent only $1.3 million or $1.24 for each vote.

Among female candidates, Democrat Barbara Boxer spent the most to gain her California seat—$10.3 million or $2.12 per vote. Murray spent the least.

The first black woman senator, Carol Moseley-Braun, Democrat from Illinois, spent the most of any minority candidate—$6.5 million or $2.55 per vote.

House Seats: No Bargain There, Either

Constitutionally speaking, representatives are on a par with senators. Yet Senate races as a rule are more competitive and more expensive. To reach all the voters in his or her state, a Senate candidate may have to buy commercial television spots in a major market at high rates, whereas a House candidate in the same state may be able to reach the whole district from a local station. And traveling over a large state is much more expensive than covering a district within that state.

The added prestige of the Senate also brings out more candidates and drives up the costs. A House member may represent half a million people—still a lot—but the two senators from California speak for thirty million people.

It is still possible for a popular incumbent to be reelected on a shoestring in the House. For example, in 1992 veteran William Natcher, Democrat from Kentucky, won another term by spending only $6,000 or five cents for each vote he received. In contrast, Michael Huffington, Republican from California, spent $5.4 million or

Rep. William Natcher of Kentucky—5 cents a vote.

Rep. Michael Huffington of California—nearly 45 dollars a vote.

$44.80 per vote to win his first term.

In all, fifty House candidates spent more than $1 million in 1992, compared with fourteen two years earlier. Six exceeded $1.75 million in 1992; none did in 1990.

Heavy spending does not guarantee success. Two of the top ten spenders in 1992, Tom McMillen of Maryland and Linda Bean of Maine, were defeated. McMillen, an incumbent Democrat, spent $1.5 million or $14.10 per vote. Bean, a Republican challenger, spent $1.4 million or $11.22 per vote.

The Whole Enchilada

Overall, congressional campaigns spent a record $678 million in 1992—and went in the red doing it. The 2,956 House and Senate candidates raised a total of $659 million—$19 million less than they doled out. Ten years earlier the reverse was true: 2,240 candidates raised $354.7 million and spent $342.4 million, for a surplus of $12.3 million.

Closest Senate Race

The saying "My vote doesn't count" isn't really true. Consider the 1974 Senate race in New Hampshire between Republican Louis Wyman and Democrat John Durkin. When the polls closed, Wyman led Durkin by only two votes out of 221,850

Senate Election Firsts

✳ To serve in the Senate from three states—James Shields (Democrat), Illinois, 1849–1855; Minnesota, 1858–1859; and Missouri, 1879. In those days, senators were elected by the state legislatures. Because Shields, a native of Ireland, had not been a U.S. citizen long enough, his first election in 1849 was voided. He was reelected and seated later in the year after he met the citizenship requirement.

✳ To be elected to the Senate on a write-in vote—Strom Thurmond of South Carolina, 1954. Former governor Thurmond, then a Democrat, received 143,442 write-in votes to defeat his party's endorsed candidate. He has been in the Senate ever since—but as a Republican since 1964.

✳ To go from space to the Senate—former astronaut John H. Glenn, a Democrat, was elected from Ohio in 1974. In 1962 astronaut Glenn was the first person to orbit the Earth.

cast—110,926 to 110,924. Durkin's challenge of Wyman's right to the seat spawned a long, bitter, and embarrassing Senate dispute that ended when the Senate for the first time declared itself unable to decide an election winner. In a special 1975 rematch, Durkin won the seat with 53.6 percent of the vote.

The narrowest final vote in a Senate contest was recorded in 1912 in Nevada by

Key Pittman, a Democrat, who won by only eighty-nine votes. His total of 7,942 votes in the four-way race also was the smallest in Senate history.

Direct Election

Besides being the closest Senate election, the 1912 victory of Sen. Key Pittman was notable for another reason: it ended the era of Senate elections by state legis-

latures. Pittman was not actually elected until January 28, 1913, by the Nevada legislature, which had agreed to select whoever won the popular referendum. Several states had adopted this two-track system because of mounting demand for direct popular election of senators.

The Seventeenth Amendment, ratified April 8, 1913, instituted direct election nationwide. The following November, in a special Maryland election, Democrat Blair Lee became the first popularly elected new senator.

Representative, er, Senator Sparkman

The only person elected to both chambers at the same time was Alabama Democrat John Sparkman, who simultaneously was reelected to the House in 1946 while winning a special election to fill an expired Senate seat. Senator Sparkman was the Democratic nominee for vice president in 1952.

Congressional First

Two House Democrats, Majority Leader Hale Boggs of Louisiana and Nick Begich of Alaska, were reelected in 1972 after

This political cartoon, which appeared in *Puck* magazine in 1905, depicts contemporary popular sentiment favoring the direct election of senators.

they disappeared on an Alaskan airplane flight. Boggs was still listed as missing when the new Congress convened in 1973. His wife, Lindy, was elected to succeed him after he was declared legally dead later in the year. Begich was declared legally dead in 1972, before the new Congress was sworn in. A special election to fill the vacancy was held in 1973.

■ Congressional Campaign War Chests

Money has been a major issue in American politics since colonial times. In his race for the House of Burgesses in Virginia in 1757, George Washington was accused of campaign irregularities. He was charged with dispensing twenty-eight gallons of rum, fifty gallons of rum punch, thirty-four gallons of wine, forty-six gallons of beer, and two gallons of cider royal during his campaign. A large expenditure indeed—there were only 391 voters in his district.

PACs vs. Fat Cats

Corporate, labor, and other political action committees (PACs) contributed thirteen times more money to congressional campaigns in 1990 ($159 million) than the $12.4 million they gave in 1974. Nevertheless, rich individuals gave even more than PACs—$164.0 million.

Top of the PACs Pack

The ten political action committees (PACs) giving the most money to congressional campaigns in 1991–1992 were, according to the Federal Election Commission:

☞ 1. National Association of Realtors	$2,950,138
☞ 2. American Medical Association	2,936,086
☞ 3. International Brotherhood of Teamsters	2,442,552
☞ 4. Association of Trial Lawyers of America	2,366,135
☞ 5. National Education Association	2,323,122
☞ 6. United Auto Workers of America	2,231,917
☞ 7. American Federation of State, County, and Municipal Employees	1,950,365
☞ 8. National Automobile Dealers Association	1,784,375
☞ 9. National Rifle Association	1,738,446
☞10. National Association of Letter Carriers	1,714,777

According to a Federal Election Commission study, PACs stepped up their donations in 1991–1992, giving $205 million to congressional campaigns. Most (72 percent) went to incumbents, with the rest going to challengers or candidates running for vacant seats.

The biggest increase over 1989–1990 (132 percent) came from the National Rifle Association, which was under increasing fire in Congress for its unyielding opposition to handgun controls. The NRA, with donations of $1,738,446, was one of twenty-seven PACs giving more than $1 million to congressional campaigns in the 1991–1992 election cycle. Six PACs gave more than $2 million, topped by the National Association of Realtors at $2,950,138.

Growth of PACs

The Congress of Industrial Organizations (CIO) founded the first PAC in 1943. By 1974 there were 608 PACs, but their number began to shoot up a few years later when Congress passed campaign reform legislation that limited the amount

THE BOSSES OF THE SENATE.

individuals and organizations could give to candidates for federal office. For example, an individual could give more to a PAC ($5,000) than to a candidate ($1,000).

By the end of 1990, there were 4,677 PACs registered with the Federal Election Commission (FEC). Of those, 3,044 made contributions in the 1990 elections.

The number of registered PACs dropped somewhat, to 4,025, in 1992 according to the FEC. The number of PACs contributing to the 1992 elections was not available.

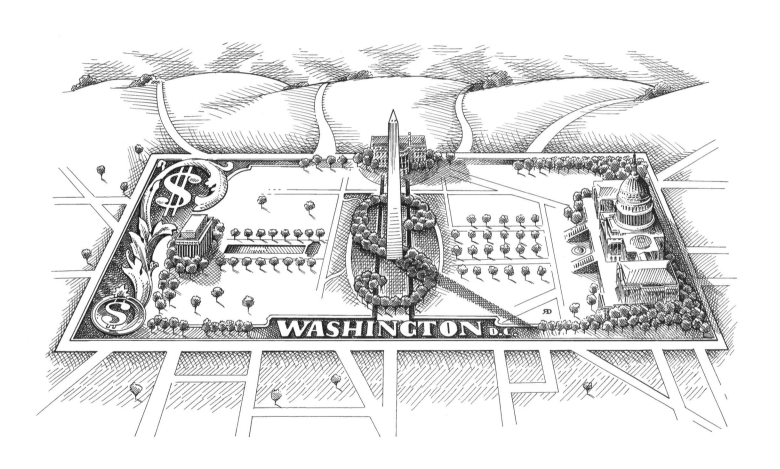

Unelected Power Brokers

Some of the most important people in Washington have never been elected to anything. They are the lobbyists, journalists, and pollsters whose work helps determine what the public thinks of the current occupants of the White House, Capitol, and Supreme Court, as well as the other individuals and institutions that make up the U.S. government.

In turn, the president, members of Congress, justices, and others in positions of authority are influenced in their decisions by what the public thinks of them.

Lobbying: Not a Dirty Word

Washington is full of lobbyists—people paid to help mold laws or executive actions into shapes favorable to the interest groups that employ them. On the whole, lobbying is an honorable profession, but abuses by a minority have from time to time soiled its reputation. When it has been taken too far

and bribes, kickbacks, and other illegal methods have been used to get what lobbyists want, lobbying becomes "influence peddling," a shady activity that has ruined many reputations.

The Crédit Mobilier, "Koreagate," and Abscam scandals all stemmed from real or "sting" lobbying operations. But legitimate lobbying is protected by the Constitution as free speech and the right to petition government. And, unsurprisingly, the forceful presentation of conflicting points of view helps to ensure that legislators know what they're doing when they pass new laws.

Madison's Warning

Although he sponsored the Bill of Rights, James Madison warned against the power of pressure groups, which he called "factions." It didn't matter that the faction represented a majority, Madison wrote in the *Federalist*, No. 10, it could still be dangerous if its members were "united and actuated by some common impulse of passion, or of interest, adverse to the rights of other citizens, or . . . the community." A strong federal government was needed to counterbalance interest groups' influence, he argued.

Origin of Term

Etymologists, who trace words back to their beginnings, disagree about where *lobbyist* comes from. One theory is that it originally referred to the journalists who waited in the lobbies of the House of Commons in London. A variation is that the people standing around were not journalists but citizens hoping to plead their causes with lawmakers.

In Washington, the word *lobby* first appeared in 1808 in annals of the Tenth Congress. By 1829 favor-seekers at the New York capitol in Albany were being called "lobby-agents."

Lobbyists congregated in Washington during the passage of the civil rights bill in 1866.

were registered with Congress, but that included inactive registrations; the registrations still active were believed to be only the tip of the iceberg. Between 1946 and 1980 there were only six prosecutions under the lobbying act, which the Justice Department called "ineffective, inadequate, and unenforceable."

Washington has some 47,000 lawyers,

ARTHUR G. NEWMYER & ASSOCIATES
SUITE 601 EVANS BUILDING, 1420 NEW YORK AVENUE, N.W.
WASHINGTON 5, D. C.

DISTRICT 9200

May 22, 1945

Dear Senator O'Mahoney:

Thought you might enjoy looking over these pictures taken at the hearings of your Committee yesterday.

Incidentally, when you have about five minutes to spare, I would welcome the opportunity of giving you a little information which may be of value as time rolls on.

Sincerely,

A. G. Newmyer

Hon. Joseph C. O'Mahoney,
232 Senate Office Building,
Washington, D. C.

The subtle give and take between members of Congress and lobbyists takes many forms as shown in this letter.

Sam the King

One of the first Washington lobbyists of note was Sam Ward, the so-called King of the Lobby. Ward made a fortune during and after the Civil War, when the government's expansion drew an army of advocates. Known for his lavish dinner parties, Ward lived by the motto "The way to a man's 'Aye' is through his stomach."

How Big Is It?

Lobbying in Washington is big business, but no one knows how big. Although lobbyists are supposed to register with Congress under the 1946 Federal Regulation of Lobbying Act, there is no enforcement mechanism or any systematic way to weed out inactive registrations. And the act, which has been called "more loophole than law," allows some organizations to avoid registration by claiming that influencing legislation is not their "principal purpose." For years, the powerful National Association of Manufacturers refused to register on those grounds.

By 1992 some eight thousand lobbyists

many of whom are at least part-time lobbyists. Uncounted thousands of consultants and other types of professionals also are directly or indirectly involved in some form of lobbying of Congress or executive departments. In the absence of tighter controls, the best indicator of lobbying's scope may be the so-called lobbyists' phone book, *Washington Representatives,* which has fifteen thousand listings.

The Clinton Push

In 1993 Bill Clinton became the first recent president to call for stronger lobby disclosure laws. When speaking to Congress on February 17 about his economic program, Clinton challenged the members "to deal with the undue influence of special interests by passing a bill to end the tax deductions for lobbying and to act quickly to require all the people who lobby you to register as lobbyists, by passing the lobby registration bill." He added: "Believe me, they are cheering that last section at home."

Two days earlier, in a speech to the nation, Clinton warned that the special interests who profited from the status quo would be "out in force" to oppose his proposed budget cuts and revenue increases.

This demonstrator from the National Campaign Finance Reform Coalition made his pitch for change in lobby laws outside a Bush/Quayle fund-raiser in Washington.

Where the Action Is

Another measure of the extent of lobbying in Washington is the number of organizations based there. More than 30 percent of all national nonprofit and professional associations call the nation's capital home. These two thousand organizations employ some fifty thousand to eighty thousand people, many engaged in some form of lobbying.

In a written appeal to his "PAC Pardners," Rep. Jim Hansen of Utah reminded his supporters: "I need to start building my corral for the next roundup, so I need your help rustling up some pesos. . . ." Invitations to a subsequent western chuck wagon buffet (donation requested: $500) honoring Representative Hansen contained this bit of poetry:

EMPTY OLE SADDLE BAGS IN THE HANSEN
CORRAL, AS ON DOWN THE TRAIL I GO.
LOOKING TOWARD THE NEXT ROUNDUP.
A POOR WRANGLER, I SURE NEED YOUR
DOUGH.

I HOPE TO RIDE AGAIN AMONG THE
    COMMITTEES THAT I KNOW BEST,
BUT THE JOURNEY THERE REQUIRES
    MONEY IN THE VEST.
PLEASE HELP ME TO CONTINUE TO
    REPRESENT UTAH AND THE WEST.

More than five hundred corporations have Washington offices and some, such as Mobil and General Dynamics, have moved their headquarters to the area. Others, such as Marriott, MCI, and Martin Marietta, were founded there.

PACs o' Money

Interest groups win friends and influence people with money—lots of money. Corporations and unions are not allowed to use their treasuries for political purposes, but they and other organizations form political action committees (PACs) to raise funds for favored candidates. PACs spent $358.1 million in the 1990 elections, including $159 million given to congressional campaigns. PAC spending on congressional campaigns jumped to $180 million in 1991–1992.

Foreign Lobbying

Lobbyists for foreign governments or interests are required to register with the Justice Department under the Foreign Agents Registration Act of 1938, which originally was aimed at Nazi and fascist propaganda before World War II. Registered foreign agents make up some one thousand of the Washington lobbying corps.

Grass-roots Approach

Much lobbying today is the indirect or "grass-roots" variety. Although direct buttonholing of representatives or senators has not gone by the wayside, many organizations use mass mailings to induce their members to write or call their representatives in Congress and argue for or against bills of interest to the group. The 2.9-million-member National Rifle Association is particularly adept at using grass-roots pressure to influence and even intimidate lawmakers, despite polls showing that Americans overwhelmingly favor more gun control.

The Biggest Lobby

It's called "gray power" for good reason. With 28 million members, the American Association of Retired Persons (AARP) draws strength from sheer numbers. Next to the Roman Catholic Church, the AARP is the nation's largest organization. It has its own ZIP code and eighteen registered lobbyists.

'Gucci Gulch'

Probably nothing brings out the big guns of lobbying more than proposals to change the tax laws. When big bucks are at stake, the halls of Congress swarm with corporate hired hands in expensive suits and dresses. For authors Jeffrey Birnbaum and Alan Murray, designer shoes symbolized the money behind the lobbying on the 1986 tax reform package. They called their 1988 book on the subject *Showdown at Gucci Gulch.*

Revolving Door

Many members of Congress leave by a revolving door. They come right back in as lobbyists for companies or organizations that want well-connected people representing them in Washington. Unlike other lobbyists, alumni of Congress have the privilege of strolling onto the House or Senate floor. Rules or protocol, however, bar them from the floor during debates on bills that affect their personal or business interests. Since 1990 ex-members have been prohib-ited from lobbying Congress for a year after leaving that institution.

White House Lobby

Presidents perhaps have the biggest stakes in influencing legislation. But not until the administration of Dwight D. Eisenhower was there a formal White House lobbying operation. Eisenhower's congressional liaison officers were retired general Wilton B. Persons, a deputy to Chief of Staff Sherman Adams, and Bryce N. Harlow, a former House committee staffer who replaced Persons when he succeeded Adams in 1958. Harlow was the first full-time presidential lobbyist.

Presidents, of course, hold the ultimate lobbying weapon—the veto. Through 1992, they had vetoed 2,513 bills, and Congress had managed to override only 104.

Feel-Good Politics

The saying "You can catch more flies with honey than with vinegar" describes another aspect of White House lobbying. Presidents have at their disposal some attractive goodies they can use to make members of Congress feel important and receptive to the president's program. It may be a ride on *Air Force One,* an invitation to Camp David, a seat next to the first lady at a state dinner, use of the presidential box at the Kennedy Center, a pen used to sign a bill into law, or any one of dozens of other gestures to share the prestige and perks of the presidency.

Conversely, a president can withhold little favors from political opponents while showering them on friends. Lyndon Johnson sat allies, even Republicans, at the head table of White House dinners while assigning opponents, even of his own party, to the cheap seats.

At least once a year, usually in late spring, the president tries to cozy up to the whole Congress by inviting members to share hot dogs and hamburgers under a big tent on the South Lawn. In the LBJ years the picnic featured genuine Texas barbecue.

The Fourth Estate

The press gets its name as the "fourth estate" from the three estates of feudal Europe: the clergy, the nobility, and the commoners. In the eighteenth century, British statesman and author Edmund Burke observed that in the reporters' gallery of the British Parliament "there sat a Fourth Estate more important by far than them all."

'What Hath God Wrought?'

Modern presidents might be asking themselves the same thing. That four-word question, telegraphed from Washington to Baltimore on May 24, 1844, by Morse code inventor Samuel F. B. Morse, revolutionized news reporting and marked the beginning of the end of presidential privacy.

Morse's message began the era of instantaneous delivery of words

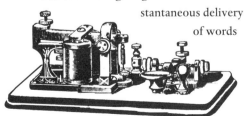

by wire, which soon stretched across oceans and linked the world as never before. Almost at once, the cables were crackling with a steady flow of stories about public figures, leading to the age of mass communications of today.

No Place to Hide

If, as they say, White House life is like living in a fishbowl, Abraham Lincoln was the first fish. He was the first president to have a reporter assigned to cover him full time. The reporter, Henry Villard of the Associated Press, had covered Lincoln in Springfield, Illinois, and accompanied the new president to Washington in 1861.

Today, about seventy-five journalists cover the White House regularly for all types of news media. Hundreds of others report on the president's activities as needed. In 1988, for example, almost two thousand reporters applied for credentials to cover President Ronald Reagan's Moscow summit with Mikhail Gorbachev.

President Gerald Ford takes questions from the White House press corps.

The White House photographers pose for a picture in 1918.

Press Relations

Although presidents before Theodore Roosevelt had little contact with the press, Roosevelt courted journalists and gave them wide access to the White House—but on his terms. It was Woodrow Wilson, however, who held the first formal news conferences, at which reporters were limited to written questions.

Warren G. Harding hired the first White House speech writer, and Herbert Hoover appointed the first press aides, George Akerson and Theodore Joslin. But FDR spokesman, Stephen T. Early is generally regarded as the first full-fledged White House press secretary. Bill Moyers, Lyndon Johnson's press secretary, was the first without a journalistic background.

First of Her Kind

Bill Clinton was the first president to have a female press secretary, thirty-two-year-old Dee Dee Myers. After Clinton appointed a new communications director, David R. Gergen, in May 1993, Myers began giving most of the press briefings while continuing her regular duties as presidential spokeswoman.

Radio

A Pittsburgh radio station reported Warren G. Harding's defeat of James M. Cox in 1920, marking the dawn of broadcast journalism. In 1923 Calvin Coolidge's first State of the Union message was broadcast, and two years later his inauguration was heard coast to coast.

By the 1930s millions of Americans were listening to FDR's "fireside chats," through which he masterfully lifted the nation's Depression-weighted morale and built support for his New Deal programs.

At the same time another skilled broadcaster, Father Charles E. Coughlin, "the Radio Priest," was effectively attacking Roosevelt from his parish in Royal Oak, Michigan. But Catholic authorities eventually silenced Coughlin, whose talks became increasingly anti-Semitic and pro-fascist. In the Roosevelt landslide of 1936, Coughlin's candidate, William Lemke, ran a distant third to Alf Landon with 2 percent of the vote.

Television

A televised picture of Herbert Hoover, then secretary of commerce, was transmitted by phone from Washington to New York in 1927, but commercial development of TV was slowed by World War II. After the war, Harry S. Truman be-came the first president on TV from the White House. He gave televised tours showing how the mansion was reconstructed during his administration.

Truman's successor, Dwight Eisenhower, gave filmed news conferences, but the broadcasts were delayed so that aides could snip out the worst of his garbled syntax. John F. Kennedy, more comfortable with impromptu speech, held the first live, unedited sessions with the press.

In 1967 all three networks televised Lyndon B. Johnson's fourth State of the Union address, inaugurating complete coverage of the presidency.

Taking Questions

In the not-so-olden days, when the entire White House press corps could crowd around Franklin D. Roosevelt's desk to ask him questions, presidential news conferences were frequent and informal. Richard Nixon held the fewest press conferences, 37, or 0.5 a month. Although he was called the "Great Communicator," Ronald Reagan held only 46 press sessions in eight years, or 0.4 a month.

Today's formal news conferences are major events, with reporters jamming the White House East Room for sessions televised around the world. John Kennedy, who held the first live conferences (Dwight Eisenhower's were filmed and edited), averaged 1.9 a month. Recent presidents met the press somewhat less frequently in full-fledged news conferences, but George Bush in particular responded to reporters on almost all occasions when they were close enough to ask him questions. As he settled into office, Bill Clinton seemed inclined to be accessible in the same fashion.

What Malaise?

Given the spontaneity—and thus the inherent danger—of press conferences, presidents today are fond of informing, and sometimes even lecturing, the American public from the safety of their perch in the Oval Office. It was during the troubled year of 1979 that Carter shook up his cabinet and spoke to the American people about the nation's low morale. The speech quickly became known as Carter's "malaise speech," even though he never actually used the word *malaise* in his televised address.

A Republican to the Rescue

In a drastic move similar to Carter's— but at a lower level and sooner in his presidency—Bill Clinton shook up his communications staff in May 1993 as he sank in the polls and his economic recovery program

Franklin Roosevelt still holds the record for the most press conferences. He held 998 news conferences, averaging 6.9 a month during his twelve-year presidency (1933–1945).

Care and Feeding

Just as there is an army of journalists camped in Washington, so is there a corps of men and women assigned to assist reporters, protect officials from bad press, and publicize their agencies' work. The White House Office of Management and Budget has estimated that the federal government employs five thousand federal information specialists (writers and editors), not counting hundreds more classified as "public affairs" people. Estimates of the cost of government publicity programs range from $400 million to over $2.5 billion a year.

Opened Doors

The first Congresses, and especially the Senate, took slowly to the idea of having the public look over their shoulders as they wrote laws. Reporters were barred from House of Representatives meetings until the second session, in April 1790. The Senate met in closed sessions until 1795, when galleries for the public and press were opened.

Committees, where Congress conducts most of its business, remained closed for much longer. Public hearings on proposed legislation did not become standard practice until the early 1900s. In the 1970s, "sunshine" reforms opened so-called

was foundering on Capitol Hill. Clinton replaced his thirty-two-year-old communications director, George Stephanopoulos, with a more experienced hand, David R. Gergen, a Republican. Gergen, a columnist and TV commentator, had held the same job under Ronald Reagan and had worked

for other GOP presidents as well.

Clinton's decision to relieve, but not fire, Stephanopoulos underscored the importance that presidents attach to effective use of the news media to put their message across.

UNITED STATES
Senate and House of Representatives
N E W S   G A L L E R I E S

R. MICHAEL JENKINS
CONGRESSIONAL QUARTERLY

103D CONGRESS 1ST SESSION
EXPIRES FEBRUARY 28. 1994

markup sessions where committees draft the final language of bills. In the 1990s, reporters complained of a backlash and a return to more secrecy on Capitol Hill.

Capitol News Galleries

About six thousand reporters, photographers, and technicians are accredited to cover Congress from the news media galleries overlooking the House and Senate chambers. The galleries (press, press photographers, radio-television, and periodical) are maintained at public expense and staffed by superintendents. Telephones and writing materials are provided, but today computers link many correspondents directly to their home offices.

Credentials for the galleries are granted by the standing committees of correspondents, which are elected by gallery members. Only bona fide correspondents are admitted. Spectators in the visitors' and other galleries are not allowed to take notes. Photography is not permitted except on special occasions, such as the president's State of the Union message, and then only by accredited photographers. Regular sessions are televised by House and Senate employees and broadcast on C-SPAN (Cable-Satellite Public Affairs Network).

Press tables at committee hearings are reserved for correspondents—and are therefore off limits to lobbyists and spectators.

Many congressional correspondents also have White House credentials, which are issued separately and require FBI security clearances.

First Female Correspondent

The first woman admitted to the Senate press gallery was Jane Gray Swisshelm, an abolitionist who wrote for Horace Greeley's *New York Tribune.* She was admitted on April 17, 1850, with the grudging permission of future president Millard Fillmore, who as vice president was also president of the Senate. On her first day, Swisshelm witnessed a historic episode, when Sen. Henry S. Foote of Mississippi pulled a pistol against the approaching Sen. Thomas Hart Benton of Missouri, who shouted, "Stand out of the way and let the assassin fire!" The two men were separated, and heated debate continued on the Compromise of 1850.

First Black Correspondent

The first black correspondent admitted to the Senate gallery in modern times was Louis R. Lautier of the *Atlanta Daily World,* who was accredited on March 18, 1947, when the Senate Rules Committee overruled the standing committee of correspondents. After the Civil War some black journalists, including the prominent editor Frederick Douglass, had access to the galleries. But in 1879 House and Senate correspondents set up the standing committee system to keep out lobbyists and other nonjournalists. The rule also excluded weekly newspapers, which meant most of the black press. Lautier argued successfully that he reported for a daily paper as well as several weeklies.

'Smile, You're on Congressional Camera'

Members of Congress go to great lengths to stay in the public eye, knowing that at election time it pays to be better known than your opponent. Most members today employ press secretaries to field reporters' questions and gain maximum favorable publicity. Federal agencies funnel announcements of new grants or projects through congressional offices, and the lucky Senate and House members race each other to break the good news and get the credit.

The House and Senate and their Democratic and Republican party organizations provide well-equipped broadcast studios so that members can go on camera with the Capitol dome in the background, hoping to get a taped sound bite used as "film at eleven" on the TV news back home. Satellite feeds beam the clips directly to the stations, which can also pick shots from televised hearings or floor debates.

Members also appear on radio and TV talk shows, give interviews, write columns for local papers, and hold briefings on bills they are sponsoring.

Speaking Frankly

Much of the outpouring of newsletters, statements, and other publicity materials from congressional offices goes to the voters postage free thanks to the franking privilege—the members' right to send official mail with only their signature instead of a stamp.

Members soon learn that the frank is one of their strongest political tools. According to former representative Bill Frenzel, Republican from Minnesota, members are taught by the parties three rules: "Use the frank. Use the frank. Use the frank."

Congress appropriates money to pay the U.S. Postal Service for carrying the franked mail—but it must be delivered even if the appropriation falls short. In fiscal 1990 franking costs exceeded $100 million, about $40 million less than in 1988 when some 600 million pieces of franked mail went out.

Restrictions on pictures and repeating the member's name limit the use of newsletters to gain reelection, but still the frank is widely criticized as a campaign subsidy.

■ Pollsters: The New Gurus

Like their modern counterparts, early presidents tried to gauge how the wind was blowing politically. To do that they had to depend on their own instincts and a limited number of public opinion indicators, primarily feedback from grass-roots party organizations. Other sources of information about the mood of the country included Congress, newspaper editorials and letters, and public demonstrations.

Presidents today use some of the same methods to avoid being blindsided by adverse reaction to some proposal or appointment. But presidents now have the added advantages of high-tech public opinion polling to reinforce their own gut feelings about what's on the country's mind. The polls are not always right, but they are a better navigation aide than the old seat-of-the-pants method.

FDR: The First Poll-Watcher

Franklin Roosevelt was the first president to take polling data routinely into account when weighing decisions about his administration's policies and actions. With war looming in Europe in the late 1930s, FDR received advice from George Gallup, the founder of modern polling, on how to frame his rhetoric about possible U.S. involvement in what became World War II. By the 1960s, public opinion polling was an accepted White House tool.

Media consultant Peter Fenn advises Democratic candidates.

Albert Cantril:
First White House Pollster

Lyndon Johnson was the first president to hire a pollster, Albert Cantril, for the White House staff. Cantril, son of Princeton University pollster Hadley Cantril, provided LBJ with polling data from every state. Johnson used the polls both to defend his escalation of the Vietnam War and his decision in 1968 not to seek another term in the face of mounting opposition to the war. His successor, Richard Nixon, said polls showed there was a "silent majority" of Americans opposed to vocal antiwar demonstrators.

Gallup Polls

Outside polling continues to be a major factor in presidential decision making, despite a growing tendency—particularly since the Reagan years—for presidents to have their own polling professionals within the White House. From a White House perspective, the most important of the traditional measures of the president's standing with the public is the Gallup presidential approval survey. Since 1945 the Gallup Organization has asked members of the public monthly—and sometimes more often—whether they approve or disapprove of the president's handling of the job.

How Low Can You Go?

Harry Truman and Richard Nixon are tied for having the lowest public approval ratings while they were president. Truman dipped to 23 percent in Gallup's presidential approval poll in November 1951, when the Korean War was in its seventeenth month. Nixon hit the same bottom in August 1974 just before he resigned because of the Watergate scandal.

The only other president to score in the twenties was Jimmy Carter, who fell to 29 percent at several points in 1979, a year marked by farmers' demonstrations against low prices for crops, gasoline shortages, the Three Mile Island nuclear power plant accident, and transfer of the Panama Canal to Panama. Carter's ratings rose dramatically after Iran seized the American embassy in November, but they fell again in 1980 as Carter failed to gain the hostages' release.

Public dissatisfaction with George Bush's handling of the recession dropped his approval rating to the 30 percent level in mid-1992 and contributed to his reelection defeat.

In early 1993 Bill Clinton, plagued by a series of missteps—including a $200 haircut aboard *Air Force One* and his withdrawal of a major civil rights nomination—registered the lowest approval ratings for any new president. They stayed, however, above the Nixon-Truman record low of 23 percent.

High Scorers

All presidents get high approval ratings just after they are inaugurated, but most ratings fall as disenchantment sets in and the honeymoon is over. The most consistently popular presidents since the Gallup presidential approval poll began in 1947 have been Dwight Eisenhower, John Kennedy, and Ronald Reagan. George Bush has the distinction of having the highest rating, and some of the lowest. In March 1991 after the Persian Gulf War victory, Bush scored 89 percent, surpassing the previous peak, Kennedy's 83 percent in April 1961. But by the summer of 1992 a lagging economy pitched Bush's approval rating to the near-bottom 30 percent level.

Party Loyalties

Pollsters for hire tend not to cross party lines. They have either Democratic clients or Republican clients, not both. For example, Patrick Caddell polled for Democrats George McGovern, Jimmy Carter, Gary Hart, and Joseph R. Biden, Jr. Richard Wirthlin and Robert Teeter polled for Republicans Ronald Reagan and George Bush, respectively.

Congress and Its Public

A May 1991 Gallup poll found that Americans don't think too highly of their members of Congress. Only 19 percent of the voters polled gave their senators and representatives a high or very high rating for their honesty and ethical standards. Forty-four percent rated their representatives average; senators fared a little better at 48 percent. The remaining voters sampled took the dimmest view, rating their representatives (32 percent) and senators (30 percent) as low or very low.

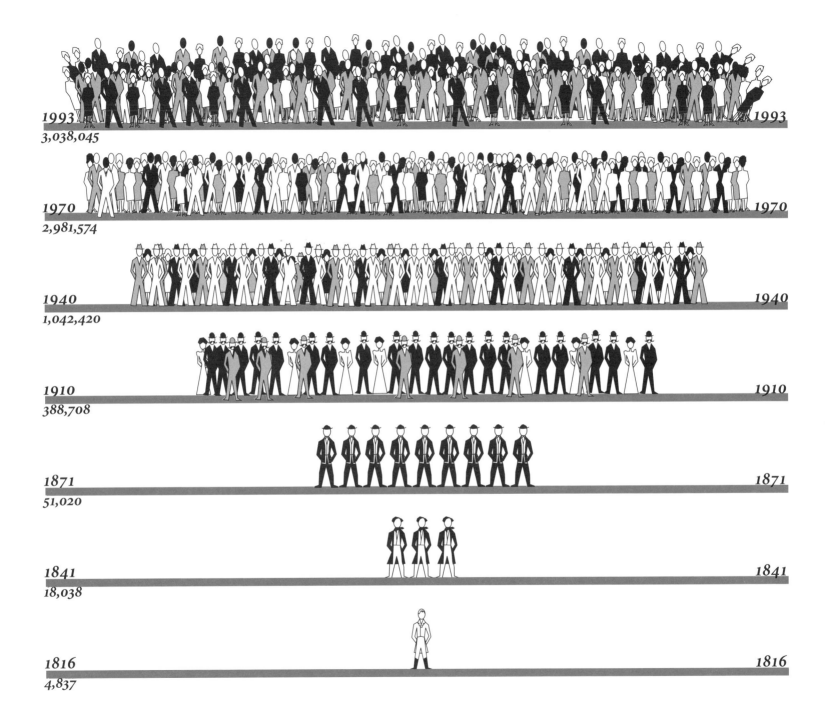

1993
3,038,045

1970
2,981,574

1940
1,042,420

1910
388,708

1871
51,020

1841
18,038

1816
4,837

The Entrenched Bureaucrats

The federal bureaucracy has a life of its own. Presidents and Congresses come and go, but hundreds of thousands of government employees hang on administration after administration, doing their jobs in obscurity, usually performing a public service but sometimes posing a major obstacle to change and greater efficiency.

Presidents soon learn that there's little they can accomplish without the cooperation of the bureaucracy. Because many officeholders have the authority to make policy, they are often regarded as the "fourth branch" of government. President Jimmy Carter said that he had been warned about the bureaucracy's rigidity but found it "even worse than . . . anticipated."

■ The Federal Monster

Factory Jobs Surpassed

For the first time, government jobs now outnumber manufacturing jobs in the Uni-

At the turn of the century women found Uncle Sam an eager employer. These women were trimming currency in 1907.

Departments' Dates of Creation

Department of State (originally Foreign Affairs)	July 27, 1789
Department of the Treasury	September 2, 1789
Department of Justice	June 22, 1870★
Department of the Interior	March 3, 1849
Department of Agriculture	February 9, 1889
Department of Commerce (originally Commerce and Labor)	February 14, 1903
Department of Labor	March 4, 1913
Department of Defense (originally War, Navy)	August 10, 1949
Department of Health and Human Services (originally Health, Education, and Welfare)	April 11, 1953
Department of Housing and Urban Development	November 9, 1965
Department of Transportation	October 15, 1966
Department of Energy	October 1, 1977
Department of Education	October 17, 1979
Department of Veterans Affairs	October 25, 1988

★ The attorney general has been a cabinet member since September 24, 1789, but the Justice Department (which the attorney general heads) was not created until June 22, 1870.

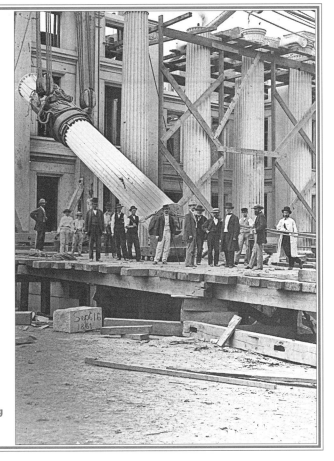

The Treasury Building is the oldest federal government departmental headquarters. Here, columns are erected as the early construction of the building begins.

ted States. That milestone was passed in October 1991 when the Bureau of Labor Statistics counted 18.41 million jobs in government—federal, state, and local—versus 18.39 million in manufacturing. There were more local government workers (61 percent) than state (23 percent) or federal (16 percent). State and local work forces grew 20 percent since 1892; federal, 8 percent.

Growth Spurts

For most of its first 150 years of existence, the United States got along with fewer than a half-million federal civilian workers. In the next fifty years, that number more than quintupled, largely for two reasons: hard times and war.

When Franklin D. Roosevelt took office in 1933, the federal bureaucracy numbered about 600,000. His "New Deal" activism created more than sixty new agencies to combat the Great Depression. By the end of 1941, when the United States entered World War II, the federal civilian work force had doubled to more than 1 million.

The war mobilization brought another wave of growth, peaking at 3.8 million in 1945. Since the 1950s, the number has

Under the resourceful direction of Harry Hopkins, a New York social worker, a succession of public agencies tackled the problem of aid for the unemployed during the Great Depression. Hopkins's solution relied on jobs rather than cash handouts. Ben Shahn's mural for the Public Works Administration captures the feeling of a New York speakeasy during Prohibition. Hopkins later became a top aide to FDR.

settled to about what it is today, almost 3 million. (Postal workers were placed under their own civil service when the Postal Service was removed from the cabinet in 1970, but they are still counted as government employees.)

Alphabet Soup

The New Deal recovery program spawned many new federal agencies known mostly by their abbreviations such as CCC (Civilian Conservation Corps), PWA (Public Works Administration), and WPA (Works Progress Administration).

Most have disappeared, but some still exist such as the FCC (Federal Communications Commission), NLRB (National Labor Relations Board), and the SEC (Securities and Exchange Commission). And, of course, many new ones have been added.

Civil Service

The Spoils System

The vast majority of the executive branch's 3 million civilian employees are protected by the civil service, which largely replaced the unsavory *spoils system*. The spoils system is called that because in an 1832 Senate speech William Learned Marcy of New York used the phrase "to the victor belong the spoils of the enemy."

Although it existed earlier and still does today, the spoils system had its heyday in the administrations of Andrew Jackson and several that followed. It was characterized by abuses of *patronage*—the power to hand out jobs. New administrations fired waves of job holders and replaced them with cronies and relatives.

Reforming the System

Pressure to reform the patronage system resulted in the Civil Service Act of 1883 (the Pendleton Act), which based hiring on

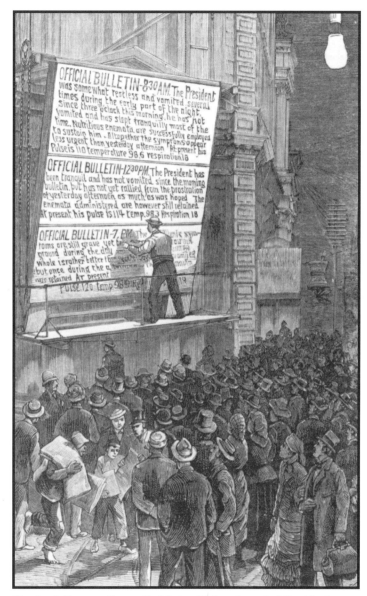

Charles Guiteau, a disgruntled federal job seeker, shot President James Garfield on July 2, 1881. Guiteau's bullet killed Garfield and gave birth to a reform movement that helped to eliminate the federal spoils system.

merit for about 10 percent of federal jobs. Amended and expanded several times, the act now covers almost all government workers. The fifteen GS (general service) job ratings pay at maximum (step ten) from $14,891 for GS1 to $86,589 for GS15.

About 12 percent (365,000) of all federal workers live in the Washington, D.C., area. Their average salary is $46,400.

Beginning in 1994 there could be twenty-nine different pay scales for federal employees. Under a 1990 act, salaries for federal jobs are supposed to be comparable to those for private jobs in the same locality by the year 2004.

Office of Personnel Management

A 1978 act replaced the Civil Service Commission with the Office of Personnel Management and the Merit Systems Protection Board. It also set up the Senior Executive Service (SES), which offers bonuses to high officials willing to forgo some job security. SES salaries range from $92,900 to $115,700; the range for executive schedule jobs is $108,200–$148,400. Cabinet members receive the top (Level 1) executive schedule salary. The president receives $200,000 a year, and the vice president receives $171,500 a year. Several hundred federal jobs are classed Schedule C (political) and are not subject to civil service competition or protection. George Bush placed more political appointees (2,435) on the federal payroll than either Ronald Reagan or Jimmy Carter.

Nepotism No-No

A law passed in 1967 (PL 90–206) prevents a president from giving a government job to a family member. The act is called the "Bobby Kennedy law" because it is intended to prevent a repetition of the situation in 1961 in which President John Kennedy appointed his brother Robert attorney general of the United States.

The law apparently did not prohibit Bill Clinton from appointing

Risking charges of nepotism, President John Kennedy named his brother Robert attorney general, despite his limited experience in the law profession. Robert Kennedy's closeness and unquestionable loyalty to his brother allowed him to make suggestions and criticisms that no one else could.

by John H. Trattner of the Council for Excellence in Government, the most recent *Prune Book* focuses on the top federal science and technology jobs and gives more information about them than the barebones Plum Book. Its subtitle is *The Sixty Toughest Science and Technology Jobs in Washington.*

■ Where Do Most Bureaucrats Work? The Executive Branch

Biggest and Smallest Departments

Measured by the size of its work force, Defense was by far the largest executive de-

his wife, Hillary Rodham Clinton, as head of his health care reform task force in 1993. There was no challenge to the appointment, presumably because it was unpaid and advisory only.

■ Plums and Prunes

The Plum Book

And how do federal job-seekers learn what's available? Certainly no bulletin board is large enough, so Congress publishes the so-called Plum Book—officially known as *Policy and Supporting Positions*—issued near the end of every presidential

election year. Although it lists the several thousand executive branch positions that presidents fill by appointment, it doesn't give a whole lot of information—just the title, grade or salary, type of appointment and location, and the name of the incumbent and the expiration date, if any, of his or her appointment.

The Prune Book

A prune is a plum—only tougher and shriveled up. The *Prune Book* is a privately published (Madison Books), expanded version of the so-called Plum Book. Written

WE NEED OUR BOOKS TO UNDERSTAND YOUR BOMBS

partment in 1991, with 1,014,212 civilian employees. Next biggest was the newest department, Veterans Affairs, with 249,957 employees. The smallest department was Education, with 4,676 employees.

Departments That Are Not

Within the Defense Department, the Army, Navy, and Air Force are still called "departments," but in truth they're not real departments. The National Security Act of 1947 combined the old War and Navy departments into something called the "National Military Establishment." Two years later, the National Security Act Amendments of 1949 created the Department of Defense and placed all the military services under its wing.

Departed Departments

Besides War and Navy, departments that no longer exist include Post Office (changed to an independent agency in 1970), Commerce and Labor (divided into two separate departments in 1913), and Health, Education, and Welfare (split in 1979 into the Health and Human Services Department and the Education Department).

Independent Agencies

The federal government gets its regulatory power from Article I, section 8, of the Constitution, which empowers Congress "[t]o regulate Commerce with foreign Nations, and among the several States." While a handful of agencies were created within executive departments before 1887, it was Congress's formation of the Interstate Commerce Commission (ICC) that year that furnished the model for today's regulatory agency.

The ICC, charged with taming railroad competition, was the first "independent agency," intended as an arm of Congress but with commission members appointed by the president for staggered terms. Today, besides the fourteen cabinet depart-

Postal employees sort through hundreds of millions of packages each year.

Deposit Insurance Corporation (FDIC), created in 1933 to regulate banks and guarantee individuals' deposits.

Social regulation dates mostly from the 1960s and includes enforcement of laws to protect civil rights, highway safety, environmental quality, consumer products, and workplace safety. Some of the important agencies in these areas are the Civil Rights Commission, National Highway Traffic Safety Administration (NHTSA), Environmental Protection Agency (EPA), Consumer Product Safety Commission, and Occupational Safety and Health Administration (OSHA).

In both employees and budgets, social regulation is about three times larger than economic regulation. Almost 90,000 federal workers spend about $9.8 billion a year on social regulation, compared with about 27,000 workers and $2.4 billion devoted to economic regulation.

Deregulation

Beginning with the administrations of Jimmy Carter and Ronald Reagan, regulation of businesses was eased in the 1970s and 1980s. On the theory that more competition would lower prices and improve efficiency, many industries were partly or completely deregulated, including the airline, banking, bus, cable

ments, there are more than sixty independent regulatory agencies or government corporations. Among the largest are the U.S. Postal Service (792,000 employees), Tennessee Valley Authority (31,000), Federal Trade Commission (25,000), National Aeronautics and Space Administration (22,000), and the ICC (21,000).

Types of Regulation

Basically, there are two types of federal regulation: economic and social. Economic regulation began during the New Deal and was designed to ensure the health of banks and other financial institutions and to protect consumers from their excesses and collapse. A prime example was the Federal

television, railroad, and trucking industries.

One measure of bureaucratic red tape and regulation is the number of pages in the *Federal Register,* where all new regulations are published. From 5,307 pages in 1940, the *Register* grew to 87,012 pages in 1980. By 1990, the total was down to 53,618 pages, with most of the decrease in economic regulation. Continuing pressure for environmental and similar protection kept social regulation from shrinking.

Backlash

Deregulation caused serious problems in some industries. Increased competition led to the bankruptcy and disappearance of several major airlines, including some of the oldest and best known such as Braniff, Eastern, and Pan American.

In banking, deregulation of savings and loans (S&Ls), backbone of the home mortgage industry, proved to be extremely costly. Freed to lend money for commercial structures, many S&Ls made risky investments. But then, hit by a real estate recession and overbuilding of office complexes, hundreds of S&Ls collapsed, requiring the most expensive federal bailout in U.S. history. Estimates of the final cost reached as high as $500 billion.

Ironically, Congress had to create five new regulatory agencies to deal with the consequences of banking deregulation. Chief among them was the Resolution Trust Corporation, empowered to close or merge the failed S&Ls and pay off the depositors.

In 1992 Congress moved to reregulate the cable TV industry because of subscribers' anger at rising fees. The pressure for reregulation was so intense that President George Bush suffered his first and only defeat in forty-four veto battles with Congress. A two-thirds majority vote of each chamber is needed to override a presidential veto.

■ What Do Bureaucrats Do?

Produce Paper, Tons of It

Each year the intelligence directorate of the Central Intelligence Agency publishes about a hundred national intelligence estimates, as well as enough major studies to fill an eighteen-wheeler truck. Study subjects have ranged from offensive weapons capabilities in the Middle East to AIDS in Africa to narcotics in Burma.

Build Pyramids—Paper Ones

In 1991 the Agriculture Department was all set to come out with a "Food Guide Pyramid" to replace the "Basic Four Food Groups" that had been around since the 1950s. But the department held up the graphic for restudy and reworking, at a cost of $855,000, after the meat and dairy industries objected that the original version urged consumers to go easy on their products. As finally released in 1992, the Food Pyramid suggested eating two to three servings daily of meat, poultry, fish, dry beans, eggs, and nuts. It did not say how big a "serving" should be.

Too Much Paper—Not a New Problem

In March 1887 a Senate select committee established to examine and analyze why it took the executive departments so long to conduct public business found that "there were large masses of files of papers, which have been accumulating for a long series of years and now occupy much room."

The solution was vintage bureaucracy. On February 16, 1889, an act was approved to authorize the heads of government departments that had an "accumulation files of papers, which are not needed or useful in the transaction of the current business . . . and have no permanent value or historical interest" to send a report

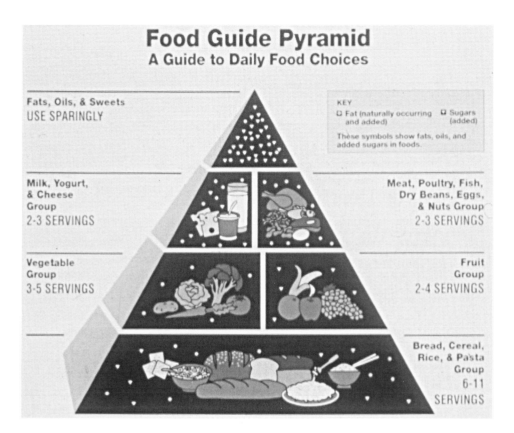

Food Guide Pyramid
A Guide to Daily Food Choices

Fats, Oils, & Sweets
USE SPARINGLY

KEY
□ Fat (naturally occurring   □ Sugars
and added)   (added)

These symbols show fats, oils, and
added sugars in foods.

Milk, Yogurt,
& Cheese
Group
2-3 SERVINGS

Meat, Poultry, Fish,
Dry Beans, Eggs,
& Nuts Group
2-3 SERVINGS

Vegetable
Group
3-5 SERVINGS

Fruit
Group
2-4 SERVINGS

Bread, Cereal,
Rice, & Pasta
Group
6-11
SERVINGS

to Congress about the papers. Congress would then appoint a joint committee to consider and report on the report. The "report" filled fifty-three feet of shelf space, and forty-five years later, when the National Archives was created, it was given the job of deciding which records were worth keeping.

Crunch Numbers

The Labor Department's Bureau of Labor Statistics (BLS) is one of the most important numbers-crunching operations in the country because it produces the Consumer Price Index, the country's leading indicator of inflation.

To develop the index, BLS sends its field collectors into retail and other business establishments once a month to collect price data on the thousands of goods and services offered to American consumers. Then it processes the data, and, within three weeks after the data were collected, releases the resulting index to the White House—or more specifically, to the chairman of the president's Council of Economic Advisers.

Because a new index is such sensitive information, even the secretary of labor—the agency's big boss—doesn't get to see it first.

As it does for the Consumer Price Index, the Bureau of Labor Statistics keeps its monthly findings on the unemployment rate highly secret, and it announces the new rates at times when the information will have the least impact on the world stock markets.

Pay Homage to the Hill

Federal Aviation Administration head James B. Busey once claimed he spent 20–25 percent of his time dealing with Congress—and even more during budget hearings, which, according to the *Prune Book,* Busey called "the slow dance on the killing grounds." Busey and his staff also testified frequently before the FAA's oversight committee, spent a lot of time trying to educate members of Congress and their staffs about aviation matters, and, last but not least, answered telephone calls daily from members about the airports in their districts, all of which seemed to require some new piece of equipment or runway extension.

■ High Profiles

The image of a bureaucrat is that of a man or woman shuffling paper day after day, just putting in time until he or she retires with a generous pension. But the perception is as unfair as it is inaccurate. As in any other field, some government jobs are boring and unfulfilling. But the vast majority are necessary, and some are downright glamorous.

G-Man

Arguably the most famous U.S. bureaucrat of all time was J. Edgar Hoover, who, as its first director, molded the Federal Bureau of Investigation (FBI) into an efficient crime-fighting agency. For fifty years Hoover was in the headlines, personally arresting such criminals as John Dillinger, ferreting out spies during World War II, and never missing an opportunity to publicize the FBI or himself.

He set high standards of conduct and appearance for the thousands of FBI agents under him. After his death in 1972 his body lay in state in the Capitol Rotunda, and he was buried in Congressional Cemetery. But his posthumous reputation has suffered from allegations that he bugged the bedrooms of civil rights leader Martin Luther King, Jr., snooped on John F. Kennedy and other presidents, and may have been ho-

J. Edgar Hoover

mosexual. Some critics have demanded that his name be taken off FBI headquarters, which is named after him. But whether he was a hero or a heel, J. Edgar Hoover indisputably was a leader among bureaucrats.

What's Her Line?

Doctor. Just as women have made inroads to the highest echelons of the federal government including the cabinet and the Supreme Court, so have they captured some of the highest bureaucratic posts once held only by men. Two of the most notable were physicians: Dr. Bernadine P. Healy, the first woman to head the National Institutes of Health (she was appointed in 1981), and Dr. Antonia C. Novello, the first woman surgeon general of the United States (appointed in 1990). Both left office in 1993, Dr. Jocelyn Elders of Arkansas became the first black woman surgeon general.

Economist. Laura D'Andrea Tyson is the first woman to head the president's Council of Economic Advisers. She was appointed in 1993.

Environmentalist. Carol M. Browner, a Clinton appointee, held one of the highest ranking subcabinet positions—but it wasn't to be subcabinet for long. Acting on Clinton's proposal, Congress was upgrading

Carol Browner

her Environmental Protection Agency to a cabinet department. Browner would be the first secretary of environmental protection.

Statistician. Janet L. Norwood joined the Labor Department's Bureau of Labor Statistics in 1963 and has been its commissioner since 1979.

Lawyer. In May 1993 the Senate confirmed Roberta A. Achtenberg's appointment as assistant secretary for equal opportunity in the Department of Housing and Urban Development. Achtenberg, a former San Francisco city official, was the first openly avowed lesbian confirmed for a high federal office.

What, Me Retire?

At age ninety Emil Corwin was the oldest federal public affairs official still on active duty in 1993. He was also one of a handful of federal employees in the same age bracket. All far exceeded the federal work force averages for age (forty-three), retirement age (sixty-one), and length of service (14.1 years).

Corwin, with thirty-one years of service, had slowed down to three days a week working for the Food and Drug Administration in Washington.

■ Leak Control

Thousands of government employees are paid to keep secrets. They censor and classify all manner of information, some essential to national security and some not. With the end of the Cold War, pressure grew to save money and cut red tape by declassifying millions of documents. Even before the Soviet Union collapsed, President Jimmy Carter had started a disclosure program, but many bureaucrats

CENSURED

ignored it and the Reagan administration reversed it. As recently as late 1992, Congress ordered the Pentagon to put new locks on 200,000 safes and filing cabinets at a cost estimated as high as $500 million. The habit of secrecy does not die easily.

Lifting the Veil

In the 1990s there were signs that the federal bureaucracy was trying to overcome its almost pathological desire to hide everything. Responding to pressure from scholars, journalists, and families of missing Vietnam War prisoners, agencies throughout the government were reexamining millions of classified documents to see if they might be declassified without harming the national security.

Early in 1992, CIA Director Robert M. Gates disclosed his internal memo endorsing a move toward greater openness. He said the agency should "strive where we can to be as forthcoming, candid, informative, and helpful as possible to the public, the media, and academia, consistent with our mission and the protection of sources and methods. . . ." Ironically, the rest of Gates's memo was partially blacked out.

Later in the year, the public obtained its first look at documents related to the 1963 assassination of President John F. Kennedy, including notes of the doctors who treated

President Clinton paid a Memorial Day visit to "the wall" in 1993. The V-shaped reflective black granite is inscribed with the names of more than 58,000 casualties, missing in action, and prisoners of the Vietnam War. A diamond next to a name indicates the death was confirmed; a cross signifies the person was either missing or a prisoner at the end of the war.

extends beyond the agency to the coordination of all government intelligence gathering outside the United States. The FBI is responsible for intelligence within the country. Former president George Bush is also a former director of central intelligence.

■ Say 'Please' Three Times

Bureaucratic resistance to change is legendary. A maxim dating from the Franklin Roosevelt administration is that bureaucrats feel they can safely ignore presidents' first two requests because presidents rarely ask a third time. John Kennedy learned the truth of this when he ordered the removal of a sign pointing to the CIA's supersecret Virginia headquarters. On the third try, Kennedy called the person in charge. The sign finally came down. "I now understand," Kennedy declared afterward, "that for a president to get anything done in this country, he's got to say it three times."

■ Love It or Hate It, It's Here To Stay

Whistle Blowers

The Merit Systems Protection Board, which along with the Office of Personnel Management replaced the ninety-year-old Civil Service Commission under the 1978 civil service reforms, is responsible for pro-

him immediately after he was shot in Dallas, and the CIA's file on Kennedy assassin Lee Harvey Oswald.

In May 1993, as the first president to visit the Vietnam Veterans Memorial wall for Memorial Day ceremonies, Bill Clinton announced that he was ordering the declassification of all records pertaining to the search for prisoners of war and persons missing in action in the Vietnam War.

Speaking of Intelligence . . .

For shorthand purposes the head of the CIA commonly is called the CIA director. The full title is actually "director of central intelligence" because the director's job tecting "whistle blowers"—civil servants who expose possible wrongdoing.

The Defense Department has had a particularly notable collection of whistle blowers. One, Franklin C. Spinney, a systems analyst, even made the cover of *Time* magazine in 1983 because of his criticism of the Pentagon's habit of underestimating the cost of weapons.

Finger-Pointing by the Media

News stories about bureaucratic snafus and wastefulness range from the enraging to the amusing. No taxpayer enjoys reading stories about the $659 ashtrays and $7,000 coffeemakers purchased by the Defense Department, or knowing that the Department of Energy declassified documents showing how to build a hydrogen bomb. But who wouldn't smile upon hearing that the Department of Health and Human Services sent fifteen chimpanzees to a laboratory to start a chimp breeding program—only to find that they were all males?

Whistling to the White House

One famous whistle blower, A. Ernest Fitzgerald, tried to blow the whistle on the president and his top aides—and succeeded only in clarifying the law in such circumstances.

Fitzgerald sued Richard Nixon for damages after losing his air force job in 1970. The Pentagon procurement official claimed the White House ordered him fired in revenge for his frequent leaks to Congress and the press about weapons cost overruns. The Justice Department countersued in Nixon's behalf.

By the time the Supreme Court ruled in 1982, Nixon was long gone from office and the suit was largely academic. But *Nixon v. Fitzgerald* and a companion case, *Harlow v. Fitzgerald,* stand as an important precedent in the question of presidential immunity. The Court ruled 5–4 that the president enjoyed "absolute immunity" for his official acts and was not liable for civil damages.

In the companion decision the Court ruled that Nixon aides Bryce N. Harlow and Alexander P. Butterfield could be sued under limited circumstances. Presidential aides and cabinet officers can be held liable, the Court held, if their actions violate a person's statutory or constitutional rights.

Who Ya' Gonna Call? Fraudbusters

Two government scientists who had invented a "plagiarism machine" were reassigned in 1993 after a noted author complained that they were misusing taxpayers' money. The pair, Walter Stewart and Ned Feder, developed the computer software while sleuthing for scientific fraud for a unit of the National Institutes of Health. Using the software on a biography of Abraham Lincoln they found hundreds of phrases allegedly cribbed without attribution from other works. Historian Stephen B. Oates accused Stewart and Feder of malice, and their superiors agreed that their investigation had strayed from its authorized bounds.

Defenders of the Bureaucracy

Although critics of the bureaucracy abound, some people have come to its defense. They point out, among other things, that the U.S. bureaucracy actually performs pretty well when compared with the bureaucracies of other countries—and, of course, that no bureaucracy is free of mistakes and foul-ups. Defenders of the bureaucracy also contend that it's become a scapegoat for many of the problems of modern society—that is, it's a convenient target because it is big, powerful, hard to change, and relatively anonymous.

Attackers of the Bureaucracy

One of the most well-known attackers of the bureaucracy was former senator

Costly Monkey Business

For years until he left the Senate in 1989, Wisconsin Democrat William Proxmire made headlines with his satiric "Golden Fleece Awards" that spotlighted wasteful government spending. But in at least one case the publicity backfired and ended up hitting the senator—and the taxpayers—in the pocketbook.

In 1975 Proxmire "awarded" the prize to the National Aeronautics and Space Administration and the Office of Naval Research for giving Dr. Ronald Hutchinson of Michigan $500,000 to research how monkeys show aggression. The scientist, Proxmire told the Senate, "made a monkey out of the American taxpayer."

Hutchinson sued for libel and the Supreme Court ruled in 1979 that congressional immunity protected Proxmire's remarks on the Senate floor but not his actions off the floor to publicize the Golden Fleece Award. Proxmire agreed to pay $10,000 to Hutchinson, who had paid his own legal fees. The Senate picked up the $124,351 tab for Proxmire's defense.

William Proxmire, Democrat from Wisconsin. For years, he assumed a watchdog role, hunting out waste and wrongdoing in government agencies. Each culprit then received—with great fanfare—one of Proxmire's "Golden Fleece Awards," which not only encouraged improvements in agency performance but also gained publicity for the senator. In 1979 Proxmire gave the award to Congress itself for the growth of its staff bureaucracy.

Firing Bureaucrats

As Carter administration aide Jody Powell once put it, "it is damn near impossible to fire someone from this government for failure to do their job." The statistics support Powell: only about 0.004 to 0.01 percent (twelve thousand to thirty thousand) of the 3 million or so federal workers are fired each year.

Because it's so hard to fire bureaucrats, some agencies unofficially maintain "turkey farms" where unwanted employees can continue to collect their salaries while having little or nothing to do. Others are encouraged to take early retirement or, as a last resort, the agency is reorganized to eliminate their jobs. As Jimmy Carter remarked, it's "easier to promote and transfer incompetent employees than to get rid of them." Richard Nixon phrased it less ele-

"Think of it! Presidents come and go, but we go on forever!"

gantly. In one of the Watergate tapes Nixon is heard telling aides that "there are unpleasant places where Civil Service people can be sent. . . . Let people know that when they don't produce in this administration, somebody's ass is kicked out."

Panetta and the 'Leper Colony'

Another name besides "turkey farm" for unwanted bureaucrats is "leper colony." Leon Panetta discovered one in an undisclosed federal agency shortly after he left the House (where he served as a Democrat from California) to become Bill Clinton's budget director. Panetta expressed amazement to columnists Jack Anderson and Michael Binstein that there are such places

Air traffic controllers are a highly skilled and trained group. Their ranks were sorely depleted when striking controllers were fired by President Reagan.

than in a tongue-in-cheek memo he wrote concerning a dispute among agencies:

I agree with the Secretary of the Interior. Please have it carried out so that fur-bearing animals remain in the Department of the Interior. You might find out if any Alaska bears are still supervised by (a) War Department (b) Department of Agriculture (c) Department of Commerce. They have all had jurisdiction over Alaska bears in the past and many embarrassing situations have been created by the mating of a bear belonging to one Department with a bear belonging to another Department.

F.D.R.

P.S. I don't think the Navy is involved but it may be. Check the Coast Guard. You can never tell!

where people work, out of sight and out of mind. "That's the kind of thing you do to work around the system," Panetta said. "We have to reshape that."

Ronald Reagan and the Air Traffic Controllers

All the talk about how hard it is to fire bureaucrats meant little to Ronald Reagan in 1981 when the unionized air traffic controllers refused to work, in defiance of a law barring strikes by federal employees. Reagan promptly fired all 11,400 of the strikers. The courts upheld Reagan, and polls showed that the public over-

whelmingly approved of his action.

Reagan took his cue from another conservative president, Calvin Coolidge, who came to prominence during the Boston police strike of 1919. As Massachusetts governor, Coolidge called out the militia and declared, "There is no right to strike against the public safety by anybody, anywhere, anytime."

■ Bosses on the Hired Help

FDR: The Ideal Boss?

Unlike most presidents, Franklin D. Roosevelt seemed to enjoy working with the bureaucracy. Nowhere was that plainer

RR: No Friend of the Bureaucracy?

Ronald Reagan was no friend of the bureaucracy—and he didn't care who knew it. Because his 1980 campaign em-phasized his desire to get government off the backs of the people, he spent much of his presidency trying to curb the size and influence of the federal bureaucracy.

While he may have curbed its influence, he was not so successful when it came to its size. The number of civilians working for the federal government rose from 2.8 million in 1981, the first year of his presidency, to over 3 million in 1988, the last year.

On the Bureaucracy

There is no idea so uplifting as the idea of the service of humanity.
President Woodrow Wilson

I thought I was the president, but when it comes to these bureaucracies I can't make 'em do a damn thing.
President Harry S. Truman

The nearest approach to immortality on earth is a government bureau.
Former secretary of state James F. Byrnes

We have no discipline in this bureaucracy. We never fire anybody. We never reprimand anybody. We never demote anybody. We always promote the sons-of-bitches that kick us in the ass.
President Richard Nixon

Getting the bureaucracy to accept new ideas is like carrying a double mattress up a very narrow and winding stairway. It is a terrible job, and you exhaust yourself when you try it. But once you get the mattress up it is awfully hard for anyone else to get it down.
Arthur M. Schlesinger, Jr. Aide to President John F. Kennedy

[Dealing with the bureaucracy] is like trying to nail jelly to the wall.
President John F. Kennedy

We have excellent hard-working, imaginative workers trapped in bad systems.
Vice President Al Gore

BY MIKE LUCKOVICH FOR THE ATLANTA CONSTITUTION

And Reagan was quick to unleash criticism of the bureaucracy when he was held accountable for its blunders. One of the best examples of this happened early in his administration when Reagan appointees in the Department of Agriculture made the astonishing pronouncement that ketchup was an acceptable substitute for a vegetable in school lunches. In responding to the criticism that followed, Reagan explained that "somebody got overambitious in the bureaucracy."

■ Reform in the Works

With Vice President Al Gore in charge, yet another effort to reform the federal bureaucracy was set in motion in 1993 by

Dinosaur Fever

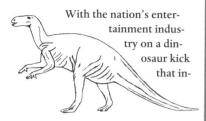

With the nation's entertainment industry on a dinosaur kick that included a purple toy (Barney) and a blockbuster summer movie (*Jurassic Park*), Congress's watchdog General Accounting Office was finding some prehistoric monsters within the federal bureaucracy.

In almost fifty papers the GAO reported its findings to the incoming team of Bill Clinton and Al Gore, who was charged with carrying out the president's National Performance Review of federal programs. Some highlights from the GAO studies:

• The government spends about $1.5 trillion—almost a fourth of the gross domestic product—and yet does "an abysmal job" on bookkeeping and government spending controls.

• The Agriculture Department is a "twentieth-century dinosaur" that badly needs streamlining.

• The Education Department's student loan program is "inordinately complex and cumbersome."

• The more than 125 employment training programs spread among fourteen agencies cry out to be coordinated.

President Bill Clinton. Called the National Performance Review, this initiative was billed as something completely different. It was to look at every federal program, evaluate its efficiency, and coldly recommend whether it should live, die, or be slimmed down.

Gore began a series of road trips to seek the views of federal employees all over the country. He was assisted by Philip Lader, author of *Reinventing Government.*

And, of course, any serious study of the federal bureaucracy needs a bureaucracy of its own. Gore and Lader assembled a staff of about 150 federal employees to work on the National Performance Review.

With President Clinton at his side and stacks of government regulations behind him, Gore unveiled his report September 7, 1993, on the White House South Lawn. It called for streamlining "old fashioned, outdated government" to save $108 billion over five years. Some 252,000 federal jobs would be cut.

Photo Credits

Special thanks are due to several people who were especially helpful during the process of collecting the images for this book. Phil Duncan, longtime political reporter and writer for Congressional Quarterly, lent his collection of political buttons, many of which were used on the pages of this book. Illustrator John Kascht provided numerous drawings, including Hillary and Bill Clinton dancing, which appears on the front cover and on the title page. Guy Lamolinara, editor of the Library of Congress Information Bulletin, lent us photos from his collection. And, finally, thanks to Dennis J. Slick of Salt Lake City, who lent the $10,000 bill on page 210.

Constitutionally Speaking: 2 and 3 Douglas Chadwick. **4** cartoon, Library of Congress. **5 and 6** Library of Congress. **7** painting, Library of Congress. **9, 10, and 11** Mason, Randolph, and Gerry, Library of Congress. **14** A project by the Iowa chapter of the Federal Bar Assoc., and the Center for Law Related Education, Drake Law School. **15, 16, and 17** Library of Congress.

Uncle Sam's Building Blocks: 20 and 21 Library of Congress. **22** Washingtoniana Division, Martin Luther King Public Library, Washington, D.C. **23** cartoon, University of Arkansas Libraries; Finney, Kassebaum, and Meyers, respective offices. **25** Library of Congress.

Government, Take a Seat: 26 Library of Congress. **27** Architect of the Capitol. **28** National Archives.

29 and 30 Library of Congress. **31** George Washington, Library of Congress; Martha Washington, National Portrait Gallery. **32** Smithsonian Institution. **33** sketches, Library of Congress; White House photo, White House. **34** Library of Congress. **35** Culver Pictures, Inc. **36** Bulldozers, White House Historical Association. **37** cartoon, Wasserman/Los Angeles Times Syndicate; Bush, Bush Presidential Materials Project. **38** sheep, Library of Congress; Clinton, White House. **39** Truman, Truman Library/Bettmann; Ford, Ford Library. **40** Bush Presidential Materials Project. **41** White House. **42** Pentagon, Department of Defense; Capitol, Library of Congress. **43** White House. **44** Library of Congress. **45** Department of Defense. **46** sculpture, Lisa Hartjens; painting, Architect of the Capitol. **47** policeman, R. Michael Jenkins; Greenbrier, Greenbrier. **48** John Moore. **49 and 50** Library of Congress. **51** Congressional Quarterly. **52** Royal Exchange, Collection of the Supreme Court of the United States; Old City Hall and Supreme Court, Library of Congress. **53** Collection of the Supreme Court of the United States. **54** Library of Congress.

The Toughest Job in the World: 56 George Tames. **57** Library of Congress **58** Reagan Library. **59** Library of Congress. **60** Johnson, Johnson Library; Coolidge, Library of Congress. **61** Lincoln, Roosevelt,

Ford, Library of Congress; Kennedy, Kennedy Library. **62** National Archives. **63** Jackson and Kennedy, Library of Congress; Carter, Carter Library; Clinton, White House. **64** Library of Congress. **65** cartoon, Oliphant/Universal Press Syndicate. **66** Library of Congress. **67** Eisenhower Library/Bettmann. **68 and 69** White House. **70** Library of Congress. **71** Nixon, Nixon Project/National Archives; Taney, Library of Congress. **72** R. Michael Jenkins. **73** McDonald's. **74** Department of Defense. **76** Library of Congress. **77** cartoon, Library of Congress. **78** Auth copyright 1992, the *Philadelphia Inquirer*. Reprinted with permission of Universal Press Syndicate. All rights reserved. **79 and 80** Library of Congress. **81** R. Michael Jenkins. **82** Library of Congress. **83, 84, and 85** Library of Congress. **86** Department of Defense. **87** R. Michael Jenkins. **88** Library of Congress. **89** Le Pelley in the *Christian Science Monitor,* ©1974 TCSPS. **91** Theodore Roosevelt, Library of Congress; Franklin Roosevelt, National Archives. **92** Reagan, Reagan Library; Borgman cartoon, reprinted with special permission of King Features Syndicate; Washington and Roosevelt, Library of Congress. **93** Sequoia, Congressional Quarterly; Camp David, Reagan Library.

White House Personae: 94 White House/Bill Fitz-Patrick. **95** White House. **96** Library of Congress. **97** Wilsons, Library of Congress; Adams, all rights reserved, the Metropolitan Museum of Art. **98** Washington and Grant, National Portrait Gallery; Eisenhower, Eisenhower Library. **99, 100, 101** Library of Congress. **102** Theodore Roosevelt Collection/Harvard College Library. **103** pantograph, Bettmann; Monticello, Monticello; Taft, Library of Congress. **104** Eisenhower, Eisenhower Library; Clinton, John Kascht. **105** balloon, Library of Congress; Nixons, Nixon Project/National Archives. **106** cartoon, copyright 1993, John McPherson. Distributed by Universal Press Syndicate. Reprinted with permission of Universal Press Syndicate. All rights reserved. **107** Reagan, AP/Wide World; Tyler and Cleveland, Library of Congress. **108** Hayes, Library of Congress; Clinton, R. Michael Jenkins. **109** Bush, Bush Presidential Materials Project; Johnson, Johnson Library. **110 and 111** Library of Congress. **112** Truman, Library of Congress; Nixon/Cox, Nixon Project/National Archives. **113, 114, 115** Library of Congress. **117** Booth, National Portrait Gallery; McKinley headline, Smithsonian; Oswald, *Dallas Times Herald.* **118** Kennedy, Kennedy Library; presidents, White House/David Valdez. **119** Library of Congress. **120** Arthur, Library of Congress. **121** Library of Congress. **122** cartoon, Don Wright, Inc.; Qualye, John Kascht **123** cartoon, Dan Lynch, reprinted by permission of NEA, Inc.

Body Politic or Politic Body?: **124** John Moore. **125** Gerrymander (right), Bettmann. **127 and 128** R. Michael Jenkins. **130** O'Neill, AP/Wide World; Reed, National Portrait Gallery. **131** Library of Congress. **132** Byrd and Mitchell, AP/Wide World; Adams, Library of Congress. **133** R. Michael Jenkins. **135** Thurmond, Library of Congress; cots, *Washington Post.* **136** Library of Congress. **137** etching, Library of Congress; Yeltsin, R. Michael Jenkins. **138 and 139** Library of Congress. **140** McCarthy, AP/Wide World; Ervin and Baker, Senate Historical Office. **141** Synar, Congressional Quarterly; Johnson, drawing by David Levine, reprinted with permission from the *New York Review of Books,* copyright 1966 Nyrev, Inc. **142** AP/Wide World. **143** photo, AP/Wide World; cartoon, drawing by Leo Cullum, ©1993 the *New Yorker* magazine. **145** AP/Wide World. **146 and 147** Library of Congress. **148** Williams, AP/Wide World; Keating, R.

Michael Jenkins. **149** Etta Hulme, reprinted by permission of NEA, Inc. **150** Bob Englehart. **151** Library of Congress. **152** R. Michael Jenkins. **153** Library of Congress. **154** U.S. Government Printing Office. **155** R. Michael Jenkins.

The Capitol Hill Crew: **156** Lisa Hartjens. **157** R. Michael Jenkins. **158** Senate Historical Office. **159** Joseph Kennedy, R. Michael Jenkins; Robert Kennedy, Bettmann; women, Library of Congress. **160** Congressional Quarterly. **161** Bettmann. **162** Library of Congress. **163** Fong, Congressional Quarterly; Campbell, Washington office. **164** Felton, Library of Congress; Rankin, AP/Wide World. **165** Boxer, Washington office; Feinstein, R. Michael Jenkins. **166** R. Michael Jenkins. **167** Library of Congress. **168** Eisenhower Library. **169** Johnson, George Tames; Baker, AP/Wide World. **170** Architect of the Capitol. **171** Library of Congress. **173** National Archives. **174** Marty LaVor.

'USA Law': **176** R. Michael Jenkins. **177** Maryland Historical Society. **178** Frankfurters, Library of Congress; coathook, Collection of the Supreme Court of the United States. **179** Library of Congress. **180** Burton, Library of Congress; Reagan and O'Connor, AP/Wide World. **181** Bettmann. **183** Flip Schulke, *Life* Magazine, ©1964 Time Inc. **184** Library of Congress. **185** Maryland Historical Society. **187** Collection of the Supreme Court of the United States. **188** Congressional Quarterly. **189** Parks, Tommy Giles; telephone, *Washington Post,* D.C. Public Library. **190** voting rights and child laborers, Library of Congress; Japanese-Americans, AP/Wide World. **191** Brown and Bakke, AP/Wide World; McCorvey, Bettmann; electric chair, *Washington Post,* D.C. Public Library. **192 and 193** Library of Congress. **194** Reprinted by permission of United Feature Syndicate, Inc. **196** Johnson Library. **197** Riggins, AP/Wide World; bench, Congressional Quarterly. **198** Library of Congress. **199** Collection of the Supreme Court of the United States.

Justices for All: **200** composite, Kachergis Book Design from Philippa Strum, *Louis D. Brandeis: Justice for the People* (Cambridge: Harvard University Press, 1984);

portraits, Library of Congress. **201** Kennedy, Souter, Thomas, National Geographic; Ginsburg, R. Michael Jenkins. **202** Litchfield Historical Society. **203** Law school class, Bettmann; Brandeis cartoon, Library of Congress. **204** John Kascht. **205** Warren family, Collection of the Supreme Court of the United States; Taft, Bettmann. **206** National Geographic Society. **207** Rutledge and McReynolds, Library of Congress; Baldwin, Collection of the Supreme Court of the United States; Livingston, New York Historical Society. **208** Library of Congress. **209** McKenna, Collection of the Supreme Court of the United States; Sanford, Library of Congress; Murphy, Bettmann. **211** Congressional Quarterly. **212** Fortas and Johnson, Johnson Library; Douglas, Will Thomas/Yakima Valley Museum. **213** Bancroft Library, University of California.

The Political Party Scene: **215** Library of Congress. **217** *Nast,* National Portrait Gallery. **218** Library of Congress. **219** John Kascht. **220** Stassen, *St. Petersburg Times;* Debs, New York University, Tamiment Institute Library. **221, 222, 223, 224** Library of Congress. **225** *Charleston Gazette*/Kennedy Library. **226** Library of Congress. **227** AP/Wide World. **228** Library of Congress. **230** Bettmann. **231** Library of Congress. **232** Coolidge, Smithsonian; Douglass, Library of Congress. **233** Chisolm, Congressional Quarterly.

Electoral Engineering: **234** John Kascht. **235** Library of Congress. **236** R. Michael Jenkins. **237** Library of Congress. **239** Jefferson, National Portrait Gallery; Burr, Library of Congress. **240** Architect of the Capitol. **241** MacNelly/Reprinted by permission of Tribune Media Services. **242** Congressional Quarterly. **243** Truman Library. **245** Douglas, Bettmann; Lincoln, Library of Congress. **246** General Dynamics. **247** drawing by Weber, ©1992, the *New Yorker* Magazine, Inc.; Johnson, Johnson Library. **248** Truman, Bettmann; D'Amato, R. Michael Jenkins. **249** R. Michael Jenkins. **250** NASA. **251 and 253** Library of Congress.

Unelected Power Brokers: **256** Library of Congress. **257** man, R. Michael Jenkins; PAC letter, Washington office of Rep. Jim Hansen. **258 and 260** Congressional Quarterly. **261** Library of Congress. **263** FDR Library. **266** Congressional Quarterly.

The Entrenched Bureaucrats: 269 and 270 National Archives. **271** Museum of the City of New York.

272 Library of Congress. **273** Kennedys, Kennedy Library; protesters, *New York Times*. **274** U.S. Postal Service. **277** Department of Agriculture. **278** Hoover, Library of Congress; FBI building, R. Michael Jenkins. **279** R. Michael Jenkins. **280** Bettmann. **282** cartoon, Jim Berry. **283** Congressional

Quarterly. **284** Wilson and Byrnes, Library of Congress; Truman, Truman Library; Nixon, Congressional Quarterly; Schlesinger, Bettmann; Kennedy, Kennedy Library; Gore, R. Michael Jenkins; cartoon, by permission of Mike Luckovich and Creators Syndicate. **285** Tom Toles and the *Buffalo News*. ©March 8, 1993.

*I*ndex

Whittaker, Charles E., **210**
Whitten, Jamie, **157**–158
Wilbur, Richard, **153**
Wilder, L. Douglas, 24
Williams, Harrison A., Jr., **148**
Williamsport (Md.), 28
Willkie, Wendell, **232**
Wills, Frank, 76
Wilson, Don W., 16
Wilson, Edith, **97,** 109, 110
Wilson, Eleanor, 112
Wilson, Ellen, 110
Wilson, Henry, **64,** 77, 123
Wilson, James, 12, 177
Wilson, Jesse, 112
Wilson, Pete V., 131, 166
Wilson, Woodrow. *See also* Nobel Peace
    Prize
  background, 95, 96, 104, 106, 110, 218,
    226, **284**
  cartoon, **84, 203**
  Congress and, **80, 147**
  inauguration, 62, 64
  League of Nations, **84,** 102

media and, 261
as president, 37, 80, 81, 82, **97,** 105,
    118, 223
stroke, 109
Supreme Court and, **203,** 204, 205,
    207, 208
White House, 38
Wirthlin, Richard, 267
Wirt, William, 217, 222
Wisconsin, 25, **79,** 224, 237
Wolfson, Lewis, 211–212
Women. *See also* individuals by name
  African-American, 73, 227, 229, 233,
    249
  bureaucrats, 278–279
  cabinet members, 72–74
  convention delegates, **223,** 224
  employment, **151,** 269
  governors, 22–23, 236
  media, 264
  members of Congress, 159–160, 162,
    163–167, 249
  national party committee
    chairwomen, 226

Nineteenth Amendment, 14, 46
party conventions, 227, 229
poet laureate at Library of Congress,
    153
presidential appointees, **72,** 261
presidential/vice presidential
    candidates, 121, **223, 233**
Rotunda, lying in state in, 45
Supreme Court justices, 202, 203,
    204
swearing in by, 59, 60
voting rights, 166, **235**
Woodhull, Victoria Claflin, 223
Woods, Elliott, 43
Woodson v. North Carolina (1976), 191
Woodward, Bob, 76
Works Progress Administration (WPA),
    271
World War I, **85,** 99, 161, 164
World War II, 6, 84–85, 101, 161, 164,
    265
WPA. *See* Works Progress Administra-
    tion
Wright, Jim, 129

Writ of certiorari, 183
Writ of habeas corpus, **183**
Wyman, Louis, 250
Wyoming, 126

Yale University, 202. *See also* Bush,
    George; Clinton, Bill; Clinton,
    Hillary Rodham; Ford, Gerald
Yarborough, Ralph, 172
Yeltsin, Boris, **137,** 138
Young, John, **150**
Young, John R., **153**
Youngstown Sheet and Tube Co. v. Sawyer
    (1952), 190

Zangara, Joseph, 116
Ziegler, Ronald L., 76
Ziolkowski family, **119**
Zweifel, Jan, **32**
Zweifel, John, **32**